W9-BBG-849

Foundations of
Intercultural Communication

Foundations of Intercultural Communication

K. S. Sitaram
University of Hawaii
Roy T. Cogdell
Governors State University

Charles E. Merrill Publishing Company
A Bell & Howell Company
Columbus, Ohio

Published by
Charles E. Merrill Publishing Company
A Bell & Howell Company
Columbus, Ohio 43216

The book was set in Times Roman.
The Production Editor was Lynn Walcoff.
The cover was designed by Will Chenoweth. Cover photo by Editorial
Photocolor Archives.

Library of Congress Catalog Card Number: 76-7257

ISBN: 0-675-08626-4

1 2 3 4 5 6—80 79 78 77 76

Printed in the United States of America

CONTENTS

Acknowledgments

This book culminates several years of work done by the first author in the United States, Japan, and India. While preparing this book, several friends and colleagues have encouraged us and contributed valuable ideas. We would like to mention just a few of them. The faculty members of the Department of Speech at the University of Hawaii and the Area of Interpersonal Communication at Governors State University have encouraged us a great deal. Toyoko S. Yamashita of the Department of Genetics at the University of Hawaii has done a thorough job of checking the information on Japanese culture which appears throughout this book. Tom Hutchinson and Lynn Walcoff of Charles E. Merrill Publishing Company have given us valuable suggestions. Without Tom Hutchinson's enthusiasm, this book would not have appeared so soon.

To the Student

The need to understand other cultures better is both a help and a hindrance in considering the study of communication. It helps because it motivates, and one must have motivation to learn. It helps, too, because it makes the student understand how little he or she knows and how much he or she needs to know. Unfortunately, an uninformed interest in communication can lead some students to think they already know more about communication than they really do, just because they have previously taken a keen interest in aspects related to people different from themselves. Being amateur observers, such students usually have mistaken ideas about communication matters that need to be corrected.

Indeed, one of the important tasks of the study of communication is to correct the misconceptions nearly everyone acquires in the course of living in the everyday world. Hence, as you study this book you should be prepared to find that some of your opinions may be inaccurate or even erroneous.

An interest in communication may also lead students to expect the wrong things from a book such as this one. They may expect either too much or too little from it. They expect too much if they look for a few patent remedies to use in solving world problems overnight. No one learns to be a physician, lawyer, engineer, or musician in a single course. Neither can he or she quickly become a professional in intercultural communication by taking one or two courses. In each case, long years of training in the subject area and in many related areas are necessary to become professionally proficient. Thus, although you will learn much from this book that can be of value in understanding more about other peoples, you must expect to acquire only the rudiments of the subject, not profound knowledge or great skill. You should therefore be prepared to study a subject of considerable breadth—one that touches on a wider variety of problems than most people realize.

It is important for you to understand how the study of intercultural communication evolved as a discipline. Such knowledge is gathered by carefully observing and measuring events. The things and events observed are systematized in various ways, most often by classifying them into categories that describe and predict them as accurately as possible. Through the valiant efforts of many researchers and thinkers over the centuries, there is now a discipline of intercultural communication—a large body of systematized knowledge—which can be taught and which is the best foundation for developing an understanding of other people's worlds.

Although intercultural communication is a branch of communication, it is by no means the exclusive property of that discipline. Several disciplines also make the study of intercultural communication their business, including diplomacy, government, anthropology, sociology, economics, and even agriculture. Each discipline focuses its attention upon certain aspects of communication, but none has purported to pull all aspects into a single, cogent, and comprehensive treatment of the subject. Differences among them are not always clear-cut; therefore you will find some overlap.

Sociologists and social anthropologists are concerned with the behavior of groups of people. These specialists study the cultures and social structures of various societies or groups of people living together. The sociologist typically deals with modern, literate cultures such as our own; the anthropologist, with more primitive cultures. Each science has devised its own methods and acquired its own body of information. This is precisely what is occurring now as intercultural communications emerges as a discipline.

Religion and philosophy are concerned with how the individuals relate themselves to the world around them and the power that created such a world. Arts and Letters are concerned with the ways in which an artist or a poet expresses his or her feelings. Each of the areas has devised its own method of acquiring information. In intercultural communication we try to show similarities and differences in how people relate themselves to the world around them and how they express their feelings related to their world.

Finally, it should be noted that no matter how good a student has proven to be in interacting within his or her own cultural setting, it does not mean that he or she will be equally good at doing so with members of a different setting. The reason is that the communication models and theories that are applicable to one's own culture may not be applicable to other cultures.

In this book we have attempted to familiarize you with communication theories of other cultures. An understanding of these theories will help you appreciate the fact that cultural differences do exist, but it should be possible for you to adapt your communicative techniques in order to interact successfully with members of different cultures.

To the Instructor

Intercultural communication is a whole new way of looking at the art and process of human interaction. In America and other countries communication is fast becoming intercultural. People of these countries are realizing that they are not just one people and one culture, but that they are conglomerates of several people and cultures. In America, for example, the myth of American culture has all but disappeared. Americans have discovered they are ethnic and multi-cultural. In such changed situations, peoples are asking questions. How can we interact with others? How can we communicate with others without creating any breakdowns? Intercultural communication is the answer to such questions.

We do not boast that we have experimental data to support every word we say in this book. But we do believe that everything we say is verifiable by human experience, scholarly opinions, and even by empirical evidence. We are also confident that the studies to be conducted in the future in intercultural communication around the world will confirm our views.

We consider this textbook unique in several ways, especially considering the stress given to non-Western thought. You will observe that a tremendous amount of attention has been given to cultures in Japan, China, India, Africa, and other so-called third world nations which have been ignored traditionally in scholarly writings. Our intention is to provide a more balanced treatment of the subject and to recognize the existence of other cultures in which your students will be working and preparing for careers.

Hence, our thrust has been focused on pulling together in a comparative way the unique ideas from those major cultures which have more or less been played down in the past by many Western authors.

Another area to which we have given considerable attention is the thought of minority scholars within the United States. Those would include Americans of African, Chinese, Japanese, and Mexican ancestry. We have attempted to elucidate the cultural characteristics these groups have brought to America and the impact each has had on intercultural communication.

The reader will note that at times we are critical of the American cultures. Many of our examples have tended to focus upon attitudes and practices found in America. This is certainly not without reason.

Americans tend to use themselves as standards. Cultures which deviate from their standards are categorized as being backward, primitive, under-developed, and undeveloped. These labels may even be placed on cultures such as China, India, and Japan which pre-date American cultures by thousands of years. Such labeling is based on how much material wealth members of a culture have accumulated, not how much wisdom they have developed.

We see therapeutic value in isolating and dramatizing incidents of Americans' using their own cultural standards in making value judg-ments about other cultures. The examples used in this book tend to be blatant. They are not exceptions, but are general and well known to most people in other cultures who have been exposed to Americans either in their own countries or in the United States.

We also feel that, since many American authors neglect to point out self-critical aspects of the American cultures, this book should provide an honest revelation of the origin and nature of problems which give rise to poor intercultural relations on the part of Americans. We do not claim to have answers to all the problems we identify. But if an aware-ness can be created as a first step, then we feel we have initiated the battle against ignorance and disrespect for the factors which do affect communication among members of differing cultures.

1

The Study of Intercultural Communication

Human communication is strongly related to cultural backgrounds of the communicator and his audience. When a person interacts with another person he unconsciously reveals his cultural identity. We can test the validity of this statement by observing the way in which people greet their friends and relatives. Let us consider a few examples from American and Asian cultures. When an American meets a friend, he stands a foot or so away from him and shakes his hand. By standing a foot away, he is exercising his right to his personal space, which is customarily accepted in his culture. By touching the friend's hand, he is indicating his belief in the concept of equality and individuality which are very important values in his culture. He might even resent it if the other person encroaches upon his personal space and refuses to shake his hand.

A Muslim looks at friendship differently. Take the case of Arabs who are Muslims. When an Arab meets another Arab, he hugs him shoulder-to-shoulder and says, "greetings to you, brother." *Koran,* the holy book of the Muslims, says that all Muslims are brothers. There is no hierarchy among Muslims. Therefore, there is no personal space between them.

When a Hindu meets another Hindu, he stands at a distance and greets him by bringing his palms together on his chest. Basically, the Hindu believes in a hierarchical society. However, he also believes that the soul is derived from the divine and therefore all souls are equal. The soul, which is supposed to be situated somewhere around the heart, has no hierarchy. The Hindu indicates the equality of souls by bringing his palms close to his heart.

Although each person greets another according to his custom, he probably does not know why he is doing so. He greets people as he was taught by his elders, and probably does not even know that he is revealing his cultural identity by his greeting.

Cultural Expectations

When someone communicates his belief in equality, individuality, social status, or some stereotype that he has about other persons, he expects the other person to reinforce his belief or the stereotype.

When an American agricultural expert tells an Asian farmer that the latter should improve his agricultural technique, he not only reveals his Christian belief in helping the needy but also his expectation that the other person will listen to him. When a Hindu in Bombay greets the Pope from the Vatican, he not only shows his belief that all religions should be respected and tolerated but also expects the other person to show the same tolerance and respect. When a Japanese scholar greets a comparatively junior American scholar by bowing to him, he not only shows his Buddhist value of humbleness and modesty but also expects the junior scholar to be equally humble and modest. When an "Anglo" farmer in California hires a migrant laborer from Mexico, he expects the Mexican to behave like a servant. The Anglo does not expect the migrant to sit next to him in a bar and drink beer or live in a luxurious house right next to his.

Let us consider some more detailed examples. At a bus stop in Honolulu, Hawaii, a young man was waiting for the city bus. The bus had not arrived as scheduled. A few minutes later, a middle-aged man came to wait for the same bus. He looked at the young man, who appeared to be a student from Asia. The middle-aged man asked,

"You go to university?"

"I teach at the university."

"How nice, are you a teaching assistant?"

"No, I am a professor."

"You are! What do you teach, an Asian language?"

"No, nuclear physics."

The middle-aged man was trying to conceal his embarrassment when he stretched out his hand, saying, "Looks like we are in different fields. I am. . ., I teach communication at the university. As a matter of fact, I just got back from your country. I was advising your government on developing mass media there."

They shook hands. The Asian professor expected a barrage of personal questions. It would not be new to him. Almost every day he had the same stereotyped questions from students, professors, and lay people. They were inquiries about himself, his culture and when he would go back. But this time he did not have to answer those questions. The bus came. The two men got in and sat in different parts of the bus.

In an apartment building in Portland, Oregon, a white woman was going down in the elevator. A little eight-year-old black girl was going down in the same elevator.

"You live here?" the woman asked.

"Yes."

"You go to school?"

"Yes."

"What grade?"

"Third."

The elevator stopped. They got out.

That evening the white woman called the black girl's mother on the telephone.

"You are the little girl's mother?"

"Yes, I am Amanda's mother."

"Amanda, what a nice name. You have a cute little daughter. I saw her in the elevator. The reason why I called you is, I have a beautiful night-gown that I bought for my daughter. It is brand new. It's so beautiful I hate to waste it. I am sure your little daughter could use it."

"Why can't your own daughter use it?"

"It is too tight for her. Why don't I take it to your apartment?" The white woman then put down the phone with a click.

When the woman arrived, Amanda's mother opened the door and asked her to come in,

"No, I can't. I have to go. I just wanted to give this nightgown to Amanda. See you later." Without waiting for an answer the woman left. Amanda's mother opened the package. The gown was not brand new. She did not know what to do. This was the first time someone had given her daughter something that was used. Since they had just moved in, she did not want to make enemies in that building. Her husband, a medical doctor, had been hired by the Portland medical school as a consultant. She knew he would be annoyed if she told him she had accepted an old gown from a white woman. Without telling anybody, she wrote a note to the woman to say that it was nice of her to give the beautiful gown to Amanda, but it was too tight for her also. She took it and left it at the woman's door.

The white woman had probably done this before. She expected every black woman to accept a gift of used clothes.

The persons mentioned above behaved as they did almost instinctively. They were probably not aware that they were revealing their cultural expectations in the way they greeted friends or talked to strangers.

Ignorance of cultural values and communicative skills of the audience negatively affect a communicator's success. Sometimes, failure to communicate at the cultural level will lead to misunderstanding at the national level. A classic example is that of the military dictator of a Muslim country ridiculing the woman prime minister of his neighboring country by saying, "I am not afraid of that *woman.*" In Muslim cultures, the woman is not considered equal to man. But the neighboring country, although it is comprised of many cultures, is mainly a Hindu country. In Hindu cultures, a woman is not considered inferior to man. Thus, a woman could be elected prime minister. Misunderstanding that starts at the cultural level can lead to conflict at the national level.

Is Integration the Answer?

Evidently, different cultures have different value systems. The cultural differences seem to make intercultural communication almost impossible for the lay person. Individuals who would like to communicate effectively have asked how they can communicate with members of strange cultures. The answer always has been to integrate all cultures. For more than two thousand years, conquerors have tried to unify the world under their own flags. Missionaries have tried to convert people of other religions to their own. Recently, some communication specialists have started arguing for a global village. Others have been talking about a universal language. All those attempts, however, have given rise to new countries, new religions, and new communication skills. The old cultures have continued to exist. Some have absorbed values from other cultures and yet have remained distinct. Those distinctive features include values, beliefs, expectations, and customs. These features have affected not only interpersonal communication but also mass communication techniques and processes. Cultures have given rise to many schools of communicative arts. They have helped develop diverse theories of communication. The cultures that have existed for several thousand years have promoted curiosity and inquiry in man. They have added variety and charm to life. Accepting the Nobel prize for literature, Hermann Hesse, the great Swiss novelist, said that his ideal was not the blurring of national characteristics which would lead to intellectually uniform humanity. Diversity in all shapes and colors should live on the earth. The many races, languages, and variety of attitudes should continue to exist. The many wars, conquests, and annexations have destroyed the rich civilizations. Those who simplify cultures do not have any respect for quality craftsmanship and uniqueness of each culture.[1]

We believe that "the diversity of all shapes and colors" continues to exist. Therefore, we do not propose to advocate uniformity of any sort. Instead of suggesting how to dissolve the hundreds of traditional cultures, our purpose here is to accept them as reality. Rather than insisting that others understand us, we will discuss the need to understand them. Instead of teaching how to force others to accept our superiority, we propose that we respect them as equals.

College students have been told for more than a century that Aristotelian rhetoric is the only way to speak effectively with other peoples. For more than a century most Western scholars have virtually ignored the intellectual contributions of non-Western scholars. This is particularly true in the case of communicative arts. Although non-Western scholars have been developing communicative theories and techniques for over two thousand years, Western scholars have not explored these developments and contributions. The propensity of most Western scholars is to restrict their research to the Greek, Roman, and European traditions. When attention of Western scholars is focused on the non-Western cultures, their thrust seems to be aimed at analyzing and identifying ways in which their own values can be imposed on non-Western cultures. Recently, a few Western scholars have tried to analyze in depth the contributions of Asian communications specialists, but there has not been equal treatment of their African counterparts. Even these analyses are generally done in such a way as to show that Western values are superior to non-Western values.

There is a Western intellectual arrogance which is viewed by many non-Westerners as mitigating against a greater understanding of the contributions of non-Western scholars. Western scholars seem to have a tendency to reduce the value of non-Western intellectual contributions when they differ from their own. Questions are now being raised as to the degree of objectivity employed by Western scholars in their academic treatment of non-Western cultures.

What happens when these scholars educate their students? Obviously they transmit their own cultural biases and false sense of cultural superiority to their students. These students then are deficient in their understanding of the substantive contributions of the non-Western scholars. When these students are placed in situations which demand effective intercultural communication, they fail miserably.

Cultural Ways

Clearly, if a person wants to communicate in other cultures, he should develop a new insight into human communicative behavior. He needs to know that other peoples are not like what he thought they were. The most important part of his preparation for interacting with other peoples is to be ready to change his image of them. This is easier said than done. It is not easy for a conservative American politician to accept Asian and African peoples as his equal. It is not easy for an old-fashioned white homemaker to invite her black neighbor to dinner in her home. Nor would it be easy for a black man to perceive his white boss as a person interested in employees of other colors.

A person who is a highly successful communicator in New York can fail miserably in New Delhi because of his ignorance of the cultural ways of the Indian peoples. A white businessman can be perceived as insincere by his black workers if he fails to take into consideration certain cultural factors cherished by the blacks.

He who wishes to be able to communicate should study in detail the process of intercultural communication. A study of the process helps him in three ways: (1) it helps him understand the nature of the variables that affect communication between members of differing cultures; (2) he will know where he should be cautious; and (3) on the basis of his knowledge of the process, he can develop his own communicative skills to interact effectively with members of another culture.

Origins of Intercultural Communication

Although the study of intercultural communication as a discipline is comparatively new in America, elements of it are not new to historians. The enlightened ones such as Goutama Buddha and Jesus Christ, playwrights such as Sophocles and Shakespeare, philosophers such as Aristotle and Socrates, and linguists such as Chomsky and Staal occasionally mentioned the importance of speaking "the other man's" language and adapting our communicative techniques to the audience background.

The dire need for intercultural communication was not felt, however, until our own recent failures in the international scene. For example, the underdeveloped countries that received millions of dollars in foreign aid from the United States voted against the United States and even supported the Soviet Union in international meetings. The poorer countries acted as if they were ungrateful to the United States. International troubleshooters who were sent to other countries by American presidents failed to persuade the other countries to accept American military and economic policies. Heads of some countries even nationalized American businesses that had been flourishing for a long time. Hundreds of American experts were sent to underdeveloped countries to help develop their agriculture and industry, but their advice fell on deaf ears. Failures in communication were not limited to cultures outside the United States. Even within the United States there were problems between the majority and the minority peoples. Here in America, blacks rebelled against whites; Mexicans, Indians, and other minorities as well rose against the white majority.

Indira Gandhi, the Indian prime minister, inaugurating the Asian Industries exhibition in New Delhi in 1972, said, "It is about time we put an end to the Western scholars and scientists using Asians as subjects in their experiments."² Gandhi even refused to issue visas to American scholars who wanted to do research in India. She said the Americans' research findings tended to be biased and to give an inaccurate or wrong picture of Indian life and culture.

White scholars specializing in minority problems began taking another look at their earlier research findings. Black scholars wrote books explaining their views of the communication problem between blacks and whites. A few white scholars suggested bi-dialectalism as the answer to the problem, and such programs were even implemented in several states.* Black intellectuals, however, reacted angrily to such programs. James Sledd said that predators can and do use dialect differences to exploit and oppress, because the ordinary people can be made to doubt their own value and to accept subservience if they can be made to despise the speech of their fathers.³

Early Efforts

The discussions and inquiries resulted in a few universities offering courses in intercultural communication under different titles such as Cross-Cultural Communication, Interracial Communication, Communication and Culture, and Intercultural Communication. Some of the earliest attempts to study this area systematically were made at the University of Hawaii.

For many years in America, speech has been an area of study from grade school up to the university level. Traditionally, it has included Rhetoric, Public Speaking and, in some schools, Oral Interpretation and Storytelling. But these schools and universities had limited their scopes to studies of American, British, and Greek rhetoric and storytelling. A few speech departments have now broadened their progams to include subjects such as communication theory. Other schools have even changed the names of their speech departments to "departments of communication." Professional associations of speech and communication have established divisions of the so-called basic areas of communication: interpersonal communication, mass communication, and organizational communication. Recently some organizations have recognized another main area: intercultural communication.

As a result of efforts by several scholars in this area, the first professional organization was established, the Intercultural Communication Division of the International Communication Association. The first organizational meeting of the Division was held in 1970 at Minneapolis, Minnesota, after which many other professional organizations added in-

---

*A movement designed to teach minority children their own language or dialect along with standard English is referred to as bi-dialectalism.

tercultural divisions to their structures. Today there are more than a dozen organizations in the U.S. devoted to systematic study, research, and training in intercultural communication. Other countries also have organizations focusing on intercultural communication.

International Agencies

We prefer the term "international agencies" to identify the organizations in other countries since most of those have the support of their governments and are subject to their nation's regulations. These organizations are active in diverse fields such as business, communication, economic development, and social service.

UNESCO.   The United Nations has established several organizations of an international nature. The foremost of these is the United Nations Educational, Scientific and Cultural Organization (UNESCO). As early as the 1950s UNESCO conducted several studies of communication and development in other countries. Those included the study of radio rural forums in Canada and India, Teleclubs in France, cultural radio broadcasts in many countries of both East and West, and the feasibility of satellite communications for development of poor nations. UNESCO has a large program to publish books and occasional papers in mass communication.

ITU.   Probably the earliest effort in international communication was the establishment of the International Telegraphic Union (ITU). It was started in 1864 to establish some order in sending messages across countries and to facilitate communication between peoples of different countries. Later, radio and television were also included in the ITU; its name changed to International Telecommunications Union. Today, ITU has more members than the United Nations, suggesting that communication may be more important than the political maneuvering that occurs in the UN. The ITU register of radio and television stations around the world contains information as to the frequency, area of coverage, time of operations, and ownership of the stations. According to the ITU register, there are approximately 20,000 radio and television stations in the world.

Universal postal union (UPU).   The present system of carrying letters has a long history, dating back as far as the days of ancient Egyptians, Chinese, and Romans. Pigeons and other birds have been used as international messengers even in modern times. However, carrying letters between countries was not systematized and legalized until 1874. At the same time, a kind of sanctity was added to the system. A letter addressed to an individual has traditionally been considered the property of the addressee, and it is wrong of another person to open that letter.

The purpose of the UPU is "to secure the organization and improvement of the postal services and to promote in this sphere the development of international collaboration." Like ITU, the UPU is an example of cooperation among nations, here for the purpose of developing the essential service of carrying letters between countries.

INTELSAT. A recent and important effort in international communication has been the establishment of International Telecommunications Satellite Consortium (INTELSAT). INTELSAT is responsible for regulating satellite communications around the globe. One of its purposes is to allot the frequency at which a satellite should operate. The managing company of INTELSAT is the American Communications Satellite Corporation (COMSAT) which was established under a Congressional Act in 1972.

Broadcasting unions. Two very commendable efforts in the area of communication are the European Broadcasting Union (EBU) and the Asian Broadcasting Union (ABU). The purpose of EBU is to coordinate broadcasting in the European countries. It is a sort of European common market in radio-television communication on that continent. ABU membership is more varied than that of EBU. Its purpose is not only common marketing of broadcasting programs among the Asian nations but also cooperation in research, training, and technological exchange in the area of telecommunications.

Two organizations that have done excellent research in identifying cultural variables affecting communication are the British Broadcasting Corporation (BBC) and the Japanese Broadcasting Corporation, or Nihon Hoso Kyokai (NHK). NHK conducts surveys of the effects of broadcasting on the Japanese people. The NHK Radio and Culture Research Center studies several hundred thousand subjects each year. These studies give us valid information on cultural variables that the intercultural communicator should know.

Peace Corps. The American Peace Corps and its counterparts in other countries were established to train volunteers who would go to underdeveloped countries and help those peoples develop their industry, agriculture, education, etc. The volunteers gained valuable experience in intercultural communication. Studies done by objective scholars have shown that many cultural variables affect communication between the volunteers and their host peoples. Although language was an important area of training, only a few volunteers learned the language of their hosts. It has been the experience of the Peace Corps that those volunteers who spoke the native language were most successful in their work. Others were not as successful. There have been instances of volunteers being expelled by the host countries because of unacceptable behavior on the part of those volunteers. While the volunteer's behavior would have been perfectly acceptable in his or her own culture, it was unacceptable in the hosts' culture.

Foreign studies programs. In some universities in the U.S., Afro-Asian-Latino studies programs were established. The purpose of these programs was to educate and train Americans in dealing with peoples of those countries. Most of the students in these programs were members of the foreign service or were planning to go into such services. Faculty members from anthropology, history, philosophy, religion, and other related areas taught in such programs. Basically, they did not include science, industry, and communication arts of the Afro-Asian-Latino peoples.

Cultural exchanges. The U.S. Department of State and its counterparts in other countries established centers of cultural exchange. Although the announced objectives of those centers were to bring peoples of different countries together, the fact that they were sponsored by departments whose main purpose was political, raised doubts in the minds of objective scholars. To make matters worse, the experts that worked in those centers were carefully picked by the departments that sponsored such centers. Few, if any, of the "experts" belonged to any minority group, nor were they the authors of any controversial works. So, even the so-called centers of cultural exchange did not really bring in ideas from foreign cultures. Instead, they generally exported the values and beliefs of the sponsoring department.

Related studies. Some notable studies relating to the area of intercultural communication are by anthropologists such as Herkowitz and Shibutani, psychologists such as Rokeach and Segall, and political scientists such as Pye and Wright. Herkowitz has done many studies on *ethnocentrism* and cultural relativism. We will be using these terms quite often and have defined them later in this book.

Another study worth mentioning here is the one sponsored by Jawaharlal Nehru, who was prime minister of India from 1950 to 1964. Nehru was concerned about the barbaric way in which Hindus and Muslims massacred each other at the time of the partition of British India into the two countries of India and Pakistan. He wanted to find out why human beings, the highest among the creations of God, hated each other so much as to butcher even infants and old men. He commissioned a study conducted by many eminent scholars around the world. The findings of this study are highly relevant to our own discussion in this book.

The Need for Studying Intercultural Communication

The study of intercultural communication is comparatively new. The need for study of this special type of communication was realized after failures in international negotiations, particularly on issues such as the Kashmir problem, the Middle East crisis, the Disarmament Plan, the Nuclear Test Ban Treaty, and the Paris Peace Talks.

There were many blunders in intercultural communication. Host countries asked the American Peace Corps volunteers to leave. When Western businessmen offered to start new industries in African, Asian, and Latin American countries, their offers were rejected. American businessmen abroad were asked by the host-country governments to close down their firms. Some foreign governments nationalized such firms without giving compensation.

Western Solutions to Eastern Problems

In the 1940s many colonial countries became independent. Although these countries were economically poor, the intellectuals and opinion leaders of these new nations knew of their cultural greatness. They did not like Western peoples looking down on them and sometimes humiliating them with labels such as "backward," "underdeveloped," "hungry," "poor," and so on. The newly independent countries expected the Western peoples to confer with them, not dictate; treat them as equals, not inferiors; and to talk to them on their own terms.

But the Western populace, through their political "experts" and economic "specialists," continued labeling the peoples of new nations. They were not sensitive to the feelings of the economically backward but culturally advanced peoples. This communication gap widened in the 1950s as more and more countries became independent. The gap began to crystalize in the 1960s, by which time more than sixty new nations had emerged. The new nations began defying the very governments from which they had obtained political independence and economic aid. This became especially evident when new nations began demanding their rights in international meetings.

To make matters worse, scholars in the West, many times self-styled experts on "underdeveloped" countries, were proposing in the 1950s and sixties their hypothesis on modernizing the traditional peoples. Although the Western scholars said that the traditional countries should modernize, the intellectuals in the new nations soon realized that the suggestions made were Western solutions to Eastern problems. By modernization of the underdeveloped, the self-styled scholars really meant Westernization of the East. In their attempts to modernize the traditional countries, they were imposing the traditional Western ideas on the Eastern cultures. Consequently, their solutions to the problems of the "underdeveloped" countries were DDT for improving agriculture, the pill for the population explosion, and capitalism for democratic practices.

The Eastern intellectuals, in their traditional humbleness, said that probably the Western ideas were not very useful to their people. Their opinion leaders also agreed with them. But the Western "experts" on the "underdeveloped" countries did not understand why their ideas were essentially rejected. They thought that the simple-minded Easterners did not understand the highly advanced ideas. The Western experts continued proposing their hypotheses on the Eastern problems, and the Eastern leaders continued to reject them.

When even the great international troubleshooters failed, and some resigned from their jobs, a few Western scholars began questioning their communication methods. They asked "What did we do wrong?" Ambassador Chester Bowles answered on NBC's *Meet the Press* program: "We should quit labeling the Asian people and try to understand them."[4] Bowles believed that while the American failures in foreign affairs appeared to be political, they were really intercultural.

Everett Kleinjans, the Chancellor of the Honolulu East West Center, proposed that Americans should stop playing God and join the human race. It was time for Americans to rise to a new and higher ethic, a more refined conscience, and a humbler style of relating to other people.[5]

There is indeed a need for the study of intercultural communication. And such a study is needed not solely by Americans but also by peoples of other countries. What Bowles says about labeling the Asians and Kleinjans about a nation's feeling superior applies to non-Western countries also. The Western peoples cannot be blamed entirely for intercultural failures. Many Africans, Asians, and Latin Americans are partly responsible for such misunderstandings, too. In business dealings and diplomatic approaches they have demonstrated their ignorance of intercultural communication techniques. Foreign students attending American universities have been guilty of poor intercultural exchange. Studies have shown that they tend to stereotype, are ethnocentric and unduly nationalistic in their behavior. Although their friendship families in the host countries try to make them feel "at home," the students tend to make a few adaptations to the host culture.

An understanding of intercultural communication, then, is needed by all cultures. Individuals, whether they be citizens of the United States or citizens of another country, should realize that in an intercultural setting, *the communicator should adapt his communication techniques to the culture of the audience with whom he is trying to communicate.*

Approaches to Studying Intercultural Communication

Although it is possible for a person to adapt his communicative techniques to his audience's culture, the reasons he does not do so may not be always the same. In other words, a person's approach to the study and practice of intercultural communication depends upon how he looks at his audience. Does he look at them as a group of people whom he should change whether or not they want to be changed? Does he adapt his communication in order to understand and respect their culture? These questions can be better answered in a discussion of the three approaches to the study of intercultural communication.

As in psychology, three major trends can be identified in intercultural communication. They are the behavioristic approach, the humanistic approach, and the moderate approach.

The Behavioristic Approach

Based on the theories of Pavlov and Skinner, intercultural communication specialists are trying to develop techniques that will help bring about desired changes in the members of other cultures. According to some Western behaviorists, modernization means Westernization of the non-Western. Some of them even go to the extent of saying that the purpose of intercultural communication should be to bring about cultural change even in the minority communities of the same culture so that the minorities adopt the values, beliefs, and expectations of the majority. They feel, for example, that the American black man should adopt the values of the American white man; that the non-beef eater should learn to eat beef.

One psychosocial-behavioral model is based on the following assumptions, which could be applied to most behaviorist approaches:

1. Most human behavior is learned.
2. Behavior can be changed by applying reward-punishment techniques.
3. Since most behavior is learned in a social situation, it is possible to create situations conducive to bringing about desired changes.
4. Creation of mental state is a part of the situation thus created.
5. Mental states could be created by using communcative techniques.
6. Communicative techniques include verbal, nonverbal, and media messages.
7. Using such messages, a desired change, cultural change, for example, could be brought about.

The Humanistic Approach

On the other hand, the humanists' approach to intercultural communication is cognitive. They believe that communicative behavior is not learned. The individual has certain innate abilities that enable him to communicate. Depending upon his abilities, and using the traditional symbols of communication that he has learned, the individual develops his own art of communication. The communicative arts of the individual members of a culture together make up the communicative arts of that culture. It should be possible to understand communicative behaviors intuitively rather than by rigid experimental studies. Such intuition is the result of respect for and understanding of the other culture. The purpose is to study the cultural factors that affect communication.

Communicative art should be developed on the basis of knowledge of cultural factors. In other words, the cognitive approach is to understand the culture of the audience and then adapt communicative skills to that audience culture. This approach implies that the communicator and his audience are partners in the process of communication. Both affect the process. Both communicate with each other, not just one with the other.

The humanists believe that it is necessary to keep the other cultures intact. Social change, if any, should spring from within the culture, not be imposed from outside. Such a change should be relevant to the local culture. It should make use of the local resources and talent. Any change that does not respect the local values and does not utilize the local resources is unnatural and uneconomic. Imposed change is unethical.

Humanists believe that the communicologist does not have the right to use members of another culture to bring about the behavior change that only he desires, not they. The behaviorist apporach of using conditioned stimuli and applying reward-punishment techniques is not acceptable to the traditionalist. Situational variables rather than elicitation techniques are important to him.

The Moderate Approach

The third approach is moderate. It takes the best of both the behavioristic and cognitive approaches. The moderates believe that social change is represented by a continuum. Depending upon their political, economic, and social needs, all cultures change. There is no culture in the world that has not changed. Change is the response to inside and outside stimuli.

Culture change is a result of effective communication. An effective communicator is also a change agent. He studies the needs of a society's people, then tries to bring about change that fulfills those needs. In order to bring about the change he develops, depending upon his innate abilities and learned behaviors, his own art of communication. According to some moderates, several factors contribute to cultural estrangement and alienation among people within highly industrialized and pluralistic societies such as the United States. These estrangements and alienations also cause intra- and intercultural misunderstandings and hatreds.

Whatever the approach of an intercultural communicator, it is imperative that he study the fundamentals of the process of communication between cultures. We shall discuss those fundamentals in this book.

The study of intercultural communication is highly interdisciplinary. If we take a close look at any discipline in this day and age, it does not seem to be entirely independent. Like any other area of the social sciences and humanities, however, intercultural communication deserves to be considered independently, since we can clearly identify more than one approach to its study and practice. Certain variables are clearly intercultural in nature. Not only the overall area of intercultural communication, but also its highly specialized components such as interracial communication could be studied as sub-areas of emphasis.

In the present-day world, peoples of different colors, cultures, and countries must interact. In order to make their interaction easy and meaningful, they should know the basic factors that affect intercultural communication.

Who Should Study Intercultural Communication?

All the peoples of the world should study intercultural communication. Those who must study it are (1) the officials of departments who interact with members of different cultures in their everyday business; (2) the young men and women who aspire to work in such departments; (3) officials of international organizations such as UNESCO and INTELSAT; (4) business organizations which have international operations; (5) educational and religious organizations which have international clientele; and (6) the officials and others of countries other than the United States who must deal with members of different cultures.

Although some of these organizations and individuals therein are presently involved in intercultural settings, their backgrounds reflect their inadequacy in formal education and training in intercultural communication. Others do have training programs, but they are inadequate in the sense that they do not take into consideration the principles we will be discussing in this book.

SUMMARY

Intercultural communication is a whole new approach to the study of human interaction. The way in which people interact reveals a great deal about their cultural identity. People communicate with the hope of fulfilling their cultural expectations. If their expectations are not met, communication breakdowns occur.

Although the ancients did practice intercultural communication, the dire need for an understanding of this area was felt after international failures such as Kashmir, Vietnam, and the Middle East. The need for this understanding was further felt when national leaders in all countries could not solve certain problems between minority and majority groups.

Today, many national and international agencies have been established to deal with the myriad of intercultural problems.

We identify three main approaches to the study and practice of intercultural communication: behavioristic, humanistic, and moderate.

Intercultural communication is needed by all peoples of the world, especially government officials, students, teachers, businessmen, religious leaders, and others who have to interact with people of other cultures.

NOTES

1. Hermann Hesse, "Acceptance Speech," *Nobel Prize Library* (New York: Alexis Gregory, 1971), p. 237.

2. *India News* (Washington: Embassy of India, January 1972).

3. James Sledd, "Bi-Dialectalism," in *Intercultural Communication: A Reader,* ed. Larry Samovar and Richard E. Porter (Belmont, Calif.: Wadsworth, 1972), p. 167.

4. NBC Television Network, "Meet the Press" show, June 1965.

5. Everett Kleinjans, "Kleinjans Calls for Humility," *Honolulu Advertiser,* December 17, 1969, p. c-8.

2

Components of Intercultural Communication

Newspapers in the United States in 1972 printed a news story about Princess Anne of Great Britain. According to the story, she went fox hunting with her boyfriend. One gruesome account described how she enjoyed seeing the hounds get the fox and tear it to pieces. If the story had been read by a girl in Afghanistan, many aspects of it would not make sense to her. First of all, she would not understand how a girl can go out alone with a man who is not her husband. She thinks it is unwomanly for a girl to ride on horseback and go hunting. Even if the man is going to be her husband, the Afghan culture does not approve of a girl's seeing him before marriage.

If the same story is read by a girl in Tibet, she might also be shocked, but for different reasons. The Tibetan girl is a Buddhist. She thinks it is cruel to hunt fox the way the English princess did. Because Buddhism preaches nonviolence, the Tibetan believes that no animal should be treated cruelly. There are other cultural factors as well. Girls are not supposed to ride on horseback. They should not appear in public with men, particularly if they are single. If married, they should stay home. Rarely do girls and women appear in public. It is unheard of for a girl to appear with a man who is not her husband. As in Afghanistan, even if the man is going to be her husband, she should not go out with him before marriage.

The story which originated in Great Britain might shock Afghan and Tibetan cultures, but the behavior it describes is perfectly normal in English and similar cultures.

Let us consider three more examples. A group of Taiwanese students in an American university saw a television show in which a black boy visits his white neighbor who is much older than the black. The boy opens the door, walks in, shakes the hand of the white and sits right next to him.

17

The American students who saw the same scene did not think it was anything special, but the Chinese did not like it. They thought it was unmannerly of the black to sit on a chair right next to an elderly person. In the Chinese culture, younger people show respectful distance rather than sitting with them.

A senior Indian professor was visiting an American university. A young American professor wanted to see him to talk with him about a topic of mutual interest. The American called the Indian at the hotel where he was staying and made an appointment to see him one evening. When the American went to the hotel he saw the other professor in the lounge, and asked the Indian if he might buy him a drink. The Indian declined, and the conversation did not go very well. That was the first and last time the two professors visited each other. The American never understood what went wrong. To him his behavior was perfectly normal in his culture. The Indian, however, did not think so. Although he was used to drinking liquor, he did so only privately, not in a public place like a hotel lounge. Further, he did not like drinking with younger persons. He would take drinks only with professors of his age and status. The Indian therefore took the young American's behavior as an insult.

A white social worker spoke to a black audience. He made statements such as "I have always liked black people," "when I was little, my black mammie used to tell me Uncle Remus stories," and "I want to help you people." The black audience listened to him silently and showed no reaction in their faces. The white speaker did not understand why the blacks showed no enthusiasm. But the blacks knew why. He had made statements that a hundred other "whiteys" had already bored them with. They perceived all whites who used those old clichés as highly insincere.

Defining Intercultural Communication

Intercultural communication is interaction between members of differing cultures, such as the Afghan-English, American-Indian, and black-white. Intercultural communication would be studied under different headings. It could be interethnic, interracial, intracultural, intercultural, or even international. The categorizations depend upon cultural differences and similarities between the interacting members. The study of intercultural communication is obviously highly multidisciplinary. The scope of this broad area can be better understood if we first arrive at acceptable definitions of terms such as culture, communication, and message.

Culture

Anthropologists, sociologists, psychologists, historians, and others have each tried to define culture for their own purposes; what they have not mentioned is the fact that one individual could belong to several types of cultures. What we generally refer to as culture is really the traditional culture of a people. Then there is the youth culture, the national culture, and so on, to which the same person might belong.

The *traditional culture* of a people may be defined as a social system consisting of learned behaviors, artistic traditions, technological achievements, communicative techniques, religious beliefs, philosophical concepts, and even genetic characteristics of that people that are transmitted from generation to generation as their heritage. Culture is developed by a people living in a geographic region to make their life in that region and interaction among themselves easy and meaningful. Culture changes slowly but gradually depending upon the needs of its people. Learned behaviors include factors such as values, beliefs, expectations, and customs. Artistic traditions are the different schools of dance, drama, music, painting, and architecture. Technological achievements include tools such as tractors, automobiles, and computers. Religious beliefs are the faiths peoples have in God, salvation, sin, and punishment. Philosophical concepts deal with the individual's relationship with his fellow man, nature and God. Genetic characteristics are the biological variables such as color of skin, width of eyes, and straightness of hair. Several traditional cultures might exist in the same nation, but there will be only one national culture.

The *national culture* of a people may be defined as a system of values, beliefs, expectations, and customs of the people of a particular nation. National value systems are determined by political leaders, economic experts, and military strategists of the nation. For example, although the United States is a secular democracy, its national values support dictatorships in Spain and Portugal and kingships in Thailand and England.

National culture is not static; in fact, it changes several times in the lifetime of an individual citizen of that nation while his traditional culture might remain the same. While the traditional cultures of Americans and Canadians are not much different from each other, their national cultures are certainly different. Traditional cultures of several East Asian peoples are not much different from each other, but their national cultures are far apart. It is well known that most Western traditions are derived from ancient Greco-Roman and Judeo-Christian cultures. Those of East Asia originated from Confucian-Mahayana Buddhist cultures. The cultures of South and Southeast Asia have their roots in Hindu-Hinayana Buddhist cultures. Middle-Eastern cultures are mostly Muslim. The more than one hundred and fifty nations that exist in these areas of West and East, however, have an equal number of national cultures.

Political and other national situations change more rapidly than religious and other traditions. Until 1972, communism was of negative value in the United States. That year, President Nixon visited Communist China and the Soviet Union. The two communist nations came closer to the United States. Until the President's visit Americans knew little about Communist China. Then, American mass media began giving more and accurate information about Chinese medicine, commune system, farming techniques, and other aspects of everyday life in that nation. Several missions of scholars, students, and politicians were sent by the American government to Communist China. Many businessmen and scholars took crash courses in Chinese studies to become overnight specialists on Chinese business. Some medical doctors approved acupuncture as a method of treatment in American clinics.

Although the changes in American national values were due to political and economic demands, communication played an effective role in bringing the changes. A study conducted at the University of Hawaii showed that the live satellite television coverages of the Nixon visit to Communist China were mainly responsible for changing several negative stereotypes of Chinese people to more positive ones.[1]

Communication

Communication has been defined differently by different specialists. Some of them have developed models to explain the process of communication. We shall consider a few definitions and models to help us define intercultural communication.

The mathematical model.   This model is also known as the Shannon and Weaver model, and is often referred to as the Information Theory. Shannon and Weaver focus on the mechanical and mathematical aspects of communication process. They are concerned with the quality and quantity of information that is transmitted from one point to another. They explain the concept of communication; the word *communication* includes all the methods by which one mind may affect another. It also includes techniques by means of which one mechanism affects another mechanism.[2]

According to Shannon and Weaver, five elements are involved in the process: (1) information source; (2) transmitter; (3) channel; (4) receiver; and (5) destination. In the case of a television newscast, the newsreader is the information source. He collects, edits, writes, and reads the news that goes on the air. Although many others contribute to the newscast, it is the newsreader who could be considered the main source of information. Television cameras, audio and video controls, multiplexers, and finally the transmitter make up the second element in the process. This equipment transforms the light and sound energy that originate in the television studio—the newsreading in this case—into electromagnetic energy, or signals, as Shannon and Weaver call them. The signals are sent into space over a particular frequency. In the case of television, space is the channel.

The television set at home is the receiver. The person who watches the newscast is the destination. According to Shannon and Weaver's definition of the term *communication*, destination is also the target of behavior change.

Concept of information. Probably the most important part of Shannon and Weaver's theory is their concept of Information.* The term Information is explained in mathematical terms, hence the other name for the theory: Mathematical Theory of Communication. According to Shannon and Weaver the word Information is not the same as what we normally refer to as information. Their concept of Information includes everything that is transmitted on a channel and received by the destination. It includes both signals and noise. Signals are the intended bits of information and noise are the unintended bits. Unintended bits could originate anywhere in the chain between transmitter and receiver. These may be due to static, mechanical, or manmade interference.

When a certain quantity of information or a certain number of words and pictures are transmitted on television they get mixed up with static and other noises. The channel that is capable of transmitting all that noise can also transmit the same quantity of signals providing the communicator and transmitter are working at optimum capacity. However, the mixing up of noise creates uncertainty about the information that is intended to be received at the destination. The person who watches television is also the destination of communication. He finds it hard to decide which is signal and which is noise, nor can he coordinate the signals that make sense to him. Mathematically speaking, if the information source tries to transmit 100 words and pictures and only 80 words and pictures are accurately understood by the destination, then we can say the signal-to-noise ratio is 8:2. Although 100 bits are seen and heard, only 80 percent make sense to one person. To another person the ratio could be 9:1.

Clearly, the main concern of the mathematical model seems to be the technical problem of communication or the accuracy with which the quantity of intended information is transmitted from information source to its destination. Shannon and Weaver talk about problems of precision with which information is transmitted and the effect the transmitted information has on the receiver, but they do not really offer solutions to problems.

Nonetheless, the Shannon and Weaver definition of communication and their concept of Information are important to the study of intercultural communication. If the information source and destination belong to different cultures, how much of the intended information is received by the destination? Is received information interpreted the way it is intended

---

*Note the use of capital "I" for the Shannon and Weaver concept of information.

to be interpreted? Does the amount of uncertainty depend upon the cultures of the source and destination? These are just a few of the unanswered questions.

A second definition of communication which is important for our purpose is that of Raymond Ross. According to Ross, communication is the process of creating meaning in the minds of audience. It involves the sorting, selecting, and sending of symbols by a communicator whose purpose will be to recreate in his audience's mind an image that he has in his own mind.[3]

Creation of meaning. Ross qualifies his definition by this statement: "We now see why seemingly obvious meanings (in *our* minds) are often distorted or misunderstood by others. Perhaps this is what is meant when we hear the saying, 'One cannot teach a man what he does not already know,' and perhaps this better explains the old teaching rule of 'Go from the known to the unknown.' "[4]

According to Ross, the communicator has a certain image in his mind and he intends to create the same image in the minds of his audience. To do so, he selects a few symbols from a number that he has in mind. He sends the selected symbols to his audience. The purpose of sorting, selecting, and sending symbols is to create the same image in the minds of his audience. Here again we have the problem of uncertainty. What happens if the symbols used by the communicator are not the same as those used by his audience? Also, are communication symbols, such as spoken words, the same as the images that Ross is talking about? Imagine a situation where the communicator is an American diplomat. He speaks the English language that he has learned in his culture. He tries to communicate with diplomats from North Vietnam who have learned their language in their own culture. Would the American diplomat succeed in creating the intended image in the Vietnamese mind? Even if he used an interpreter, would he succeed in creating the intended image?

Another problem in intercultural communication is that the sender and receiver of symbols do not use the same symbols for communication. When a man from Sri Lanka speaks he uses Sinhalese and the meanings he has in his mind are created in Sri Lanka using the Sinhalese language. That language was developed to make the interaction among Sri Lankayites meaningful. But when an American speaks to him he speaks the English which is supposed to help the Americans interact. When members of these two cultures speak, can each of them really create the intended meanings in the minds of the other? Let us consider the following examples of problems in creation of meaning.

At the University of Hawaii campus, an American and a Sri Lanka student were talking. The conversation went like this:

"Where are you from?"

"I am from Sri Lanka."

"Are you the only student here from that country?"

"No, there are some Tamils also."

"What city are you from?"

"I am from Candy, you know, where the Temple of Tooth is."

The question and answer session continued. The two young men thought that they were communicating. The way the American was asking questions, it was obvious he did not know much about Sri Lanka. Finally he asked:

"What is your name?"

"Gunavardhane."

"That is a nice name."

The American was trying to be nice to the foreign student. But Gunavardhane knew that the American could not even pronounce his name, so what nice thing did he see in it?

On the other hand, Gunavardhane used some words whose meanings only he knew: Tamils, Temple of Tooth and Sri Lanka.

The point is, the two young men thought that they were communicating, but they were not. The meanings they had in their minds, even when they were speaking the English language, were not the same.

In another situation, when a white man says, "childhood is the best time in life; carefree, with no worries," he probably has in mind those beautiful days of weekend picnics, birthday presents, rides in daddy's brand new station wagon and playing with dolls and bicycles. But what does a black child think of? Ethel Waters remembers her childhood days in the Philadelphia slums. She grew up in an alley, just off Clifton Street, where prostitution was legal. It was in the center of a vice and crime area.[4]

Although the Ross definition does not resolve these problems and other questions related to intercultural communication, it has some value. It helps us develop an acceptable definition.

Meaning in the mind. A third definition that is also important for our purpose is that of Dean Barnlund. Barnlund says that communication is the act of manipulating symbols in order to create meanings in the mind of an audience. His is a meaning-centered philosophy.

Barnlund's concept of the act of communication seems to have bearing on intercultural communication. Meanings are in the minds of the communicator and his audience of the other culture. These meanings have much to do with their cultures: their values, arts, technology, philosophy and communicative symbols. The meaning that a communicator tries to create might not exist in the minds of his audience. The members of the audience have a different cultural experience. Their values, beliefs, arts, technology and even the communication symbols are not the same as those of their communicator. Symbols are designed to create the types of images that make sense in that culture. When an American says, "Today I had dinner with my family," he has in his mind the images of his electric kitchen, dinner table, plates, cups, silver, salad, dressing, meat, coffee, etc. If a farmer from Ceylon hears this, the picture he imagines is entirely different. To a Ceylonese, family means not only his wife and children but also his parents, grandchildren, uncles, aunts, brothers, sisters, and many others. For cooking, his family uses firewood. They eat on banana leaves. Their dinner consists of rice, curry, buttermilk, and hot pickles. They eat with their hands. Applying the Barnlund definition of communication, the American fails to communicate with the Ceylonese farmer when he says merely "Today I had dinner with my family." He will be able to create the image he has in mind only if he precedes his statement with an elaborate explanation of where, what and how they eat.

Audience: active participants. The definitions directly or indirectly emphasize the role of communicator and the bits of information that he tries to transfer to the audience whose behavior he wants to affect. The focus is on the images or meanings he wants to create in the minds of his audience. These definitions fail to emphasize the most important factor: the lack of commonality of bits of information or images or meanings. These are not the same for both the communicator and his audience. Also, communication is not a one-way process. The definitions imply that the audience is the receiver, or destination, of information. According to the definitions discussed earlier, audiences are merely objects whose minds are in the hands of the communicator and he can create any image or meaning that he wishes. The audience is at the mercy of the communicator, and he should be ethical in his attempts to use their minds. Another factor that is casually mentioned but not emphasized in the definitions is the act of understanding. The commonality we mentioned above depends, in fact, upon the understanding between two persons trying to communicate.

Hence, human communication is the process by which one person tries to stimulate the mind of another person. The stimulation results in a combination of bits of information* that are stored in the mind of that other person. The combination of information activated by the stimulus sender is not the same in all receivers, since each person stores different bits of information depending upon his cultural experience. It is possible, however, that a certain stimulus activates a certain combination, or a combination with certain common factors, in the majority of members of a culture since those members have common experiences. Another variable

---

*The term *information* used here is the same as the *signals* explained by Shannon and Weaver, or the meanings of Ross and Barnlund, or any memories of sound, sight, smell, touch, and taste.

that determines the nature of the combination is the situation in which the stimulus is sent. The same stimulus could activate different combinations in different situations. It is not like a computer that gives a certain output for a certain input at all times. Since individuals selectively accept or reject information, the output of each is unique.

Human communication is either intuitive or interactive. It is intuitive when the individual thinks or stimulates his faculties without the aid of any external stimulus. Individuals such as the yogis turn their senses inward and meditate; they understand things intuitively. In all cultures certain things are understood by intuition. Communication is interactive when the individual is stimulated by an external source. Activation of memory by an external source could involve one or many individuals. Interaction can also be intuitive, since two or more individuals can understand each other intuitively.

Understanding. The question is, then, how are new bits of information stored in men's minds? We cannot yet make a scientific statement. It seems, however, that each individual in any culture begins with a certain store of information and as he grows up he builds upon that base. It is like constructing new chemical compounds using the same elements. The individual and outside sources act as catalysts to activate the store of information. The aim of activation is *understanding.* We say two persons understand each other when one person activates a certain combination of expected information in another person by using a certain stimulus. In the earlier example of the American businessman and the Ceylonese farmer, the two did not understand each other because they were unable to activate common information.

Definition of communication. In an intercultural situation, understanding depends upon the intellectual levels and life experiences of the persons who are interacting. There can be several levels at which a communicator and an audience send and receive messages. Consider, for example, a Hindu philosopher talking with an American businessman. Each knows his own field very well but is not very familiar with the other person's field. The Hindu is talking about the profits a person can gain by doing good deeds, and is probably talking in terms of what the self can acquire as good Karma for its next reincarnation. The American is probably understanding it in terms of good business practice. On the other hand, if the American says that good business yields good profits, the Hindu probably understands at a different level. We can explain the different levels of communication with the aid of the figure 1.

Although different levels of understanding can occur even in intracultural situations, the probability is greater in intercultural situations. Often, however, the interacting persons will end their conversation think-

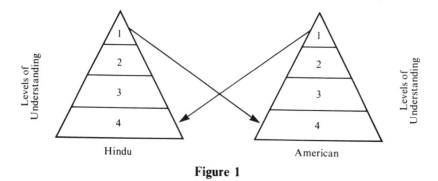

Figure 1

ing that they have understood each other. In the example, the Hindu and the American may go home believing they have understood each other, but in fact, each has reinforced his own ideas and neither has gained any new information.

The above discussion points out one very important variable in the entire process of human communication: understanding. Thus, we can define human communication as *the act of understanding, and being understood by, the audience. Intercultural communication is the act of understanding, and being understood by, an audience of another culture.*

Satisfactory communication also relies upon the attention span of the audience. Attention span is a function of the power of stimulus and selectivity of the receiver. But when does communication begin and when does it end? If we accept the concept that it begins with the sending of stimulus, it should logically end when the stimulus reaches the destination. We can say that the process of communication begins when a person sends his message or stimulus to another person and the process ends when the message activates a certain combination of bits of information in the mind of the other person. It is possible that the message never reaches the other person or, even if it reaches him, does not activate the expected combination of information. In such cases we say that communication was not successful. But once a message reaches the intended person, we can say that communication has taken place.

Message and intention. A message is the actual stimulus or signal that is sent by a communicator to his audience. It is the actual physical product that is received by an audience. It is the actual physical product that is received by an audience. In the case of a television newscast or commercial message, what is actually seen and heard on the television screen is the message. We have heard the saying, "Did you get the message?" In this case, the word "message" is equated with the intention of message sender. In our definition, however, intention is not the same as message.

This definition is particularly important in intercultural communication, for the intention with which a message is sent to an audience of another culture may be unfulfilled because of inefficient encoding. Even if the encoding is efficiently done, the message may fail to elicit the intended response for several cultural reasons. In any case, we say the message has reached the intercultural audience when the actual physical product, or information, reaches the audience.

Encoding. We say a message is encoded when a person puts his ideas, thoughts, or intentions in the form of spoken words, television pictures, or nonverbal gestures. When the spoken words are heard, pictures seen, or gestures noticed by the intended audience, the message has been received and communication has occurred. The success of communication and fulfillment of the communicator's intention is a different matter. *Intention is not the same as message.*

We defined intercultural communication as the act of understanding and being understood by an audience of another culture. We also mentioned that there are different levels of cultural difference. Depending upon the levels of such differences, we can classify at least five types of communication: intracultural, interethnic, interracial, intercultural, and international communication,[6] as demonstrated in figure 2.

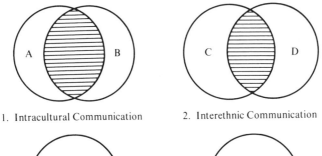

1. Intracultural Communication   2. Interethnic Communication

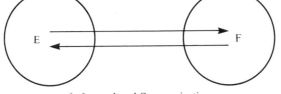

3. Intercultural Communication

Shaded areas in figures 1 and 2 show cultural similarities between A-B and C-D while figure 3 shows that E and F are culturally apart.

Figure 2

Intracultural Communication

Intracultural communication is the type of communication that takes place between members of the same dominant culture, but with slightly differing values. Some white people in the southern United States believe that blacks are inferior to whites, so they treat blacks as inferiors. This one value—that the black is inferior—sets off a series of beliefs, expectations and customs. The white man believes the black man is less intelligent because of his inferiority. The black is expected to behave as such. He should be subservient to the white man, eat in separate restaurants, refuse to marry white women, and even go to separate schools. Many well-meaning Christians sincerely believe that the black is made inferior by God Himself. Brahmins of Hindu cultures believe that harijans are not equal to them. Upper classes of Japan have for ages treated Burakumins as untouchables. Even in Hawaii, native Hawaiians have been treated as inferiors by the other ethnic groups living in the islands.

Among the majority of people in all cultures, however, there are sizable groups that do not believe anyone is inferior merely because of the color of his skin or the nature of his profession. The values of these majority groups differ from those who believe in inferiority of minorities. In addition to class values, the groups may have other differences, such as speech accent. We classify these differing groups among the majority classes, or even the minority classes, that have one or two differing values as subcultures. In these cases cultural differences are not wide enough to classify them as different cultures. Communication between members of such subcultures is *intracultural communication*. The factors that affect such communication are the one or two cultural values that differ from group to group.

Interethnic Communication

Interethnic communication is the interaction between members of different ethnic groups. Ethnicity is the result of geographic origin of the minorities of a country or culture. Although Japanese living in California, Chinese in San Francisco, Mexicans in Texas, Poles in Cleveland, or Jews in New York are full-fledged citizens of the United States, the majority of Caucasian Americans do not consider them parts of the majority culture. The minorities are deliberately identified by the country they came from. While a Caucasian from England or Scandinavia is still called an American, one from Poland is Polish American or, simply, a Polack, and one from Japan is Japanese American or, simply, Japanese. The fact that certain minorities are classified by the geographic origin of their forefathers makes a difference in their social status. These differences affect communication between the majority and the ethnic minorities or among the minorities themselves.

A Chinese-American applied for a position as a reference librarian in an American univeristy. His credentials were excellent by all standards, but he did not get the job. The reason given by the university administrators (who were white Americans) was that "he is too quiet." In the Chinese culture, quietness and respect for superiors, in this case the university administrator, is considered an important value; therefore, the Chinese was purposefully quiet. The university adminstrator, however, misinterpreted this quietness as incompetence and non-aggressiveness. Hence, some aggressiveness on the part of the Chinese and some insight into the Chinese culture on the part of the white administrator would have resulted in better interethnic communication.

Ethnic differences lead to discrimiotory actions against the minorities. Sometimes the minorities' patriotism is questioned. An example is the special laws enacted by the United States Congress during World War II to put japanese Americans in concentration camps. Spark Matsunaga, a Congressman from Hawaii, has said:

> Otherwise known as the Emergency Detention Act, Title II of the Internal Security Act of 1950 has been a source of considerable irritation to me since I learned about it because I believe that it violates the constitutional guarantees and judicial traditions that are basic to our American way of life.
>
> Although it has not been invoked since its enactment, it looms as an ominous threat to those who engage in legitimate inquiries into some of the values and assumptions of our society.
>
> This statute disturbs me for the further reason that its genesis can be traced to the tragic experiences of Americans of Japanese ancestry in World War II, an experience which most Americans now agree was unnecessary and unwarranted.
>
> To Japanese Americans, who were incarcerated in America's concentration camps during World War II, this travesty of justice is one which they fervently hope will never be visited upon any other American, indivudually or as a member of any classifiable group.[7]

Because of social or legal actions against them by the majority group, the ethnic minorities cluster together and fight for their rights as well as for their survival. The fact that certain minorities are different from the majority in physical features, and especially in language, as in the case of Japanese Americans, Chinese Americans and Filipino Americans, does affect communication. Again, as Matsunaga has said:

> Ironically, those responsible for that mass internment suspected only persons of Japanese ancestry. Others whose racial strains were traceable to nations

with whom the United States was also at war were not deemed to be sub-
versive such as to require group incarceration . . . .

It is not surprising, therefore, that the Japanese American Citizen League, a
national organization with chapters in 39 states, is found in the forefront of
the drive to repeal a law which, if enforced would inevitably lead to repetition
of that wartime blunder.[8]

A Universal Problem

The problem of ethnic minorities is not limited only to the United
States. It is the problem of all countries that imported laborers, skilled
workers, accountants and intellectuals to work on their farms, in industries, businesses, and schools. Although Hawaiians are the minority
now in their own land, more than one hundred years ago they imported
laborers from China, Japan, Korea and other Asian countries, thus inviting, along with the Asians, several ethnic problems as well. Today,
West Germany is so highly industrialized that it needs the kind of laborers that cannot be found among Germans. Germany has thus imported so-called foreign workers from Italy, Greece, Turkey, Yugoslavia and other European countries. There are now more than two-
and-a-half million foreign workers in Germany. The majority of native
Germans do not consider the foreign workers their equals. This is vividly
described by the following newspaper report:

> For years these people have been looked upon as no more than human pro-
> duction machines to do the jobs that the more affluent local worker has been
> unwilling to do. They have been just about tolerated as a temporary and nec-
> essary evil.
>
> If it had not been for the foreign workers, our economy would not have
> reached the stage where it is looked upon with respect all over the world. If it
> were not for the foreign workers, many sections of our society, ranging from
> refuse disposal to the hospital, would collapse.
>
> But most foreigners remain second class citizens. They have none of the nor-
> mal citizen's voting rights, they are treated like lepers by a certain section of
> the population and often exploited by unscrupulous landlords.
>
> Their children enter a vicious circle that can prove fateful. They are not given
> enough help at school and a Munich municipal development adviser forecast
> that they will form a large semiliterate group in years to come, a late indus-
> trial proletariat.[9]

African countries also have their own ethnic problems. Kenya,
Uganda and other black African countries that imported businessmen,
engineers, teachers, and other skilled and intellectual workers, have
sizable minorities which the majority blacks do not tolerate. In Uganda

in 1972, the government expelled many minority persons after confiscating their properties. In this case the problem is not only that of ethnic origin but also of racial factors, such as skin color and facial features.

Ethnic problems have their origins in politics also. In countries such as Great Britain, which had colonized Asian, African, and American countries, there are large minorities of peoples from those colonies. These minority peoples have immigrated to Britain. In London, it is not uncommon to see Englishmen of Asian, African and American origin walking side by side with native Englishmen. These English minorities have the same communication and other problems that are faced by the Asians of Uganda, Negroes of America and Philippinos of Hawaii.

A Problem among Minorities

Discrimination is not the monopoly of the majority people in a culture. Even among minorities there are levels of discrimination. Some Japanese of Hawaii believe they are superior to native Hawaiians and the other minorities. The Japanese think Hawaiians are less intelligent, less aggressive and less interested in public affairs. Hawaiians are expected to accept that and to act inferior to the other groups.

Although ethnic groups belong to the same overall culture and adopt many values and beliefs of that culture, some values are still derived from their parent cultures. Thus, each ethnic group has some values that are common to all the other ethnic cultures around them and other values that are unique to their group only. Among Mexican Americans, respect for elders still seems to be a unique value. Such unique values are closely guarded, thus distinguishing their ethnic groups from other surrounding cultures. These differences affect communications between the minorities and the majority on the one hand and among the minorities on the other. Some of the ethnic differences can also be racial.

A case study done in Hawaii shows how ethnic beliefs cause misunderstandings between two ethnic groups. It involved Ellen, a Chinese girl aged seventeen, who was pregnant. Her boy friend, aged twenty, was a Filipino. Her parents would not permit her to marry a Filipino. Ellen's mother thought that Filipinos were the lowest people on the Hawaiian social strata. Even a Hawaiian or a Portuguese man would be more acceptable. The family's reputation would be disgraced if her daughter married a Filipino.[10]

The reason Ellen's mother, Mrs. Quon, eventually gave permission for the marriage is also of interest to our discussion. In traditional Chinese families, it is the mother who arranges her children's marriages with the aid of matchmakers and priests. The mother is responsible for the daughter's conduct. In this case, the mother had assumed that responsibility. Because of the traditional Chinese prejudice against the Filipinos, it was not easy for young Ellen to communicate with her mother.

Interracial Communication

The racial problem is not a recent one. It is as old as the *Vedas* and the *Bible.* We read about the roots of racial conflicts in these books. The *Rig Veda,* for example, is full of stories of how the Aryan race conquered and destroyed the culture of another race that lived in the Indus valley. Aryans called the Indus valley people *dasyus* because they were of a different color, spoke a different language and worshipped strange gods. Dasyu is a derogatory term in Sanskrit, the language of Aryans, used to identify people at very low levels of the social strata. The Indus valley people who survived the Aryan destruction moved to the south. Even today the people of south India do not have a soft corner in their hearts for those of the north, but they do not know that their dislike has its roots in racial conflict that occurred more than 4000 years ago.

> The Dasas (dasyus) are described as dark and ill-favored, bull-lipped, snub-nosed, worshippers of the phallus, and of strange speech.[11]
>
> As they settled among the darker aboriginals the Aryans seem to have laid greater stress than before on purity of blood, and class divisions hardened, to exclude those Dasas who had found a place on the fringes of Aryan society, and those Aryans who had intermarried with the Dasas and adopted ways. Both these groups sank in social scale.[12]

Evidently the racial conflicts today possess all the features of the Aryan-Dasa fights.

Physical Features: Basis for Discrimination

When the Dutch sailor Tasman reached the shores of the Pacific islands now called Tasmania, he found a people that was dark and very different from himself. The white man thought the natives were ugly and not equal to the whites. There are gruesome stories of how the white man tried to destroy the natives that were often called the Tasmanian devils.[13] Even now Australia is the white-man's land.

In America blacks are discriminated against by whites. But whites do not have a monopoly on discrimination against blacks. Some blacks discriminate against each other. The basis blacks use to discriminate against each other is in degrees of likeness to the white man. That is, the more a black looks like a white man the more favor is bestowed upon him. He enjoys higher social and ecnomic status among other blacks. Whites give him preferred employment within the realm of those jobs traditionally available to nonwhites. The dark masses are heaped with scorn and disdain by both whites and so-called light-skinned Negroes. In a sense, the light-skinned Negroes are used as a buffer between the white ruling class and the black masses. The best analogy can be seen in Fanon's statement that the white man had the word; the others had the use of it. He even manufactured the native elite. This was done by picking out the most promising adolescents from among the natives.[14]

Today, in some black communities, it is the opposite, that is, the blacker a person is the more favored he is. A black with light skin does not enjoy the status formerly accorded him. When a white person tries to interact with a black person, chances are that he communicates favorably with a black with lighter skin. On the other hand, when a black person interacts with another black person, he would react favorably to a person with blacker skin. Consequently, the intellectual and meritorious qualities of a black person are virtually ignored while the shade of his skin color assumes priority.

Sammy Davis, a black comedian, writes of an incident that occurred when he was in the United States army. He recalls standing in line to use the wash basin. The soldier in front of him finished, and Davis moved to the basin. A huge Texan grabbed him and pushed him back, saying, "Where I come from, niggers stand in the back of the line." Davis angrily hit him—so hard that blood shot out of his mouth. Wiping the blood away with a towel, the Texan said, "But you are still a nigger."[15]

That scorn, "but you are still a nigger," has been heard by many blacks who have risen up the ladder as Sammy Davis did. Even when persons of the so-called lower races climb the ladder, the so-called upper race does not treat them as equals. The moment a person of another race appears, the entire communicative behavior of most people changes.

The Germans under Hitler hated the Jews because Germans of Aryan extraction thought Jewish people were inferior to the Aryans. That gave them reason to hate them. They believed Jewish people were not worth living on this earth, and even invented methods of executing Jews in large numbers.

Definition of race.   When a highly scientific people such as the Germans say that another people are inferior, the question arises: is there any basis for saying that one race is inferior to another? Is there any scientific evidence to support the argument that Jews are inferior to Aryans or that blacks are inferior to whites, or that any one race is inferior to another?

To answer these questions, we must go into some details of the genetic characteristics that distinguish one people from another. J.B.S. Haldane defines race as:

a group whose members shared a certain set of inborn physical characters and a geographical orgin within a certain area.[16]

Richard A. Goldsby's more detailed definition is that a race is a breeding population characterized by particular gene frequencies which are different from those of other populations of the same species.[17]

In 1963, UNESCO, recognizing that racism is an important phenomenon among human beings and should be examined, made some efforts to study the phenomenon. The studies took into account scientific and other evidence and came up with the following declaration on race:

1. Scientists are generally agreed that all men belong to a single species, Homo sapiens, and are derived from a common stock, even though there is some dispute as to when and how human groups diverged from this common stock.
2. Some of the physical differences between human groups are due to differences in hereditary constitution and some differences in environments in which they have been brought up.
3. national, religious, geographical, linguistic, and cultural groups do not necessarily coincide with racial groups.
4. Broadly speaking, individuals belonging to major groups of mankind are distinguishable by virtue of their physical characters, but individual members, or small groups belonging to different races within the same major group are usually not so distinguishable.
5. Studies within a single race have shown that both innate capacity and environmental opportunity determine the results of tests of intelligence and temperament, though their relative importance is disputed.
6. The scientific material available to us at present does not justify the conclusion that inherited genetic differences are a major factor in producing the differences between cultures and cultural achievement of different peoples or groups.
7. There is no evidence for the existence of so called "pure" races. In regard to race mixture, the evidence points to the fact that human hybridization has been going on for an indefinite but considerable time.
8. We wish to emphasize that equality of opportunity and equality in law in no way depend, as ethical principles, upon the assertion that human beings are in fact equal in endowment.[18]

Although some geneticists do not agree with the sixth point of the UNESCO declaration, the others cannot be easily challenged. Evidence shows that genetic differences do affect cultural achievements of peoples. The way people of certain genetic characteristics produce sounds is not the same as the way others produce it. Although this aspect of genetic characteristics and language development in man has not been extensively studied, there is some evidence to suggest a relationship between the two phenomena. One geneticist says that a person's teeth, mouth, throat, and nasal cavities affect his speech. These genetically determined characteristics affect evolution of the speaker's language. The language of Eurasian people is also linked to the 0-blood group.[19]

Even one people's concept of beauty differs from that of another. Physical features of one race are beautiful to that race, particularly when that race has not interacted at all with another.

Genes as media of communication. In order to understand the definitions and explanations put forth here, it seems necessary to go into further details of genetics. The tiny living cells in the human body are made up of several complicated chemical compounds. Among them is deoxyribonucleic acid (DNA). DNA makes up the extremely minute units called genes. Genes are lined up on the tape-like structures commonly known as chromosomes. Each living being has a specific number of chromosomes in his living cells. Man has twenty-three pairs of chromosomes. One of these pairs is involved in sex differentiation at the time of conception. Although the number of chromosomes are the same for all races—blacks, browns, whites, and others—the composition of gene groups is different. Since chromosomes are passed from parent to child, genes are passed along with chromosomes. Several biological and behavioral traits of the parents are transmitted to the child in the form of genes. Thus, genes act as "media" of communication between generations. Since genes carry hereditary traits, the child is similar to its parents, but not identical. The members of a race have similar genes and therefore have similar physical features, but no two of them are identical because they do not have the same gene combination. Further, certain traits are common to the majority of members of a race, while certain others are individualistic. These common genetic characteristics include finger prints, urine composition, blood type, and ability to taste a chemical called PTC (phenylthiocarbamide).[20]

Communication and inheritance. Geneticists also argue that if other characteristics are inherited, why not behavior also? Some of them go to the extent of saying that even intelligence is inherited. On the basis of intelligence tests, some of those geneticists conclude that peoples of certain races are inferior to certain others. These findings have been questioned. Geneticists who argue for inheritance of intelligence gave examples of illustrious families that have consistently produced intelligent persons, while their challengers give examples of individuals born into families of relatively low intelligence who have become intellectual giants. One indisputable fact, however, is that behaviors practiced for generations become deeprooted in the genes of members of a race and the behaviors are then genetically transferred. Even certain communicative behaviors are inherited. It is not easy to unlearn hereditary behaviors that have been transferred through the generations for thousands of years.

Communicability—both verbal and nonverbal—have been developed by races as a survival mechanism in their environment. Some of these communicative behaviors have become instinctive. Inherited communicative traits of one race can differ from those of another. Communication related to blackness, brownness or whiteness of a race living in one culture could become so biologically inbred that only members of that race could interact in a particular way.

Concept of beauty. A woman's beauty, which is biological, also seems to be racial. A person's height, shape of lips, width of eyes, size of breasts, and other biological features of a race seem to determine the concept of women's beauty in that racial culture. A study of the judgment of beauty of Nigerian blacks compared with both blacks and whites of America has shown:

> . . . standards for judgment of female facial beauty are essentially cultural in character.[21]

> . . . there is essentially a single cultural standard in polyracial American society for the judgment of female facial beauty: namely, the Caucasion facial model.[22]

> . . . Apparently the Africans find the more Negroid features more attractive than do American whites . . . .[23]

The above study also showed that blacks of the United States considered Caucasion features more beautiful than Negroid. It is probably because of the change in environment from Negroid Africa to Caucasoid America. A change in environment may also result in a change in biological and other characteristics. When members of a race immigrate to a different environment, continued stay in the new environment causes changes in genetic characteristics of those members. Also, changes in their environment may cause genetic changes in members of the same race. A girl in an African tribe might be light skinned, unlike the other members of her race. A Japanese boy in Tokyo might grow taller than anyone else in his community. A Chinese American girl in San Francisco might have eyes wider than her Chinese friends. These changes are called mutations. Mutations also affect the communicative behavior of the individual with others and of the others with the mutant.

When a black cannot communicate with a white, one reason can be his genetic features. The moment a person notices that another person is genetically different, his entire communicative behavior may change in comparison to his behavior with one of his own race. In Japan, there are separate tourist buses for foreign tourists. In China, people of other races have been identified as "foreign devils." Even in Hawaii, the so-called Aloha state, it is not uncommon to notice communication problems between peoples of the several races that live there. Most students in foreign universities have the common experience of sitting alone in restaurants while the local people avoid the foreign face.

This discussion is intended to show that interracial communication is affected mainly by genetic characteristics that are racial in origin. Cultural differences in this kind of communication are more intense than in a case of intracultural or interethnic communication.

Intercultural Communication

Intercultural communication is interaction between members of entirely differing cultures. The value systems of the interacting members are so different from each other that even when one is sincere in trying to communicate, the other may find it hard to perceive him correctly. Let us consider the following examples.

An American businessman is interested in investing in the oil business in Iran. All his life, he has done business only with Americans. Now he flies to Teheran to meet his Iranian counterparts. When he meets them and tries to interact with them, he finds it impossible, because of the strange customs he notices. The Iranis also fail to do business because of the strange way the American behaved. They know of other Americans who conduct themselves very well and do business successfully. But what about this particular American?

A French movie maker who has great respect for Eastern philosophy decides to produce a documentary on India. He goes to that country, talks with people, reads a lot, and sees places. He is fascinated by the variety of life and richness of culture, but is surprised by the ignorance and poverty of the Indians. Finally he makes a series of films on India. When the documentary is shown, the Indians are upset. Although the documentary is supposed to be an artistic reflection of real life, the Frenchman's documentary is called biased. The documentary is banned by the Indian government. Despite his sincerity, efforts, time, and money, where did the Frenchman go wrong?

An English scholar decides to study Japan's amazing progress in the twentieth century. He goes to Japan, talks with English-speaking Japanese scholars, studies many books on Japan written in English, and sees many places in Japan with the aid of an interpreter. The English scholar finds that the Japanese people learned Western ways so fast and substituted them for their old ways so well that they now equal any western country. He is pleased with the way the little people became the world's second most industrialized nation. He goes back to England and writes a book. The book is well accepted by reviewers and scholars in England, but it creates a furor in Japan. The Japanese condemn it. What did the English scholar do wrong?

A German girl doing graduate work at the University of Bonn decides to specialize in French politics. She visits France in order to get firsthand information. When she visits Napoleon's grave she hears all the glorious tributes the Frenchmen give to Napoleon. This bothers the German girl. She thinks of Hitler. To her, Hitler and Napoleon do not seem different. Hitler did the same thing that Napoleon did. Why condemn Hitler and glorify Napoleon? She returns to Germany disappointed in the French people and with greater respect for her own people and leaders. She decides not to waste her time in French politics. What did the French people do to the German girl to disappoint her so much?

An American movie star goes to Thailand to entertain American soldiers stationed in that country. In his comedy hour he makes a few jokes about the Thai people. He says that when he visited a Thai temple he was asked to remove his shoes outside the temple. When he came back from the temple he found a Thai family living in his shoes. The American boys burst with laughter. The story is reported in Thai newspapers. It makes every Thai angry. They say it is an insult to the Thai people and culture. What was so insulting about the American's joke?

A graduate student from Pakistan has a friendship family in the American city where he is going to school. One day he is invited by the family to dinner at 6 o'clock. The Pakistani does not want to be late, so he goes one hour early. After dinner, he stays in the host's home until about 9 o'clock. Then suddenly his friendship family members say that they have plans to visit some friends. They tell him he can stay as long as he likes, but to close the door when he leaves. Then, they leave. The Pakistani stays until midnight and leaves only when the friendship family returns. After that the Pakistani is never invited by the friendship family. What did the student do wrong?

If the American businessman does business in North America only, the Frenchman makes movies in France, the English scholar studies his people, the German girl does not go to France, and the Pakistani stays in Pakistan, there will be no misunderstanding. In each of these cases, the persons involved share different values, beliefs, expectations and customs. They use different communicative techniques to express the same idea. Each of them does something that is unpardonable in the other culture.

Although there is misunderstanding, no one knows why. In intercultural understanding, cultural factors such as the ones mentioned above play decisive roles. Through ignorance of other peoples' customs, a person who is a successful communicator in New York could be a dismal failure in New Delhi.

International Communication

International communication is much different from intercultural communication. Although the purpose of this book is not to discuss international communication, we will talk about it briefly since international relations are quite often equated with intercultural problems. In some countries, cultural traditions have shaped national values. Although diplomats from those countries say their traditional cultures have nothing to do with their national policies, a close look at the way their governments work shows a relationship between their traditions and governments. In Ireland and Pakistan, for example, religious influences on national policies can be clearly seen.

International communication is interaction at national, rather than cultural, levels. The purpose of international communication is to affect political, economic, and defense policies of other nations. In ancient time, kings used several methods of influencing policies of other kings. They sent envoys, invited religious leaders, married royal brides, and sent gifts. The bodhi tree sent by Indian emperor Ashoka to the king of Ceylon in the third century B.C. is still living in that island republic. The same method was repeated in 1912 when the Japanese sent some 3000 cherry-blossom trees to Washington, D.C. Modern political leaders are using all the old methods, and several new ones, to influence political policies of other nations. Cultural exchanges, voluntary organizations, sports teams, and gifts of animals are some of the new versions of the old techniques.

Symbols of International Communication

In international communication the communicators use not only the old verbal, nonverbal and mass media techniques, but other symbols as well. Peace Corps volunteers, steel plants, television stations, supersonic fighters, business plazas, and irrigation dams given as foreign aid are some of the symbols. These symbols are intended to remind the local people of the donor nation. Of the other techniques, the most extensive and expensive are establishments such as the United States Information Agency (USIA), Voice of America, British Broadcasting Corporation's External Broadcasts and English Language Teachings, British Councils, Japanese Broadcasting Corporation's Overseas Broadcasts, and Soviet

Information Agencies. In a memorandum regarding USIA, President John F. Kennedy said:

(the purpose of USIA is) influencing public attitude of other nations . . . by overt use of various techniques of communication.[24]

Explaining the American efforts to sell Uncle Sam in foreign countries, Kenneth Sparks, who is a former USIA official, vividly describes how, at a given time, the various American diplomats in foreign countries will try to influence the officials of the host government. In Moscow, it could be a dance performance by an American company, in front of Soviet dignitaries; in New Delhi, it could be the presentation of a book written by an American author to the Indian prime minister; and in Bangkok, a John Wayne movie could be shown to a large Thai audience.[25]

Colonial Influence

Probably the most effective method of political influence is to help the intended nation develop its communications system using modern technology. Colonial powers such as France and England are quietly using this technique in some of their former colonies. As a result, in some underdeveloped countries the operation of communications systems still depends upon the colonial powers. This type of colonial control is striking more in Africa than anywhere else in the world. The Anglophone of London controls the former British African colonies' telecommunications, while the Francophone of Paris controls the systems in the former French colonies in Africa. When a disruption occurs in London or Paris, its consequences are experienced in the colonies.[26]

The Politics of Satellite Communications

Although the big powers and the old colonial countries do not have any political control over most of the underdeveloped countries, they still would like to maintain some form of control. They have come to realize that transportation and communications are two of the most important areas where they should exercise control. Another example is the control over communications satellites. Right now, only two countries have the know-how and capability to build and launch communications satellites—the United States and the Soviet Union. In the free world, the U.S. is the only country with the potential to help the less developed countries use communications satellites.

In the International Telecommunications Satellite Consortium (Intelsat), a business organization, the U.S. has the controlling shares. The

U.S. National Aeronautics and Space Agency (NASA) is the only organization with the capability to launch such satellites. The U.S. Communications Satellites Corporation (ComSat) is the manager of Intelsat. With these U.S. organizations controlling the key jobs in the Intelsat, the U.S. virtually controls international space communications. Even Communist China in 1972 purchased American equipment for its ground stations for the satellite hookups. China is now using Intelsat IV for international communications.

On the other hand, the Soviet Union is helping Eastern European countries use its Molniya satellites for international communications. The Soviet Union is also helping India develop satellite communications. All these efforts by big powers and colonial countries show that space and other types of communications are important means of international political influence. The big powers are particularly competing with each other for the minds of the international audience via communications satellites. Two of the most spectacular events of international communication seen via satellite by millions of people around the globe were President Nixon's visits to Communist China and the Soviet Union. He opened up communication with the two nations. Why did he do it? One answer is that by establishing communications with China, the American government made the Soviet Union jealous, and eager to hold the Moscow summit conference with the Americans.[27]

After its launching, the first optimum traffic via the Intelsat IV was this communication between China and America. The American president's visit to the communist nation was watched live via satellite by millions of people around the globe. This spectacular show influenced the political thinking not only of several communist nations but also of many of the free world.

Communist China is openly antagonistic to India, and while the United States is showing "benign negligence" to India, the Soviet Union is quietly making the Indians feel they are a special people. According to one writer, India presents "a relatively easy target for Soviet influences." India is still a recipient of a torrent of Soviet propaganda.[28]

The political nature of international communication is probably most obvious in the case of communications satellites. As mentioned earlier, the big and technologically superior powers are using communications know-how as a strategy to influence the political actions of weaker and technologically less developed nations. One such case came up when NASA was admonished by the U.S. Department of State for agreeing to help the Indian Atomic Energy Commission launch a communications satellite.

The United States has a vital interest in the beneficial development of Satellite broadcasting.

Furthermore, since satellite broadcasting is expected to have so profound and widespread an effect on people of the world, the United States must be involved in order to maintain its position of leadership.

Although the United States has much at stake in the international political decisions which soon may be made regarding satellite broadcasting, the subcommittee found an appalling lack of Government policy.

The lack of policy guidelines was nowhere more clear in the arrangement made between the United States Government and the Government of India to allow the latter to use an ATS-F satellite, scheduled for launching in 1972, as the basis of an instructional television system.

As the world's first community TV broadcasting service using a satellite, this experiment is of great international significance and undoubtedly will be a model which other countries will study carefully.

While the Indian project has much to recommend it, it is disturbing that the negotiations were handled almost entirely by the technical agencies involved: the U.S. National Aeronautics and Space Administration and the Indian Atomic Energy Agency.

Although (the U.S.) State Department approval was required, the matter was presented virtually as a "fait accompli" to officials there, the subcommittee's hearings disclosed.

Nothing indicates that the implications of the American commitment to this project were fully considered by those responsible for our foreign policy.

It was another case in which the technology and technicians raced ahead of the policy and the policymakers.[29]

However well-meaning the United States or other nations are, no one will argue the point that sharing the know-how of satellite technology with other nations deserves careful consideration of the governments involved. Today, knowledge of communications by satellite technology has the same importance as had the so-called atomic secret in the early 1950s.

National Culture

We mentioned earlier that a country's national values are shaped by political, military and economic policies of that country's government and leaders. Communication between that country and others is affected by its national values. Even when the traditional cultures of that and another country are similar, their national interests may affect communication between them at the national levels. On the other hand, national interests may force two countries with entirely different cultural traditions to become closer. The discussion of how Communist China and the

United States came closer shows that international communication is designed to influence the political, economic and other policies of the communicating governments. Although China and India have been traditionally closer ever since Fa-Hien and Yon Cheng visited India in the fourth and seventh centuries, their national policies have thrown them apart since the war between the two nations in 1962. Cuba and America have similar traditional cultures, but they are nationally apart from each other. While it is easy for Chinese and Americans to communicate at their national levels, it is not so easy for Cubans and Americans to do so.

External Broadcasts

The Soviet Union has many radio stations whose only purpose is to jam the signals of Radio Free Europe (RFE). The RFE is mainly financed by American businessmen to broadcast information about free enterprise to the peoples behind the so-called Iron Curtain. During World War II, Hitler and the Japanese broadcast information to support their national policies. Until recently, listening to Voice of America's (VOA) broadcasts was an offense in the Soviet Union and Communist China. The two countries feared that the VOA's broadcasts might influence the minds of their peoples against their own national cultures.

Each country's so-called external broadcasts are designed to support the country's political, economic, and defense policies, and influence those of the audience countries. In countries where broadcasting is not directly controlled by the governments, the governments either own broadcasting stations for the purpose of external broadcasts or subsidize existing stations for that purpose.

In the United States, any film made by the federal government or any broadcast produced by VOA for foreign audiences is not shown to Americans. It is believed that the films and the broadcasts are designed to influence the foreign audience to view favorably the policies of the ruling party's government. The ruling party can use government resources to influence foreigners, not Americans. As a result, a film on the life of John F. Kennedy made under Lyndon Johnson's administration was not shown to Americans in the United States. VOA broadcasts are not directed to Americans; they are only for foreign audiences.

Clearly, the purpose of international communication is to influence the political, economic and military decisions of other nations. The variables that affect such communication are not the value systems of the traditional cultures. We have tried to show the difference between international and intercultural communication to enable the reader to distinguish clearly between the two types of interaction, but our purpose is not to discuss international communication in detail.

After a discussion of the need for and the components of intercultural communication, it seems appropriate to arrive at a model which depicts the process of and the elements involved in intercultural communication. The following model will form the basis for the ensuing chapters.

A Model of Intercultural Communication

We have discussed how a person's cultural values affect his communicative behavior. Here we shall discuss the elements involved in the process of such communication, and the stages in which the process takes place.

Communication is largely a learned behavior. The innate ability to communicate is developed to various degrees by the environment in which the communicator is born and raised. Environment is a part of the individual's culture, and a person's mind is largely a product of his culture. It is the individual's mind that is the starting point of all communication. That is where all ideas are formed. Once the ideas are formed, they are encoded in the person's own verbal, nonverbal, and/or media language. They are then conveyed through one or more of his senses and, finally, transmitted through a medium. The message is received by the audience in the reverse order: medium, senses, and mind. It is decoded by the audience in their own verbal, nonverbal, and/or media language. If both communicator and audience share the same language, there is a better chance of understanding taking place.

Man lives in two worlds: one is the external world and the other is the internal world. In the internal world he communicates with himself. This is also known as intrapersonal communication. His internal world is also his store of information about the external world and about himself. Stimuli for communication may come from the external or internal world. In other words, communication may begin as a result of the contact of his senses with the external world, or without any external contact and within his internal world. In any case, the process of communication involves three elements: mind, senses, and medium. The process consists of three actions: perception, retention and expression, as we see in figure 3.

We can better discuss the process of intercultural communication with the aid of a model, the *MSM Model*. Since no two persons are alike even in the same culture, the MSM model could be applied to any communication within the same culture.

Intercultural communication has been defined as the act of understanding and being understood by an audience of another culture. The process of understanding involves three elements: the sense-organs of the persons

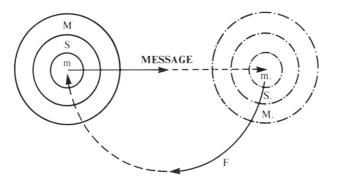

m = mind of the communicator

S = senses of the communicator

M = medium used by the communicator

F = feedback

m. = minds of the audience

S. = senses of the audience

M. = medium of the audience

Figure 3. *The MSM Model of Communication*

engaged in the interaction, the minds of those persons, and the medium of communication they use. Each of the elements is responsible for a certain function. The sense organs are responsible for perception, the mind is responsible for retention, and the medium is the channel of expression.

Input of information about the world must pass through the three elements, each of which acts as a gatekeeper. The nature of each element is such that it cannot pass all the information intact to the next element; some information is withheld and other information added. We shall consider the nature of each of these elements.

Mind

The minds of the communicator and his audience are the starting points of all communication. A person's mind is largely the product of his culture. It is also his storehouse of information about his own and his audience's environments. It is in the mind that all cultural values exist, and where all other cultures are perceived as different or similar. It is in the human mind that all external messages are received and stored. Messages originate there. Since a person's mind is shaped largely by the individual's culture, the messages that originate are also cultural. Those that are received and stored are also shaped by the receiver's culture.

Sense Organs

The individual perceives the world around him through his sensory organs: eyes, ears, nose, tongue and skin. The nature and functions of these organs are conditioned by the individual's physical and cultural make-ups. An excellent example is that of the results of optical illusion tests given by Segall et al. to members of African, American, and Filipino cultures, in which they showed that peoples perceive straight and crooked lines according to the environments in which they grew up.[27] To give another example, if a Hindu saw a cow walk into his house, he would consider it a good omen since the cow is a sacred animal. He would worship it even if it were old, nonfunctional and bothersome. If an American farmer has an old and nonfunctional cow on his farm, however, he considers it a waste of money to keep it, and slaughters it.

Sense organs are responsible for an individual's perception of the world around him. They act as channels for input and output of information. In the process of input and output, they also change some information.

Medium

The message is conveyed through a medium or several media which are also cultural. An idea that originates in the mind of the individual is encoded in a verbal, nonverbal, or media language. A person uses several types of languages to communicate in his daily life, both interpersonal and mass media. Languages are important aspects of a person's culture. They are also filters between a person's ideas and his expression, since ideas in their entirety cannot possibly be encoded and transmitted in any language. Any language fails to convey an idea exactly the way it originates in the mind. In addition to the inadequacy of the language, the communicator's culture restricts certain expressions. Some linguists even say that language is culture.

Sometimes, the message or the idea encoded in a language is further encoded in the language of a medium such as television. Mass media are also highly cultural. Media are only mechanisms used to convey signals or electromagnetic waves, but the symbols and techniques used to convey the ideas through the media are entirely cultural. While it is possible for an engineer in any part of the world to transmit the television signals, it is not possible for any two people in the world to encode ideas the same way. The nature of the transmitted message depends upon the culture of the sender of that message. The way it is understood depends upon the culture of the receiver.

Each of three elements, mind, senses, and medium, is responsible for a certain function. The senses are the media through which a person perceives the external world. Then he retains the information that comes through the senses. Retention of information takes place in his mind. When he interacts with people, he expresses his ideas through one or more media. We shall discuss the three stages in the process of intercultural communication in the next three chapters on perception, retention and expression.

SUMMARY

We can identify two types of cultures: traditional and national. The extent to which traditional cultures affect intercultural communication depends upon the degree of similarities and differences between them. While traditional cultures affect intercultural communication, national cultures affect international communication. In this book our focus will be on intercultural rather than international communication. The degree of cultural difference between interacting persons, assuming they are from different cultures, determines the type of communication: intracultural, interethnic, interracial, or intercultural.

The process of intercultural communication can be explained better with the aid of the MSM model. This model identifies three elements in the process: mind, senses and the medium. The three elements of the interacting person are largely influenced by his culture. The model also identifies three stages in the process of intercultural communication: perception, retention and expression.

NOTES

1. K. S. Sitaram and John Hwang, "The Chinese Image: Some Effects of the Live Coverages of the Nixon Visit to China," Unpublished paper presented at the International Communication Association, Annual Meeting, Atlanta, Georgia, April 1972.

2. Claude E. Shannon and Warren Weaver, *Mathematical Theory of Communication* (Urbana, Ill.: University of Illinois Press, 1964), p. 3.

3. Raymond Ross, *Speech Communication: Fundamentals and Practice* (Englewood Cliffs, N.J.: Prentice Hall, 1974), p. 10.

4. Ibid.

5. Ethel Waters, "His Eye Is on the Sparrow," *Growing Up Black,* ed. Jay David (New York: Pocket Books, 1969), pp. 155-56.

6. K. S. Sitaram, "Some Approaches to Research and Training in Intercultural Communication," Unpublished paper presented at the American Association for the Advancement of Science, Philadelphia, December 1971.

7. Spark Matsunaga, "Emergency Detention Act," *Honolulu Advertiser,* April 15, 1970.

8. Ibid.

9. *German Tribune,* Bonn, West Germany, 2 November 1972, p. 5.

10. Katherine N. Handley, *Four Case Studies* (Honolulu: University of Hawaii, 1961), p. 36.

11. Bhasham, *The Wonder That Was India* (London: Sidwick and Jackson, 1968), p. 33.

12. Ibid., p. 35.

13. "Supplement," *American Journal of Human Genetics,* 24 (November 1972).

14. Frantz Fannon, *The Wretched of the Earth* (New York: Grove Press, 1961), p. 7.

15. Sammy Davis, Jr., "Yes, I Can," *The Negro in the City,* ed. Gerald Leinwand (New York: Washington Square Press, 1968), p. 104.

16. J.B.S. Haldane, quoted in J.K. Brierly, *Biology and Social Crises* (Rutherford, N.J., Fairleigh Dickinson University Press, 1970).

17. Richard A. Goldsby, *Race and Races* (New York: Macmillan, 1971), pp. 18-19.

18. "UNESCO Declaration on Races," quoted by Michael Lerner, *Heredity Evolution and Society* (San Francisco: W. H. Freeman and Company, 1968), p. 226.

19. Brierly, *Biology and Social Crises,* p. 88.

20. Goldsby, *Race and Races.*

21. James G. Martin, "Racial Ethnocentrism and Judgement of Beauty," *Intercultural Communication: A Reader,* ed. Larry Samovar and Richard E. Porter (Belmont, Calif.:Wadsworth, 1972), pp. 76-78.

22. Ibid., p. 77.

23. Ibid., p. 78.

24. "Selling Uncle Sam," *Annals* (Philadelphia: American Society of Political and Social Science, November 1971), p. 114.

25. Ibid.

26. F. S. Arkhurst, *Arms and African Development* (New York: Praeger Publishers, 1970), p. 108.

27. *Annals,* November 1971.

28. Ibid., p. 135.

29. U.S. Government, *Satellite Broadcasting: Implications for Foreign Policy.* Hearings before the Subcommittee on National Security Policy and Scientific Developments of the Committee on Foreign Affairs, House of Representatives (Washington, D.C.: U.S. GPO, 1969).

3

Perception of the World

Until the early part of this century, scientists, particularly physiologists, believed that perception was purely sensory. They thought messages were processed only by the senses and then passed on to the brain. For example, if just one message is being passed through a given sense, then that message is processed and transmitted by the sense and received by the mind. However, "it is harder to understand two messages arriving simultaneously than two messages arriving one after another."[1] According to some recent findings, even if a number of messages are arriving at the same time, only that message which is of greatest interest to the receiver is best perceived, and the others are less perceived or even rejected. In other words, eyes and ears see and hear what the perceiver likes to see and hear. We will elaborate this point later on in the chapter. Let us first discuss the concept of Sense.

Sense

As early as the fourth century B.C., Aristotle said there were five senses and that men perceive through them. Many centuries later, Mueller and Helmholtz explained the physiological function of the senses as taking place in the center portion of the brain where the nerve fibers terminate, while perceiving a color. A person perceives only a condition of his central nerve.[2]

Evidently, Aristotle and the physiologists believed that men perceive the external world through the five senses: sight, sound, smell, taste, and touch. Although the physiologists said that in the final analysis it is the nerve ending that is responsible for the perception, they still emphasized the sensory or physiological aspect of perception. According to them, nerve ending is the final factor in deciding how the world appears.

Later on, physiologists began to doubt if perception was really sensory. For example, does a mere touch of skin result in pain or pleasure? Is there anything other than sensation that is a factor in deciding whether or not the touch is painful or pleasant? In order to answer these questions, we might consider a few learned opinions and examples, such as one physiological explanation of pain. Evidence indicates that pain is influenced by cognitive activities. An individual's cultural background and early experiences have a great effect on the experience of pain and the Hendant response.[3]

Here is an example of a person's cultural background affecting his concept of pain. Some peoples of Asian-Pacific cultures walk on red-hot stones and charcoal in order to please the gods. They believe that the superior powers protect their feet from burning. Some of those peoples have even demonstrated their beliefs in front of Western audiences. Some representatives of Fiji often visit the United States and demonstrate fire-walking to American audiences. Another example is that of Jain and Buddhist monks in Asia, who believe in penance, sitting naked on cold stones for many hours to meditate. They pick the hair from their bodies by hand because they believe that will please the Lord.

Perception is an extremely important variable that affects a person's communicative behavior. We have defined communication as a process involving a person's understanding of his audience and the way he tries to make them understand him. Both understanding and being understood involve the perceptive behaviors of the two parties.

The two examples above indicate that cultural beliefs do influence sensory perception. We shall discuss in detail the influence of culture on perception.

Influence of Culture

Members of different cultures look differently at the world around them. Some believe that the physical world is real. Others believe that it is just an illusion. Some believe everything around them is permanent while others say it is transient. Reality is not the same for all people. Depending upon the emphasis they place on their reality, they decide their relationships with men, machines and the materialistic world. In this chapter we shall discuss how the four major systems of philosophy explain the concept of reality and the influence those concepts have on the individual's communicative behavior.

Philosophy and Communication

The purpose of philosophy has been to explain how man should understand the world around him and how he should react to that world. At a given moment the world might not appear the same to all persons. We all look at the same world differently. With our eyes wide open, we are all like the blind men who touched the same elephant but perceived it differently. To each one of them what he perceived was real.

What is real and what is illusory? What do we know, and what ought we to know? These questions have occupied the minds of philosophers for several thousand years. None has been able to answer the questions to everyone's satisfaction.

We all believe we know that something is true. On the basis of our concept of truth we react to the men, machines and the nature around us. We even react toward ourselves on the basis of that truth. Our concept of reality forms the basis of our intuition within ourselves and interaction with others. If you ask a Hindu farmer why he got only ten bags of corn from his land while nearby farmers got much more he would say it was the wish of God. An American farmer's answer to the same question would be: "Hell, I didn't work hard enough." The two farmer's perceptions of the results of their year's hard work is so different for good reasons. The Hindu, despite his hard work, believes that the divine power destined it to be so. He accepts it. The American farmer does not depend upon anything but his own ability. He does not even know his reactions are really shaped by a philosophical system that has influenced the lives of his people for generations. Nor do they know that the philosophical system shapes their values and customs, which in turn influences their communicative behaviors.

Communicative behavior begins with the individual's understanding, or perception, of the world. The Americans' and most Westerners' perception of the world has been influenced to a large extent by ancient Greek philosophy. Those of the south, southeast and east Asian and some Pacific peoples have been shaped by Hindu and Buddhist philosophies. The Arabs and Muslim peoples' outlook on life have certainly been the outcomes of Islamic philosophy. We shall briefly discuss the concepts of perception of the four systems.

The four systems are: Greek, Hindu, Buddhist, and Islamic. There have been many schools of thought in each of these four systems. Some schools have completely disagreed with every other school in the system; others have been developed on the earlier ones. For the purpose of our discussion, we have selected the most commonly accepted theories by the majority of the members in each system. The purpose here is not to judge which system is the right one. We are only trying to explain how different peoples look at the same phenomena and may react differently.

The Greek Concepts

Since the Greek theories are discussed quite thoroughly in most colleges, we shall not go into greater detail of these theories. We will discuss salient points of the most well-known philosopher, Plato. Plato's philosophy has been the basis for most western thought. His *Republic* explains in detail his concept of the right way to acquire knowledge. There are many references to Plato by other great philosophers such as Socrates. Some are in the form of dialogues between Plato and his students, others are commentaries, and there are the allegories attributed to Plato. The allegory of four men in a cave is an example of how Plato tried to explain his concept of perception.

The Four Stages

While discussing his theories of perception Plato, like Hindu and Buddhist philosophers, was referring to the ultimate goal of life. According to him, the individual should proceed step-by-step to acquire knowledge. What appears to be the truth could well be merely appearance and not truth at all. Only intelligence can show what is truth and what is illusion. There are four stages in the process of acquiring knowledge, or perception. First, at the lowest level is *illusion*. The images that the individual perceives are not real. They are like shadows or reflections on water. Still, imagining is the beginning of understanding. The second stage is *belief*. The images the individual sees are compared with the real objects around him that he can see and believe. His imagining and belief together help him think about the object. *Imagination* is the third stage. This stage relates closely to the modern concepts of perception. The fourth stage is *intellection*. It is like reaching the top of a mountain after climbing many steps. This stage is real. It is the best way to understand things and acquire knowledge.

In the final analysis, Plato emphasizes the individual, who is the perceiver of the object. It is his intelligence that is responsible for his understanding of things around him. He is responsible for the cognition of reality.

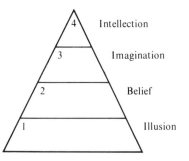

Figure 4. *Plato's Explanation of the Process of Perception*

As we shall note later, the Hindu, Buddhist and Islamic philosophies also talk about the individual's place in acquiring the right knowledge. In Hinduism, what the *Vedas* say is most valid, in Buddhism the *Sutras* speak the truth, and in Islam what the *Koran* says is the ultimate. But Plato puts the responsibility on the shoulders of the perceiving individual. He must go up the steps and understand the reality. In other words, individuality is more important than the authority of an outside source.

American Perception

In this context our operational definition of American perception is how the American white man perceives the world around him. His perceptive behavior is influenced by his primary values, such as individuality, money, skin color and aggressiveness.

Individuality and Money

In America, the individual and his rights as such transcend considerations of the welfare of others. In his pursuit of happiness as an individual right, the American tends to ignore the happiness of others. A classic example of this can best be seen in the American divorce system. It is legal for a woman to divorce her husband for reasons of cruelty, incompatibility and sexual inadequacy, but considering those who suffer as a result of the divorce, the woman seems to be placing her individual desire over the family's happiness. Moreover, she also has a right to demand alimony at the expense of her husband. In this particular case the woman might perceive her husband and children as objects of exploitation.

Let us consider how the American woman might perceive a woman in Thailand who is placed in a similar position. The Thai woman's husband is also sexually inadequate and perhaps even cruel. Instead of divorcing him, which is also perfectly legal in her country, she might hang on to him in the interest of her children's welfare and the happiness of the joint family. The American woman might certainly look down at the Thai woman because she feels the Thai woman should exercise her individual rights in pursuit of her own individual happiness.

On the other hand, the Thai woman perceives herself as a person who is doing her duty to her children and her family. She is even respected by her family and her community for bearing with a cruel husband. The Thai woman would also look at the American who divorced her husband to pursue her own happiness as a selfish, immoral, and immature person.

Let us consider another example. An American owns several acres of land on which there are large, tall and old trees. His financial advisors suggest that if he constructs a large building complex on that land, he could make several million dollars. He has the legal right to destroy the old, construct the buildings and make money. Therefore, he chops down the trees, constructs a building and enjoys the wealth. The other businessmen in his area would perceive the American as smart and successful. He will be respected for his achievement.

In the East, however, chopping down ancient trees to construct a building to make money is perceived as a negative value. One who would do so no matter how much money he makes, would be considered a menace to society. Despite the riches acquired in the process, he loses the respect of his people.

Skin Color and Aggressiveness

In America there are immigrants from many countries of the world. Some of these immigrants will always be considered aliens; others are invariably considered Americans. The length of time in America has little, if anything, to do with this consideration. Rather, the determination is based primarily on which part of the world one has come from and what color one's skin is. For example, a person of western European extraction, no matter how long he has been in America, even if he does not yet have American citizenship, may be automatically considered an American over another person, particularly one whose ancestry is Asian, African, Latin American, or even Eastern European.

The following example highlights this situation. A white American was talking with a Japanese in New York. After a few minutes another white man joined the coversation. Let us call the first man Smith; the second one, Tanaka; and the third, Jensen. Soon after Smith introduced Tanaka to Jensen, Jensen asked:

"Are you from Japan?"

"Yes," answered Tanaka.

"You like it here?" asked Jensen.

"Yes, very much," said Tanaka.

"When do you go back to your country?"

"I don't know," said Tanaka, smiling.

Then Tanaka asked Jensen, "Where are you from?" At this point Smith interrupted by saying, "Jensen is an American."

"Yes, I know," said Tanaka," but where is he from?"

Jensen said, "I'm originally from Sweden."

"How long have you been here?" asked Tanaka.

"I came to this country ten years ago," said Jensen.

It so happened that the Tanakas had been Americans for three generations. This Tanaka was born in one of the concentration camps in America in which Japanese were incarcerated during World War II. Although his physical features are Oriental, Tanaka's cultural values, educational institutions, and political party affiliations are all American. Yet Jensen and Smith perceived him as an alien.

Smith's attitude was based on the belief that the color of the skin is important and therefore all people whose skin is white can integrate into the American society. His belief that the white man has complete freedom of expression prompted him to support Jensen's questions to Tanaka, while he did not grant the same freedom to Tanaka when he asked where Jensen was from. Therefore, Smith and Jensen perceived Tanaka as an alien because he is not white. No matter how long Tanaka's family has been in this country and contributed to its culture, he is not granted the basic assumptions accorded other whites.

Earlier, we mentioned that aggressiveness is an important value of the white man. In this case, Smith and Jensen were aggressive enough to ask Tanaka when he would go back, while Tanaka smiled and said he did not know. Because of their aggressive behavior, Jensen and Smith failed to know the truth about Tanaka.

Hindu Concepts

We shall discuss the other three philosophical theories in greater detail because few students in Western universities are familiar with Eastern theories of perception. Hindu theories of perception are probably unknown to Western communication specialists. Although there has been a great interest in Indian philosophy in the West, communication specialists in this part of the world have not made any attempt to study systematically the beginnings of Hindu communication theory, which are really parts of Hindu schools of philosophy. Attempts have been made by some Indian scholars to trace the origin of Hindu psychology to the schools of philosophy. Even these are unknown to Western communicologists. Since communication theory itself is in its infancy it is no great surprise that Hindu and other ancient theories are overlooked by these specialists.

Schools of Perception

The oldest Hindu discussions of perception can be seen in the *Vedas*, which are at least 3500 years old. There have been many Vedic schools, each of which has tried to give its own definition of perception. We should remember, however, that each member of those schools first speculated within himself and then discussed his speculations with other scholars and his students. The *Upanishads* are notes taken by participants during those discussions. There are also commentaries on the Vedas called *Bhashyas*. Some scholars wrote down their thoughts in the form of *Sutras*. We might give an example here just to acquaint the reader with the levels of the Vedic students: Shankara, the great philosopher of the seventh century, be-

gins his Commentary on Brahma Sutra's by saying, "Now let us begin
our discussion of Brahman." Shankara took it for granted that his pupils
already knew something about Brahman, the all Pervading Power. If they
did not have the prerequisite, they would not have participated in that
seminar.

Our discussions here are based on the theories of three Hindu schools:
Nyaya, Mimamsa, and *Charvaka.* The Nyaya and Mimamsa schools believe in the existence of the universal spirit called Brahman. The Charvaka school does not believe in any superhuman power, but relies on the
individual's ability. Mimamsa is comparatively new. It was revived in the
seventh century by Shankara, who was mainly responsible for making
Buddhism less popular and Hinduism more powerful. The three schools
are all at least 2500 years old, and many scholars have contributed to the
development of each one of them for over twenty-five centuries.

The main purpose of the several schools has been to explain the nature
of the so-called Self and its relationship to the universal power called
Brahman. While trying to explain such a relationship, the schools have
also discussed the process of perception, or how the individual understands the world around him. They say knowledge or understanding
comes from four sources: perception, inference, comparison, and testimony. The three schools agree that these four sources are necessary to acquire valid knowledge, but each of the three schools has its own definition
of perception.

Definition of Perception

Both Nyaya and Mimamsa schools define perception as "the non-illu-
sive cognition which is produced by the contact of the senses with external
object."[4]

The sense-object contact presupposes the existence of *Manas* or consciousness. Manas comes close to the concept of mind as explained in
modern psychology. Perceived information is transmitted to the Self
through the manas. The input of information begins with the contact of
one or more of the senses with an external object. It is then transmitted to
the manas. Manas finally informs the Self. The Self decides whether or
not the input is valid. This process is represented by a diagram in figure
5. It should be noted that Manas or consciousness or the mind is also not
the final element to decide whether or not the information received by the
senses is valid. The mind acts as a gateway between the five senses that
are outside and the Self that is inside. Thus Mind is the sixth sense. It is
also referred to by some philosophers as the internal sense. Even the
Manas can make mistakes. It is only the Self that accepts or rejects information as valid knowledge. When such a decision takes place, perception

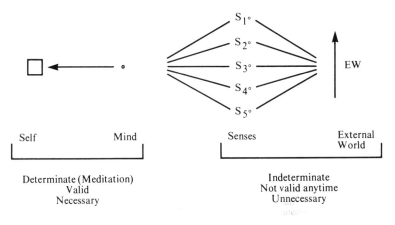

$S_{1°}$

$S_{2°}$

$S_{3°}$ EW

$S_{4°}$

$S_{5°}$

| Self | Mind | Senses | External World |

Determinate (Meditation)
Valid
Necessary

Indeterminate
Not valid anytime
Unnecessary

Figure 5. *Ancient Hindu Concept of Perception*

becomes *cognition*. Cognition, according to Hindu philosphers, is the valid knowledge. It is the input that is accepted by the mind and the Self as valid.

To prove that sensory perception may not be accurate, the Hindus give the example of the appearance of a stick in a glass of water. When we see a stick half immersed in a glass of water, it appears to be crooked. That is not how it would appear if it were not in water, since the stick is not really crooked. But the crookedness appears to be real at the time of perceiving it. Sensory perception is like seeing the stick and believing that it is crooked. Only if the perceiver applies his own cognitive powers can he know that the stick is straight. The *Manas* and the Self can determine reality, not the five senses. Therefore, sensory perception is secondary to cognition of the Self.

Information received through senses is not the most valid knowledge. like the crookedness of the stick, it may not be real. Hindus called this uncertain input of knowledge *indeterminate perception.* Only when the mind and the Self decide whether or not the sensory input is valid does it become *determinate perception,* as seen in figure 5. Determinate perception is the same as cognition which we mentioned earlier. This type of valid understanding does not come easily. Only a person with a powerful mind can achieve it, and then it will require several years of work.

The Nyaya and Mimamsa schools believed in the existence of a universal power called Brahman, which is equivalent to the concept of the Almighty in Christian theology. They believed the Brahman is the divine spirit and somewhere inside the individual there is a piece of the divine. It is that divine part or the Self that tells the individual whether or not what he is perceiving is valid.

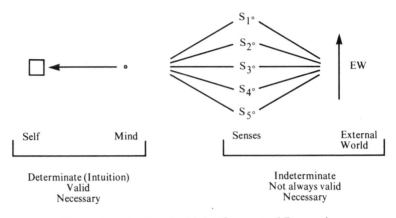

Figure 6. *Ancient Buddhist Concept of Perception*

Materialistic School

The materialists, also known as Naturalists or *Charvakas,* defined perception as knowledge acquired through the five senses only. Anything not perceived through the senses does not exist.[5]

The Charvakas said there were two types of perception, external and internal. External perception is derived from the five senses, and internal is derived from the operation of the mind. The five senses are important, however, since these are the receivers of information for the mind. So the external perception is more important than the internal. These two stages of acquiring knowledge are somewhat similar to the determinate and indeterminate perceptions of the Nyaya and Mimamsa schools. But the Charvakas said that all inputs are done by the elements of the individual's body, not by the divine Brahman.

The Charvakas believed only in the individual and his physical existence. They claimed there was nothing beyond the human body and mind. The world around us is real, not illusory. There is no such thing as the supreme power or Brahman. The goal of life should be to enjoy. "If you do not have butter today, borrow it from your neighbor and eat it." Today is important. Nobody knows what will happen to you tomorrow. The Charvakas were materialists, or to use a modern terminology, naturalists.

The Charvakas were disappointed with the ancient Vedic philosophy that gave more importance to an unseen power than to the individual person. They wanted to see people happy and healthy in this world. They emphasized this world and life today. They did not care what happened in the hereafter. The naturalists existed as early as the sixth century B.C., but were made unpopular first by the Buddha in the sixth century B.C., and then by Shankara in the seventh century A.D. The Charvakas are even credited with developing the fourth Veda called *Atharva Veda,* which was highly scientific and depended upon empirical data. Even this Veda was discredited as the agnostics' Veda. Belief in the existence of the Supreme Power and acceptance of Divine Control was so deep-rooted that not even the greatest scholar of the Charvaka school could change that belief.

In addition to the Charvakas, several independent scholars believed that happiness in this world is necessary and that it serves an important step to moksha, or salvation. These scholars delineated four steps to moksha: (1) the duties of the individual to his profession; (2) achieving wealth in his profession; (3) enjoying life, including sex; and, (4) moksha. In the fourth century, several scholars wrote books on their materialistic philosophy. Vatsyayana wrote his famous *Kama Sutra* at this time. But all these attempts were unsuccessful and the powerful *Karma* theory was firmly established in the Hindu cultures. The Karma theorists believed that despite the individual's efforts, it was the divine power that gave him material success. That power decided an individual's happiness or sorrow on the basis of what he had done in his previous life. Therefore, whatever happened to the individual in his lifetime was the result of his actions in his previous birth. What he does now will have consequences in his next birth. If he wants to be happy in the next birth, he should do the right things now. He could even get out of the cycle of birth and rebirth and unite with the Divine by acquiring the right knowledge and understanding of the Self. Shankara in the seventh century was the main proponent of the Karma theory. Thus, traditional outlook of life was again established in the Hindu cultures.

Illusory World

The traditional schools believed that the Almighty had given man his five senses and the mind to perceive His presence inside the human body and outside it in nature. Man's perceptive powers should be used to know the Self. Self-realization should be the goal of life. Therefore, although there is nature around them and humans can perceive it, it is only an illusion or *Maya* created by the Almighty to test them. The power that created nature is more important than nature itself. Exercising his cognitive powers, man can know that power in himself as well as outside. Shankara gave an analogy to bring home this point. He took one of his students to a dark room and asked him to look at a corner. There he could see five lights.

"What is it?" Shakara asked.

"Of course, they are five lights."

"Go closer and see."

The student went closer and saw a big pot with five holes on its side. Light was emanating from inside the pot. On examination he found that there was just one bright light inside whose rays were going out in the five directions.

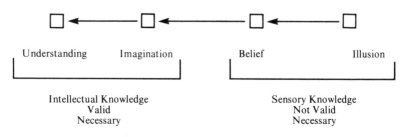

Figure 7.   *Ancient Greek Concept of Perception*

"What is the significance of this?" the student asked.

Shankara exclaimed that the human body is like the pot. The five holes are the five senses. When we look at a man's bright eyes we think that the eyes themselves have the power to perceive. In reality the five senses are only the outlets or inlets for the inner self. It is the Self that has the power to perceive. So, whatever goes in through the senses is not valid until it is accepted by the Self.

Through such analogies and his powerful rhethoric, Shankara was able to defeat the Charvakas on one hand and the Buddhists on the other.

Meditation and Intuition

Modern behaviorists and humanists are fighting over their philosophies of experimentation and intuiton. But ancient Hindus and Buddhists had gone a step further. Hindus say that not even human intuition is free from subjectivity. Intuition is affected by perception of this world, which is really an illusion. Meditation is the only way to acquire real knowledge. Meditation is a result of the mastery of Self over mind, and is therefore more important than intuition.

The Buddhists also tried to explain the undependability of sensory per-ception. They said that sensory perception implies a dual relationship be-tween the perceiving individual and the world he perceives. Believing what he perceives is true, the individual suffers in this world.

> Sensory perception is the root of all misery of this world. We perceive forms with our eyes, hear sounds with our ears, and get attached to them. But the things we get thus attached to are constantly changing, they disappear like bubbles at the slightest touch. The constant change has no permanent reality. Its existence is purely relative, and is dependent upon the activities of the senses.
>
> The world of sense perception has no independent reality. Hence, attachment to it causes sorrow. As far as the individual is concerned, therefore, he should aim at putting an end to the pursuit of knowledge by way of senses, and strive at the attainment of a more stable happiness.[6]

Early Buddhists believed that even empirical knowledge, acquired from sensory perception, was not valid. Objects in the external world are nothing but the creations of the mind of the perceiver. Therefore, intuitive knowledge derived by adopting the methods as taught by the Buddha is valid.

As Buddhism progressed, there were new developments in the study of perception. Many theories were offered which influenced even the Hindu schools. According to these theories, human thought was a continuum. Mental phenomena such as attention, assimilation, discrimination, and cognition are not separate faculties. They are stages in a process which is extremely rapid and are functions of one consciousness.

> There is no agent or director who, after the object has impinged on the sense-organ says, "you perform the function of attention or you perform the function of cognition." Each of the various acts such as attention assimilation and discrimination, function according to their own law, and the whole process is recognized as the law of operation of the mind.[7]

The greatness of Buddhist concepts of perception lies in the fact that they tried to explain the process scientifically. They did not discredit the knowledge derived from sensory activities, although they did not say it was the only way to understand the world.

We should not forget some very important facts. The Hindu and Buddhist philosophers that we are referring to lived more than two thousand years ago and did not have any scientific theories or instruments to test their hypotheses empirically. Further, their main purpose was religious: to explain the relationship between man, the world around him, and the power that created man and his world. Although the Buddhists were more scientific than the Hindus in their explanations, the powerful Hinduism defeated Buddhism in India. When it was adopted by people in other cultures, however, it was changed considerably to meet the needs of its new followers.

The Buddhist Concepts

By the time Shankara appeared on the philosophical scene, Buddhism in India was over twelve hundred years old. It was divided into two major schools. The Hinayana and the Mahayana schools were struggling to exist in India. Hinayana was also accepted by the peoples of Sri Lanka, and other southeast Asian countries, while Mahayana was adopted by the peoples of East Asia.

The Hinayana School

Hinayana or Theravada is the original school of Buddhism. According to this school, intuition is the highest source of knowledge. Knowledge derived from self-enlightening intellect is most valid. As an avenue of knowledge, sensory perception is inferior to intuition. Buddha recognized the existence of the external world. He said the world was real, not illusory, as most Hindu schools said. The senses do give some knowledge, but they are influenced by the feelings and desires of the perceiver. Those influences should be eliminated. Only Buddhist doctrines can help the individual eliminate those influences and attain enlightenment. Although sensory perception is not perfect, it is important since,

> ... sense-impressions are to be, not ignored, but recognized for what they are and perfect equanimity attained respecting them. In other words, he who can see and hear first sees and hears, then recloses eye and ear. But for one who is in the way, the rising of any sense-awareness as such causes him loathing, abhorence and disgust.[8]

Emphasizing the importance of the physical world around us and that each thing has name and form the Buddha told his favorite disciple Ananda that names and forms of objects were the cause of contact between the senses and the objects. The name of an object indicates the aggregate of its features. If the features did not exist, the name would not exist either.[9]

Since sensory perception is not valid and intuition is most valid, only the Buddha can teach self enlightenment. Buddhist books contain many stories of the Buddha explaining this point. The following story clearly tells us how he felt about the importance of his own teaching.

A harlot had stolen several valuables belonging to some young men. The harlot tried to run away and the young men chased her. They saw the Buddha and asked him if he had seen her. The Buddha asked:

> Now what you think, young men? Which would be better for you; that you should go in search of a woman, or that you should go in search of yourselves?
>
> That, Lord, would be better for us, that we should search of ourselves.
>
> If so, young men, sit down, I will preach you the Truth. . . .[10]

The Hinayana school drew ideas from Nyaya, Charvaka and other Hindu schools, but developed its own concepts of perception. By the time Buddhism reached China, Korea and Japan, however, even the Hinayana concepts had changed considerably. In China, Confucianism was already popular. In Japan, Shintoism was being practiced. The Dhyana (meditation) type Buddhism of India became Chen Buddhism in China. Through Korea, the Chen reached Japan and became Zen Buddhism. All these new forms of Buddhism are studied under one school called Mahayana.

The Mahayana School

Our discussion here is based on the Japanese view of Mahayana Buddhism. This includes Zen, Nichiren and other schools of Japanese Buddhism. We will understand the Japanese view better if we began this discussion with a reference to Shinto, which is the original religion of the Japanese.

Shintoism recognizes the world as real. A spirit known as *Kami* exists in everything, probably something like the Brahman of the Hindus. Therefore nature is sacred and real, not just *Maya* as the Hindus believe. The universe functions through the harmony created by Kami by its existence in all living and non-living things.

Man is a child of Kami and so is inherently divine. The Japanese islands were born as a result of the union of the god Izanami and goddess Izanagi; therefore, the land of Japan is sacred. The various emotions of man are natural; they need not be denied. Shintoism is neither written nor has it a founder. It is a faith of direct experience. It does not have any formal prayers. Its followers pray only for their health, happiness and prosperity. There is no prayer for forgiveness or salvation. As a religion of this world, it does not force the Japanese to look at the nature as illusion or the human body as sinful.

With such a religious background, the Japanese would reject the philosophies of the Hindus and the Hinayana Buddhists, both of whom emphasize the importance of the hereafter rather than world right here. A philosophy that is optimistic, this worldly, and interested in man-to-man relationships would be most welcome to the Japanese. By the time the Buddhism that originated in India reached China and Korea, it had undergone several phases of development. This Mahayana version of Buddhism was probably best suited to the Japanese.

Prince Shotoku who brought Mahayana Buddhism to Japan in the sixth century developed it further to suit it to the needs of his people. He rewrote Buddhist books. When Buddhism was introduced to the Japanese people, it was introduced as a friend, not as a conquerer, and as a supplement, not a replacement to Shintoism. It was accepted by the Japanese since it made them feel proud, not ashamed, of their existing cultural values.

The Japanese version of Mahayana also accepts the world as real. It emphasizes the importance of today in a man's life, not the tomorrow as does Hinduism. Today leads to tomorrow, therefore today is important. Sensory perception is more important than pure intuitive knowing, since the former leads to the latter. It is the materialistic world that helps man to understand the Absolute truth. Unless there is sense-object contact, we cannot know what created that object. Therefore man should go from the known to the unknown.

According to Shotoku, reality "is no more than today's occurrence of cause and effect.[11] The human body is sacred, it is not decaying and disgusting." In order to keep this body healthy and his life happy, man should acquire wealth. But acquisition of wealth should be according to the laws of the Buddha. Thus Shotoku focused on the utilitarian value of life and world. The practical part was considered more important than the speculative part.[12]

Mahayanists believe that there are three forms of knowledge: Illusion, Relative Knowledge, and Absolute Knowledge.

Illusion is the subjective understanding of the world. It is not verified by objective reality and critical judgment. Relative knowledge is based on the law of relativity or the belief that everything in this world has a relative and conditional existence and nothing can claim an absolute reality free from all limitations. The third type of knowledge is clear of illusions and assumptions. At this stage, the individual understands the truth like a dust-free mirror. All the three stages are necessary, because one stage leads to the other. Suzuki explains the Japanese mind when he says that Mahayana Buddhism does not look down at scientific investigation or religious beliefs. Science alone cannot satisfy all the inner cravings of man, but it certainly is a step toward enlightenment.[13]

In the pursuit of Moksha, or salvation, the Hindu neglects this world, while the Mahayana Buddhist in his pursuit of Nirvana goes through this world. The Hindu wants to take a giant step straight to Moksha while the Buddhist goes step by step through this world. Kumaraswamy sums up the Mahayana Buddhist view of life as follows:

> Thus the new Buddhist law was in no way puritanical and did not include an absolute detachment. Pleasure indeed is not to be sought as an end in itself, but it need not be rejected as it arises incidentally.[14]

Clearly, Mahayana emphasized all the joys of this world, but it directed its followers to think of a goal in life other than mere material happiness. The joys of this life and those later on were two stages in the same effort. But another Asian philosophy, the Islamic, did not direct its followers that way; it clearly separated the here and the hereafter.

The Islamic View

Islam is probably the only religion that says the world is totally real. The world is not mere illusion, as the Hindus said. Nor is it necessary for all men to *seek* enlightenment, as the Buddhists said. Islam recognizes two realities: the Creator, or Allah, and the created. Allah created the world, its animals and everything else for the enjoyment of man. The divine reality is revealed to a few men as an act of kindness by Allah. This happens only a few times in human history. Thus, all men cannot at all times see the divine even if they try to do so. That does not mean that life for those who cannot see the divine is futile. They can still believe in the divine reality, which is entirely different from the real world in which they live.

> Nature is not transcendent and constitutes an autonomous realm. There is no divinity either in its material or in its forces. It is totally real, totally a creature, totally belongs to the realm of the actual, the objective. It contains no mystery. None of its phenomena may claim to be secret, none beyond man's searching eye or hand. It is all profane, and nothing in it or of it is or can be sacred. It is utterly closed to any penetration of, fusion with or contact by, the holy. Its relationship with the latter has always been, and will always be, that of a creature to its creator, of artifact to its maker. Only such dissociation of nature from the transcendent can safeguard its autonomy.[15]

Since "God brought you out of the bosoms of your mothers knowing nothing, but gave you the faculties of hearing, sight and perception,"[16] man and god are not one and the same. In other words, man can neither be Brahman nor can he attain Buddhahood. Islam, however, places the responsibility on the shoulders of each individual to know the truth. He can do so by reasoning, of which there are two types: natural and acquired.

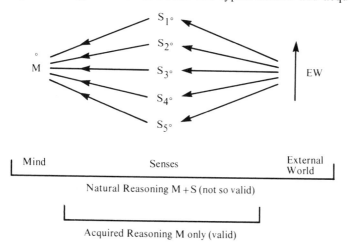

Figure 8. *Ancient Islamic Concept of Perception*

Natural reasoning is necessary, of course, to know the truth. Truth could be derived through man's senses or in his own mind. Reasoning in his own mind and knowing the truth is preferable, since it controls man from his instincts and passions. Acquired reasoning is really the step after natural reasoning, and guides man in striving for complete knowledge. This type of reasoning grows as man develops it and weakens as he neglects it.

The Islamic philosophy is not complicated like Hinduism or Buddhism. It recognizes the existence of this world as very real and that it is created for the enjoyment of man. Man does not have to struggle for salvation, nor does he have to consider himself a part of the divinity. The divinity chooses the individual that it wants to enlighten. Since the chosen ones are so special and come once in many thousand years, they should therefore be respected and their preachings should be implemented. The *Koran* is the word of the Prophet Mohammed inspired by Allah. It tells how a man should conduct himself in this world. It specifies the duties of man and woman. The Koran tells the Muslims what their values should be. Whenever he has doubt about what he should do, a good Muslim should consult only the Holy Koran. Basically, the Islamic view of this world enables the Muslims to look favorably at material progress. An expert on Indonesian Islam says that a strong parochial school system in Indonesia is not an enemy of modernization. It allows an established religious tradition, with a hold on the minds of its students, to accept the modern world and become a part of it.[16]

Philosophy and Selectivity

Perception is selective. The information that is opposed or insulting to the philosophical system or cultural values of a people does not stand much chance of being perceived. Any information that gives the remote impression of opposing a person's philosophy and religion is shut off, sometimes automatically, by that person. As an example, a student from an Arabian country was studying in an American univeristy. He was invited to dinner by a friend. The Arab student did not know that the American friend was an orthodox Baptist. The first day he presented the friend with a copy of *Ummer Khayyam*. He thought the book was well known in all countries, and that the American would be glad to receive a copy of it. A few days later the student asked his Baptist friend if he had read the book. Now, although the American had politely accepted the book, he had not cared to read it. He wasn't sure he still had it; he might have tossed it away. He knew the Holy Bible was the only religious book he should read. Books on other religions, he thought, did not support Christianity. It is sinful to read a book on another religion. So he evaded the Arab student's question.

While one culture believes that nature is sacred and should be worshipped, another may perceive it as a servant of man and a means for his enjoyment. Consequently, a person from the former culture looks at a tree as more important than an apartment house. He might still build a house, around the tree. On the other hand, a person from the latter culture might look at the lot where the tree is and think the lot is too valuable to leave it open. He may chop down the tree and build a highrise. The highrise builder perceives the nature worshipper as a backward person.

Sex is sacred in one culture and sinful in another. The result is that nudity can be looked at as something natural, a part of god's creation. In some Asian temples, the idols of gods and goddesses are in nude human form. Outside the temple walls, there are carvings of nudes and sex acts. But in cultures where sex is sinful, such carvings would be considered shameful.

Cultures that consider man as part of the divinity look at the human being as sacred. They respect his ideas. They believe in understanding him. Intuition is considered to be the best way to know the world. Innate abilities are respected. Cultures that do not consider man a part of the divinity do not encourage considering all men as sacred. Instead of knowing by intuition, they believe in manipulating nature and understanding natural phenomena. Instead of letting man do his own thing, they tend to change his behavior by artificial means. Some religious conquerors have tried to change their captives' behavior at sword point.

The result has always been the same: information that contradicts their philosophical concepts and cultural values is not accepted by most people.

Cultural differences and preconceived notions affect successful communication. When blacks of America hear a white speaker babble the same cliches, they tend to perceive him as insincere. People of one culture have an inherited disbelief in people of other cultures. With such beliefs, any communication is seen as deceitful. Muslims and Hindus, Koreans and Japanese and American blacks and whites have always looked at each other with mistrust.

Environmental factors also affect perception. African tribal people can perceive crooked lines more accurately than people in urban America, since they are used to seeing crooked trees in their environment.

We have attempted to show how the people of each culture have a basic philosophy of life. Each philosophy has given rise to a set of values and beliefs, which in turn have created a set of expectations and customs. A person may not know that his cultural expectations and customs are based on certain values and beliefs, but most persons in each culture know its expectations and customs. Only those who have deeply studied their culture know the beliefs that have shaped their customs and expectations. Nonetheless, the majority of members in each culture blindly follow their customs and expect everybody else to do the same. Many, particularly the elders in each culture, are considered to be transmitters. They advise others whenever they have doubt about their customs, but often the elders do not know why they should follow particular customs.

Modern psychologists and communicologists have tried to study the reasons for certain cultural behaviors around the world. It seems, however, that the modern empirical findings of human perception and retention have not advanced much farther than the old philosophical speculations. While studying the perceptive activities of the "external" senses and the retentive activities of the "internal" sense, the scientists begin with the basic assumption that the Self does not exist. Some of them equate the Self with the mind. They agree, however, with the ancient philosophers that there are two types of consciousness: the conscious and the subconscious. They also agree on the existence of memory or what we in the next chapter refer to as *retention* or experience. To the modern scientist, what is capable of being confirmed by experimentation is real. Since the existence of the "external" senses could be experimentally proved, they think it is worthwhile to study the senses. According to one modern definition, perception is the process by which sensory input is interpreted in the light of past experience. The input is converted into meaningful experience.

The problem concerning the communication specialist is that what is "meaningful experience" to the people of one culture may not be meaningful to people of another culture. Specifically, what is meaningful to a white man might be meaningless to a black man, or what makes sense to a Westerner may not make sense to an Easterner. Consider the ancient Greek philosophy we discussed in the last chapter. According to a Western scholar, Greek culture is marked by contrast to the self-abregation of the Eastern cultures, and an awareness of the individual's personal freedoms. These have become the tenets of Western culture.[17]

Self-sacrifice and staying away from the glamors of the materialistic world is basic to Hindu and Thervada Buddhist cultures. This attitude has resulted in the acceptance of social responsibility rather than personal freedom as a primary value. Therefore, any sensory input that opposes the value of social responsibility is not acceptable to peoples of Eastern cultures. Also, any message that opposes the concept of individual freedom is not welcomed by Westerners. It is now accepted by psychologists and communicologists that perception and retention take place in a state of mind shaped by the individual's value system.

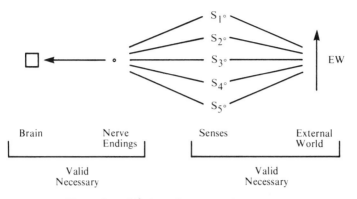

Figure 9. *Modern Concept of Perception*

Communication specialists should take special note of the fact that perception is not merely sensory. Messages are not perceived the way they are intended to be perceived. People perceive messages in relation to their cultural values and philosophical concepts.

SUMMARY

Perception is not entirely a physiological process. Some modern scientists are beginning to recognize that a person's perception is greatly influenced by his culture. The concept of perception has been explained differently by philosophers of different cultures. The ancient Greek philosophers, mainly Plato, said the process consists of four stages: illusion, belief, imagination and understanding. Ancient Hindus said the process consists of two stages: indeterminate and determinate. While indeterminate perception is sensory and influenced by external stimuli, determinate perception is internal and is influenced by the self. Hindus considered the determinate stage important, while Buddhists gave equal importance to both. Islamic philosophy also identifies two types of perception: natural and acquired. Natural perception is innate to all humans and influenced by the perceivers' emotions. Acquired perception is developed by each individual through constant effort. Therefore, acquired perception is more important than natural perception.

Modern scientists explain perception as the input of information from the senses through the nervous system and into the brain. This explanation tends to ignore the influence of cultural values on perceptive behavior. The ancient theories do reflect the cultural values of the proponents of those theories. The ancients' emphasis on mind-object contact in the process of perception indicates the importance they placed on the mind as opposed to the senses.

NOTES

1. Robert B. MacLeod, "What is a Sense?" in *Psychological and Behavioral Aspects of Taste,* ed. Morley R. Kare and Bruce Halpern (Urbana, Ill.: University of Illinois Press, 1961), p. 3.

2. Donald Broadbent, "Attention and Perception of Speech," *Scientific American* (April 1962).

3. K.L. Casey and R. Melzak, "Neural Mechanisms of Pain: A Conceptual Model," in *New Concepts in Pain and Its Clinical Management,* ed. E. Leong Way (Philadelphia, Pa.: F. A. Davis Company, 1967), pp. 13-14.

4. Chandradhar Sharma, *A Critical Survey of Indian Philosophy* (London: Rider and Company, 1960), p. 130.

5. Dale Piepe, *The Naturalistic Tradition in Indian Thought* (Seattle, Wash.: University of Washington Press, 1961), p. 59.

6. E. R. Sarathchardra, *Buddhist Psychology of Perception* (Colombo: The Ceylon University Press, 1959), pp. 11-12.

7. Ibid., p. 105.

8. C.A.F. Rhys Davids, *The Birth of Indian Psychology and Its Development in Buddhism* (London: Luzan and Co., 1936).

9. Piepe, *The Naturalistic Tradition in Indian Thought,* p. 126.

10. T.W. Rhys Davids and Herman Olderberg, *Sacred Books of the East,* Vol. 3 (Oxford: Clarendon Press, 1899).

11. D.T. Suzuki, *Outlines of Mahayana Buddhism* (New York: Shaken Books, 1963), p. 77.

12. Ibid.

13. Ibid., p. 97.

14. Ananda Coomaraswamy, *Buddha and the Gospel of Buddhism* (Hyde Park, N.Y.: University Books, 1964), pp. 222-58.

15. Ismail R. Faruqui, "Islam," in *Great Religions of the World,* ed. Wing-tsit Chan et al. (New York: Macmillan, 1969), p. 320.

16. Robert N. Bellah, "Modernization in a Muslim Society: The Case of Indonesia" in *Religion and Progress in Modern Asia* (New York: The Free Press, 1965), pp. 106-7.

17. Ignatius Brady, *A History of Ancient Philosophy* (Milwaukee, Wis.: Bruce Publishing Co., 1959), p. 28.

4

Retention of Information

The input of information into the human mind begins with perception. The next stage in the process of intercultural communication is retention of that information. In this context, we define retention as the receiving, processing and storing of information in the human mind. Although the physiological process of information storing is the same for all normal human beings, the type and amount stored are not the same. Storing depends upon the cultural values of the individual who receives the information. The information that is culturally relevant to one person may not be so to another. We shall discuss the views of retention as explained by ancient Greek, Hindu, and Buddhist philosophers, and compare these with modern concepts of retention.

Some Ancient Views of Retention

The Greeks, particularly Plato, believed that the highest level of understanding occurs at the intellectual level, which is free of sensory contaminations, as shown in figure 10. In the allegory of the cavemen, Plato shows that the individual has the ability to see things clearly, as if in bright sunlight. At the sensory level are the individual's opinions. They are the result of the shadow knowledge and beliefs that man acquires in darkness, as if in a cave. Then, at the intelligible level, the individual reasons, which leads to understanding.

But it seems that most people do not rise above the level of belief. We are concerned with communicative behavior at the belief level. This barrier, or the darkness, as Plato calls it, is created by the individual's culture. Most of us, including internationally known politicians and scholars,

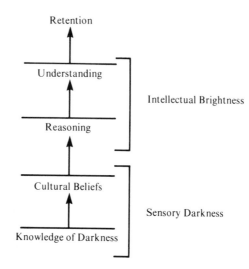

Figure 10. *Plato's Concept of Perception Leading to Retention*

are bound by cultural beliefs. Our behavior stems from those beliefs. Most of our knowledge, the information of the world we have retained, is based on those beliefs. When we rise above our cultural beliefs and reach the intellectual level of understanding, then we can see that all people have their own basic values which direct their behavior, and tend to be oblivious to behavior or ideas reflecting values inherently different from their own.

Indeterminate and Determinate Stages

As mentioned in the last chapter, the Hindus and Buddhists said that there are three ways of acquiring valid knowledge: perception, comparison, and verbal testimony. There are two stages in perception, the sensory stage and the intellectual stage. This is somewhat similar to Plato's concept of the four stages. But since the Nyaya school existed at least four hundred years before the platonic Academy was established and the Buddhists came at approximately the same time as Plato, we can hypothesize that the Hindus and Buddhists thought independently of the Greeks. The sensory stage is also known as indeterminate perception. In this stage the individual sees for the first time through the senses. What he perceives is not definitely accepted, since it could be illusory. The information then reaches the second stage, at which the individual "sees" the same object a second or a third time. Using his wisdom, he accepts or rejects the input. (See figure 11.)

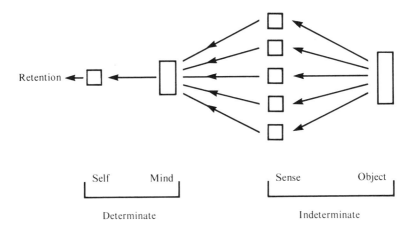

Figure 11. *Hindu and Buddhist Concepts of Perception Leading to Retention*

It is at the determinate level that the individual tallies the new input with the previously existing store of information. Acceptance or rejection depends upon the cultural values of the perceiver.

Consider an example from contemporary American culture. A young American professor was visiting Japan. He was invited by a Japanese friend to a dinner, at which there were several senior Japanese professors. The young American watched how the junior professors were separated from the senior ones. The seniors were accorded special treatment compared to that which juniors received. The young American was not an exception. He saw the same custom everywhere in Japan. The struggle of the younger ones to climb up the ladder to get recognition was pitiful, according to the young American. As we show in figure 11, there are two stages in the input of information. The first stage is when information on anything that the individual is exposed to is transmitted through the senses. This stage is the indeterminate stage. At this stage it is not certain whether or not the information is acceptable to the perceiver. The young American was at this stage when he perceived the strivings of the young Japanese. In his American university he had been elected to several positions. Wherever he went he was given special treatment. It was different in Japan; when he inquired, he was informed that the young Japanese accepted such a system. Some of them felt there was security for a young man under such a system, for once he has a job he will not be fired. He is always protected by his patron. He does not have to struggle, as in the more competitive United States, to keep his job. If a young Japanese makes a mistake, his patron takes the blame for it, but in America, when an employee makes a mistake nobody comes to his rescue. He has to defend himself. But despite all the Japanese arguments in support of their system, the young American was not impressed.

To the young American professor, equality was a positive value, and a hierarchical system was negative. The concept of patronizing was loathsome. He rejected the idea. The rejection occurred after the foreign information was tallied with the information already stored in his mind. After processing, the information on the Japanese system could not be fitted into the young American's mind. This second stage we refer to as determinate perception.

Memory Is the Standard

What a person remembers is valid knowledge to him. He uses that as a standard to test new inputs, which are accepted or rejected depending upon how they tally with his memory. Unless there is strong reason for believing it is no longer valid, the old information stays in the memory. The individual is reluctant to reject already stored information, believing it to be correct. The resistance to new information is very strong when it comes to cultural values. As did the young American professor, a person fights to prove that his information is right. In the case of values, nobody accepts a new value without fierce resistance. Despite all the wars and other persuasive acts, we still cannot say the primary values of any culture have changed.

Memory plays an effective role when something similar to the existing information is put in. When an African tribal member sees a five-foot-long, black, ropelike thing lying in front of a snake pit, even from a distance he can tell it is a snake. He has seen many snakes basking in the sun in front of their pits. That is not a new sight for him. But an American who has never seen a snake would immediately take it for a black rope. If the African goes close to it and examines to find that it is really a rope and not a snake, that is sufficient proof for him to say that everything that looks like a rope and lies in front of a snake pit is not a snake. On the other hand, if the American finds out that it moves and has a deadly hood and hiss, he would run for his life. He has also found sufficient proof to alter his stored information. In intercultural communication the persons involved perceive other people's worlds with the aid of their own memories.

Some Hindu and Buddhist Views

Memory or retention of information is important in illiterate or less literate cultures. The nature of memory has been studied and discussed in detail by the Hindus since the time when the Vedas and other works were orally composed but writing had not yet been invented. It was important to remember the right words and the right pronunciations. It is also probable that the Easterners' ability to remember, to store information, is greater than that of the Westerners. Staal gives the reason:

> The Vedic Indians looked down upon writing and considered it as impure. It is very probable that the Indians came into contact with writing only when they had possessed for centuries a vast literature transmitted orally. In India, where people have a memory vastly superior to ours, it may not be necessary to assume that "I" organization "meme du canon veduque ne se guere quere sans le concours de l'ecriture." But it is obvious that under such circumstances very much depends upon memory. This does undoubtedly explain at least partly the extraordinary importance accorded to memory by the Indians. Forgetting of what one has learnt before is like slaying a Brahman. "Honour Memory: says an Upanishad."[1]

One school of Hindu and Buddhist scholars said that memory is knowledge of a person's past. It is representative cognition. What was perceived in the past is presented again. It is not the same as recognition since the object is not presented again. In memory there is a revival of past images and other forms of perceptions. These past perceptions have been retained by the Self. Hindus believe there are at least twenty-three causes of retention. Memories are either true or false. They are true when related to something valid or real. False memory is caused by erroneous cognition.

Dreams can also be perceptions of the past. Organic disorders, unfulfilled desires, and past activities interfere with these perceptions. They do not have the clarity of perceptions that occur when a person is awake. Some dreams also have moral value.

Another school of Hindus and Buddhists believes that memory is the recognition of something that was presented to the senses and perceived, not really cognition. The form and order in which the thing was perceived do not exist any more. Even when the object recognized really exists, the memory of it has been shaped by what was presented at an earlier time. Therefore, memory is not a valid source of knowledge. Other schools however, say that memory (Smrithi) is a revival of impressions of past experience. It is a repetition of the images of what really did exist. Fire is perceived as something that burns your fingers, since the burning is experienced. Therefore, memory is real. They say, in fact, that *Smrithi* is one of the three sources of valid knowledge. The other two are what a person hears from a trustworthy source (Shruthi) and what he realizes by his own experience, such as by yoga (Anubhuthi).

One must remember that whenever Hindus and Buddhists argued about valid knowledge, there was always a subtle reference to knowledge of the so-called Absolute Reality. The goal of all knowledge should be to understand that of reality, not any material object. Seeing what cannot be seen through the senses should be the purpose of perception. Hindus believed in knowing the Reality by mind-self contact and meditation, and Buddhists believed in sense-object contact and intuition, but none placed much importance on the individual's memory.

Thought and Expression

Some scholars believe that man thinks first and then expresses his thoughts. Others argue that man thinks in his language and that he cannot think without a language. The argument will probably continue forever. It began with the ancient Hindus as early as the eighth century B.C., and is still going on. A careful study of phenomena such as meditation and yoga indicates that certain thoughts are beyond expression. Earlier, we mentioned the Sanskrit expression "Ananda," which is the intellectual pleasure the Hindus and Buddhists derive when they experience self-realization and knowing the Absolute Truth. The thoughts of such pleasures are indescribable, since each person should experience them and they cannot be explained to another person. Such rare phenomena lead us to believe that thought and expression are different factors. A person does not think in his language, he just thinks. The intensity of the thinking process and the resultant depth of thought depend upon the thinker's innate ability: the more he trains himself in activities such as meditation and yoga, the deeper will be his thoughts. A person thinks first and then develops his thoughts in language. The process could be explained by means of this diagram:

$$\text{Thought} \longrightarrow \text{Thought} + \text{Code} \longrightarrow \text{Expression}$$

The mind of the individual is the center of thought. That is, the thought and code are integrated into verbal or non-verbal expression. If the thinker's language is rich enough in vocabulary to codify the thought, all thoughts can be expressed. Otherwise, they remain in the person's memory and are never transmitted.

Thought and Intuition

Sublime thoughts such as those related to Absolute Truth are not easy to express in speech, but two thinkers who have the same experience can understand each other intuitively. We mentioned that the Buddha also emphasized the importance of developing our intuitive faculties. He said that the Truth cannot be explained, but it can be understood by intuition. Those that develop such faculties can communicate without the aid of speech. Consider the story of a young American who goes to the East in search of answers to his many problems. He meets a guru who lives at the foot of a mountain in an Asian country. The young American asks many questions, but the guru does not answer any of them. Instead, he asks the young man to stay in his *ashram*. The young man, being impatient of not getting anywhere, goes to the top of the mountain and stays there for several days. He enjoys the beauty of the mountain. One day he gets up early in the morning and looks at the eastern horizon. He sees the sun trying to emerge out of haze. The millions of sun-rays are breaking through the haze and falling on the mountain top. Somewhere in that haze he can see brightness of the sun. He knows that the bright sun is certainly going to come out any time. But it has to rise above the haze and penetrate it.

Then, suddenly, like a flash, it occurs to the young man that life is just like that. It is full of sorrows and disappointments. Man has to penetrate and rise above them. Then happiness appears. Sorrow and happiness exist side by side, but once man rises above sorrow, it melts away. The young man's face brightens. He has found answers to his questions. He runs down the mountain to the ashram and sees the guru. The guru looks at his face and says, "Son, you have found the answer, haven't you?" The guru can understand the pleasure the young American is experiencing since he has experienced it several times in his own life. They can understand each other by intuition, but cannot communicate their experience verbally.

One reason some people do not like to answer questions about their religion and philosophy is that they think the questioner cannot understand their religion. Religious experience is beyond expression, and to them, very personal. It cannot be shared with anyone else. When an American asks a Hindu or a Buddhist questions on Hinduism or Buddhism, they may evade answering or give answers that do not satisfy him. The American may think the Asian's religion is inferior to his own and that therefore the Asian is afraid to answer. On the other hand, the Asian may think the American does not have sufficient experience to understand the sublime Truth. Although there has recently been a great interest in studies of parapsychology and extrasensory perception, these studies have not yet explained the phenomena of intuition. Intuition is part of the system of the individual's retention that only another person with similar retentive power can understand. A detailed discussion of intuition probably belongs in the realm of philosophy. Scholars such as Suzuki and Huxley discuss in more detail the nature of intuition. Extrasensory perception related to intuition is now being studied, perhaps most, by scientists in the Soviet Union and Canada. It is not our purpose in this book to explain these studies, but we wish to stress that intuition plays an important role in intercultural communication, and individuals with intuitive powers can understand this phenomena much better than those without.

Some Modern Concepts of Retention

Now we shall consider some modern concepts and research findings in the area of retention as it relates to intercultural communication.

A group of students in an American university was asked to identify figure 12, which is the outline of something they might have seen or heard of. One said it was the outline of clouds; another said it was a picture of an African head-dress; it reminded a third student of an animal. The students were finally told that it was the outline of a picture of a Hindu temple. They said they would never have guessed, since they did not know what a Hindu temple looked like.

Figure 12

Just as the study of any other aspect of man's mental activity is elusive, so is the explanation of memory. Different ideas and approaches to uncovering the mystery of memory have led to the conclusion that inside man's head is a brain which controls all his activity. At a stage in his quest for enlightenment, man turned to the study of phrenology, going so far as to attempt to assemble, classify and relate to definite cranial areas those faculties which control certain aspects of behavior. Although today we have reached a higher degree of sophistication in building upon those earlier concepts, there remains much more to learn about memory. We do have some notions about the structure of the brain. We can even associate with some measure of confidence certain bodily functions with certain parts of the brain. Let us first briefly examine one aspect of the brain in terms of structure.

The brain has five major divisions, the medulla, pons, cerebellum, thalamus and the cerebrum. The crowning structure of the central axis, the cerebrum of the human brain contains more neurons than all the rest of the nervous system. The cerebrum is that part of the brain considered to be the storage and retrieval station for memory.

Neuron Function as a Cultural Factor

The physiologist is most likely to restrict his study of the brain to structure, nomenclature and functions. In discussing the functions, he describes *how* the different parts of the brain, particularly the cerebrum, are responsible for communicative activities such as receiving, processing, storing and conveying information. Such information might be received through any one of the five senses and transmitted to the parts of the cerebrum. Take, for example, the receiving stimuli such as the smell of incense, the sound of music, the taste of food, the touch of skin, and the sight of beauty. While the physiologist can point out which part of the brain is responsible for receiving information through which sense, he is unable to explain *why* the organism likes or dislikes a certain smell, sound, taste, touch or sight. As discussed earlier, these likes and dislikes are culturally based and not physiologically incurred. The functions of the brain are subject to peculiar cultural imports. When dealing with the functions of the brain, each physiologist is oblivious to his own or other cultures. Perhaps what we really need are experiments concerning the relationship between cultural values and brain function.

The study of intercultural communication also points out the need to understand the relationship between the functions of neurons and cultural variables. We would be remiss not to acknowledge current efforts to show the correlation between cognitive behavior and ethnic background, such as some controversial studies of intelligence in America, which have attempted to correlate intelligence to biological characteristics. The physiologist or geneticist tends to apply his own values as standards and, while doing so, use his own frame of reference as universal; to use his own expectations of an intelligent person; and to ignore the fact that the amount of information an individual retains is directly related to his familiarity with his own culture. The point here is that the geneticist is testing his subjects using his own cultural expectations as measures of intelligence, while his subjects are answering using their own cultural values as their frames of reference. When the expectations and answers do not match, the geneticist tends to brand his subjects as less intelligent and gives the ethnic background as the reason for the low intelligence quotient. With an understanding of the cultural values of the subjects, and assuming that he intends to be objective, the geneticist would refrain from correlating intelligence solely to ethnic or racial background.

If a Western psychologist or geneticist administers an intelligence test based on his own cultural information to non-Western subjects, the latter group will probably be branded as less intelligent. On the other hand, if a non-Western psychologist or geneticist administers an IQ test to a group of Western subjects, he may also brand the latter group as less intelligent. Because both scientists develop their IQ tests based on their own cultural milieu of information, we would say the results of both tests are invalid by definition, since results do not take into consideration the cultural base of determinants.

Sensation, Perception, and Memory

It is difficult to discuss memory without illustrating the relationship of sensation and perception to memory and the brain. Sensitivity to stimulation is a necessary condition to living. Stimulation is directly related to environmental conditions capable of igniting a response in the organism. In higher organisms such as man, this energy change excites specialized receptors or cells. These specialized receptor cells have become sensitive to variant energy changes, albeit relatively insensitive to other energy changes.

The special sensitivities are commonly grouped into five catagories: visual (sight), auditory (hearing), olfactory (smell), gustatory (taste), and cutaneous (touch). Although these five classes are believed to have several clearly defined subclasses, for our purposes it is sufficient to add as general categories kinesthetic, equilibrium, and organic sensitivities. The sensitivity of the receptors and the subsequent reactivity of the organism involve many paradoxes. The relations between the physical intensity of the stimulation and the awareness and interpretation afforded by the organism seem to depend upon many factors. As relates to memory, these factors include sensation and perception.

Many scholars ignore differences between sensation and perception. The same phenomena are classified under sensation in one text and under perception in another. However, all schools of thought admit there is a sensory core to all effective stimulation. Illusions, figure-ground relations, transpositions, and contextual relations may make the understanding of stimulus energy changes and the resulting responses a more difficult subject. The fact remains that organisms respond in terms of their interpretations of the stimulus situation, regardless of the "true" nature of the stimulus.

The activities of organisms are based on observed relations of objects and events within a framework of space, intensity, description and time. The study, from a genetic perspective, thus proceeds from the simple sensitivity to the highly developed integrations of reasoning and conceptual thinking.

Piaget's Views on Concept Development

Turning from a purely physiological approach, let us now consider other approaches to understanding the phenomenon of memory. Piaget, the famous Swiss psychologist, has perhaps gained more insight into memory than any of his contemporaries. He observed, classified, codified and systematically recorded behavioral observations of children. Piaget has described the stages in an infant's development of cognition of the external world and has described the parallel developments of cognition and goal-directed behavior. He developed a construct in which he categorized infant behavior into six stages, beginning with stage one, occurring just after birth, and progressing through successive stages to the sixth stage, which is at approximately 16 months and 5 days. He observed that the preschool child, although he is past the sixth stage, does not show all the characteristics of maturity. But at that age, the child does develop a memory, enabling him to manipulate objects in his environment in order to attain those things which satisfy his needs or give him pleasure and entertainment. Piaget also noted that differences in intelligence varied among children and relate to the amount a given child will remember. He believes the more intelligent a child, the more information he can absorb and retain.

Essentially, Piaget refers to two types of intelligence. One is the innate intelligence, which is probably constant in each child and is the property of that child. The second is a variable kind of intelligence that evolves from the constant. These variables consist of abilities such as recognizing objects, adding numbers and manipulating actions. But the point the Swiss psychologist does not mention is that both the constant and variable intelligence are culturally derived. The concepts in the mind of a Swiss child for example, are not the same as those of a Nigerian child. Even in Switzerland, the concepts of a French Swiss child can differ from those of a German Swiss child. We cannot consider Piaget's findings as having universal implications since they are not based on universal observation of children. In this case also we see the need for comparing and synthesizing the data on concept development in children from around the world, which in turn demands effective intercultural communication and comparison.

The Erikson Approach

Yet another study of memory is that of Erikson, who assumes a sociological approach. He believes that some children's views of the world are distorted views, views which may give rise to deviant behavior. If we assume that all behavior is purposive and aimed at coping with environment, deviant behavior and normal behavior must follow the same principle.

When its environment is too demanding or unpredictable or overly un-rewarding or cruel, the organism, bearing the scars of many unfortunate experiences, comes to expect the iminent recurrence of similar events or conditions. Erikson believes one may view life as a lovely garden—or as a "jungle filled with wild beasts, where one devours or is devoured."[2] Through early experiences, each of us develops attitudes and expectations which we carry throughout life. We all assume postures that we believe necessary to get along in particular circumstances or with particular people, and often these attitudes continue long after the original memo-ries causing them have disappeared. Erikson's studies deal with some of the anxious behavior patterns developed by children in order to secure comfort and avoid pain, patterns adaptive at one period in life but mal-adaptive and ineffective at later periods, or patterns which never were adaptive. Several of his articles contain emphatic and insightful descrip-tions of unrealistic expectations and feelings in disturbed children as a result of memories. Some discuss the people and situations to which a particular child was forced to adjust, with crippling results. Erikson rea-sons that if antisocial behavior is to be controlled and the ability to han-dle stress effectively increased, understanding of the nature, causes, and possibilities for altering distorted perceptions is necessary. Added to these complications growing out of perception and memory, the situa-tion becomes even more complex in an intercultural milieu. For example, Erikson cites the case of Peter whose mother had difficulty understand-ing how her child's masculine behaviors had taken on unusual propor-tions, as a result of his Chinese babysitter's influence. In Chinese culture, the female nurtures and encourages, even in very small boys, the domi-nance of males over females. It is considered a way of life in China.[3]

In this case, we have an American white woman whose son at the time was four years old. Up to this point she had entrusted her son to an Orien-tal nurse, whose memories of cultural aspects of her homeland were shap-ing the perceptions of the four-year-old boy. It was during a period of budding, provoked, and disapproved masculinity that the nurse left. Whether she left or was sent away hardly mattered to the child. What mattered was that he lived in a culture which provides paid mother sub-stitutes from a different culture.

In chapter 2, we tried to show that human nature and cultural values are not one and the same. In fact, cultural values are imposed by a society on its members to control human instincts. A male child, even at the age of four, is not only attracted to the female, but tries to show his masculin-ity in relationship to the female. Such instincts are handled differently by different cultures subject to their values. In the Orient, for example, the male is considered the provider and protector of the family. Since he has such responsibility, he is treated as more important than the female members of his family from childhood. In the case of the four-year-old and his nurse, who was many years his senior, his male superiority is reinforced by her. In other words, in the Oriental cultures, the male superiority and responsibility to the family are the important values. In those cultures, the male child starts his training at birth in order to fulfill his male role. On the other hand, in Western cultures the male child does not begin his training for the male role at such an early age. Also, the concept of male superiority is not as dominant in the Western cultures as in the Oriental. In the Western cultures the concept of equality and individuality counter such overt behavior of the male child.

The point we are attempting to convey here is that the images in the minds of the Chinese nurse, the American child and his mother are all culturally different and culturally derived. Each has different expectations of male and female roles. Therefore, the American mother punished the Chinese nurse for not reinforcing American cultural expectations. Chances are the Oriental nurse would have been rewarded had she reinforced the American mother's expectations.

Memories developed as a result of association with one culture have profound influence in an intercultural situation. An individual's memories are natural derivatives of cultural determinants. To the extent that these memories are drawn upon as a background to be applied to new situations in an intercultural setting, the likelihood of the "right" conclusions being reached to fit the intercultural situation are remote, unless the two or more cultures are inherently similar. In examining major cultures, one invariably finds that the beliefs, values, habits, and traditions of one culture are almost the opposite of those of another. This is especially true in East-West comparisons of cultures.

Some Related Factors

In this section we shall discuss some factors related to the ancient and modern concepts of retention which directly or indirectly affect our interaction with others. These factors include symbols, stereotypes, and images.

Cultural Symbols

Symbolizing is probably the easiest way to store information. It enables a person to simplify complicated information. The Japanese word

Cha shithsu for the traditional tea house does not mean just a tea house in the modern western sense, but symbolizes a great tradition called *Chanoyu,* or the tea ceremony:

> It was originally a monastic custom introduced by Japanese Buddhists who had gone to China for study. It is forgotten in the land of its origin, and survives in Japan as an esthetic pastime, a cult in which the beverage is idealized. Devotees of Chanoyu appreciate art and worship nature through the medium of the indescribably delicate and refreshing aroma of powdered tea.[4]

The pipul tree which is commonly known in Asia as the *bodhi* tree represents the divinity attached to it in two great religious systems, Hinduism and Buddhism. In Hinduism it is supposed to be the abode of the Trinity: Brahma, Vishnu and Shiva. No Hindu would want to see a bodhi tree chopped down. In Mysore City in south India, a rich businessman purchased a large lot of land in a prominent business district. He wanted to build a block of buildings consisting of a movie house, a theater, a restaurant, stores and offices. But right in the center of the lot there was a bodhi tree. Word spread that he was going to chop down the tree. That tree had been there for generations. Children had played under it and elders had worshipped it. It had become a part of their cultural lives. They demonstrated against cutting it down. The businessman said it was his property and he had the right to do whatever he wanted with it. But the people in the neighborhood did not agree. Both the businessman and the people were adamant. The fight lasted at least a year until finally the businessman gave up and built the new buildings around the tree.

We have a tendency to remember great amounts of information or complicated concepts with reference to just one item. This one item serves as an index to the complex of information or concepts. Tannenbaum believes that an index is a single stimulus element or a stimulus complex which may serve to predispose a particular interpretation or meaning.[5]

When we mention the city of Paris, some may recall first the Eiffel Tower, then all the other things they have seen and heard about that city. One Asian scholar still remembers all about an American university with reference to a girl he first saw on that campus. He had just gotten to the campus from the airport after a three-day flight from his Asian country. To him the sight of girls wearing shorts was new, and this girl was unusually fat besides. She was wearing tight shorts and a thin blouse. It was raining on the campus that day. When he saw the girl he just stood there staring at her. She was embarrassed to see a foreign student stare at her as he did, and covered her bare legs with a long raincoat. He realized it was unmannerly of him to stare at the girl as he did, but the sight was stamped in his memory. Whenever the name of that university is mentioned, the first thing he remembers is that fat girl in tight shorts. For the Asian student the picture of the girl serves as an index to open up the entire memory of the university.

Indexes are also cultural symbols. Communicators use cultural symbols in order to interact successfully with their audiences. A picture of a cow and her calf reminds Hindu of motherhood and sacredness. A picture of a family man symbolizes a good guy. These symbols help candidates win elections and succeed in business. Indira Gandhi's political party used a cow and calf as its symbol in India's general elections in 1971. Her party won. In the United States, political candidates are often pictured with their families so the voters will tend think the candidates are good guys. In Hawaii in 1970, John Burns presented himself as a leader benovelent to the Hawaiians, but would not appear in public with them to ask for their votes. The predominantly Oriental voters of Hawaii were reminded of the images of Asian maharajas, emperors and leaders that are benevolent to their people but rarely appear in public. Burns was elected.

Communicators in each culture have developed their own dialects and have conditioned their audiences to those dialects. They have also developed their own symbols for making communication easy and vivid. The dialects and symbols are designed to uphold the cultural superiority of the communicators. Their people remember the symbols, which reinforce their belief in the greatness of their culture. Some of these symbolizing techniques are stereotyping and ethnocentrism.

Stereotyping

Stereotypes are symbols intended to identify ethnic groups or races. They are usually standardized mental pictures used to oversimplify the characteristics of members of another ethnic group, race, subculture or culture. These oversimplifications can stem from the opinions and observations of a broadcaster or a reporter in just one or two situations. A snake charmer wearing a big turban represents any Indian. A sly-looking fellow with a long pigtail is identified as Chinese.

A study conducted by Radio Free Europe has shown that the people of Poland had certain stereotypes of themselves and others, most of them formed as a result of input by mass media. They had positive stereotypes of themselves and usually negative ones of other people. Another study conducted in Hawaii showed that the students of Hawaii had certain stereotypes of mainland Chinese. These stereotypes were formed primarily as a result of input from radio and television. But after watching the live broadcasts from China at the time of President Nixon's visit to that country, their images of the Chinese changed slightly toward a positive direction. The American black is stereotyped as lazy, shiftless, stupid and a thief.

Stereotyping is a useful tool. Used effectively, it can cast a certain image in the minds of those who need it in order to elevate themselves. Certain cultures, especially colonizers, have been known to employ stereotyping as a tool for projecting the image they wish to have of the people over whom they have control. The tool can also be used to dehumanize, deface and to reduce self-concept. The art of stereotyping becomes most effective when everyone, both the stereotyper and the stereotyped, begin to conform to the belief that certain images represent certain people. This, of course, is the ideal end of the art of stereotyping.

We have up to now discussed mainly the negative use of the term, but it should not be overlooked that stereotyping can be used in the positive sense. Furthermore, we might classify stereotypes under two distinct headings: auto-stereotype and hetero-stereotype. The former is the image one has of his own people; the latter is the image of another people. Obviously the auto-stereotypes tend to be positive, and to flatter the individual in whose culture it occurs. Hetero-stereotypes could be either positive or negative, depending upon how culturally close or remote the hetero-stereotype is to the culture in which it is occurring.

Stereotyping makes communication easy. Once an image is created in the minds of a people, it will be easy to communicate any information related to that image. The mere presentation of the appropriate stimulus evokes in the perceiver a total comprehensive image of the subject under communication. Take, for example, the facility with which the American mass media, particularly television, transmit information related to members of foreign cultures such as Mexicans. The moment we see a man with an over-sized hat and a carpet on his back who looks lazy and speaks with a funny accent, we know he is Mexican, and we immediately associate everything we know about Mexicans with him. Conversely, the image of an Englishman created by the same mass media is positive. The Englishman also wears a hat and has an accent, but these details are presented in such a way as to create respect and admiration for the British.

The studies show that although stereotyping makes it easy for the media men to communicate with their audiences, they create misunderstanding about the people they are stereotyping. We tend to look at all Mexicans as lazy, Chinese as sly, blacks as shiftless and East Indians as snake charmers.

Fragrance and Music

Appreciation of any new fragrance or musical sound depends upon the smells and sounds the individual remembers. These remembrances tend to be ethnocentric. Two ladies from Kansas who were visiting Hawaii passed an Oriental store at a shopping center in Honolulu. The smell of burning incense was coming from the store. One lady told the other, "I hate the smell of incense, I've never smelled anything like it before." They did not go into the store.

A music teacher in Oregon received a Christmas gift from her son who was going to school in California. It was a recording of a concert conducted by an Asian instrumentalist. The music teacher played the record to discover the Asian instrument was called a sitar. After listening to it she said, "It sounds like a bunch of noise. I've never heard such a thing before."

Literate or illiterate, people remember most information in the form of symbols, images, smells and touch. Any symbol that is close to one's own culture has a better chance of retention than a symbol that is not close.

The American Image

At the outset, we should make a clear distinction between the images we are going to talk about here and the values and stereotypes we have discussed elsewhere.While stereotypes are based on selected,one-time real experiences, images are based on what a person would like another to be.

Going a step further, we might say that while stereotypes apply to selected observations of members of another culture made one or two times, cultural values, although also observations, arise among the majority of a people over many generations. This could be represented as follows:

Cultural value	*Stereotype*	*Image*
True most of the time for more than 50% of a population for many generations	True only once or twice for less than 1% of a population in just one generation	Not true at any time for any generation

In America, the way in which a member of one cultural group interacts with a member of another cultural or ethnic group depends upon the image he has of the people of that other group. Interaction also depends upon the current relationship the American government may have with the parent country from which his ancestors emigrated. If the skin color of members of the other group happens to be white, the image tends to be positive and favorable. If the skin color happens to be black, yellow, brown or red, however, the image tends to be negative and less favorable.

Each society develops a number of institutions designed to carry out those principles. These include variations of schools, churches, universities, armies, internal security, health care, the diplomatic corps, penal systems, mass media, etc., which, when assembled, form a government. The assemblage and arrangement, again, will vary from one culture to another. Ideally, the efforts of all these institutions are concerted to perpetuate a given culture. Through various means, at great cost of time and effort, each culture shapes the internal as well as the external image it wishes to project. The founding fathers and subsequent shapers of the United States Constitution, in writing that historic document, did not necessarily anticipate the mass immigration of peoples of other color. Although prior to and shortly after the adoption of the Constitution the slave industry was initiated, the founding fathers were dealing with the general welfare of immigrants from Western Europe who lived in the original thirteen states. They did not anticipate large numbers of immigrants from the Eastern part of the world, the so-called "Third World Nations," that we have today. Hence, during America's developmental stage and since the adoption of the Constitution, the government has purposively promulgated the image of Western Europeans as the major inhabitants of America.

Until recently, and generally with the exception of the intellectual classes in most Eastern cultures, the image generated when the word American was mentioned was that of a white man. This image tends to ignore countless members of minority groups in America, such as Puerto Ricans, Cubans, Negroes, American and East Indians, Mexicans, Japanese, Chinese, Filipinos, etc. This image does not occur by accident but by design. The five principles are employed to exact the internal and external image a culture wishes to have. And since all institutions are working toward the same general goal of reinforcing desired ends, other forces, represented by the appropriate institutions, can serve too. A case in point would be that the universities can control the number of minorities successfully completing their degree programs in diplomatic service. If a minority member happens to slip through a university program in diplomatic service the U.S. Department of State can disqualify him, and if forced to hire the minority member, the State Department can confine him to duty inside the United States, thereby achieving the goal of not placing minorities in positions of responsibility in foreign countries and projecting, with adequate support and control, the image of the American as white.

Perhaps one of the most prominent intercultural symbols in America is its written and unwritten code of law. In most jurisdictions throughout America, the written code has been modified to indicate equal application of the law to all citizens. But prior to the passage of the 1964 Civil Rights Legislation, there were not only dual laws for whites and blacks but dual application of those laws. For example, in certain southern states, such as Georgia, South Carolina and Louisiana, it was unlawful for a black to appear in the white section of town after dark without permission from a white man. It was unlawful for a black man to whistle or gaze at a white woman. Either action could lead to a sizable fine or jail sentence, if the black was lucky and escaped a lynch mob. Such behavior on the part of the black was viewed as defiant and disrespectful of local custom, and therefore worthy of punishment.

The unwritten code of law evolved from those local and regional customs and practices which both whites and blacks recognized as taboo for each. One such taboo was that under no circumstances would blacks and whites socialize together. No matter how solid their friendship, which may have developed from living or working in close proximity, social mixing of races for whatever purpose could lead to legal ramifications or simple social rejection.

The intercultural symbol which was most atrocious and devastating, and which has even survived the abolition of slavery and the establishment of the 1964 Civil Rights Legislation, is the commonly accepted, unwritten code that says if a black man murders another black man, the murderer will not likely receive more than a five years' prison sentence if apprehended and convicted. In some states, the murderer of a black man, whether black or especially if white, may not even be rigorously sought by the police authorities. As late as 1960, in the state of North Carolina, if a black who murdered another black was apprehended, tried, convicted and sentenced to prison but happened to be a sharecropper with a reputation for being a "good worker," his white boss could arrange with the sentencing judge and the prison authorities a so-called work-release program. Under this arrangement, the black convict could be released to his white boss after serving a year or two of his five-year sentence. For food, shelter and small spending change, the white boss could exact five-and-a-half days of hard labor from the black convict at no cost in wages for the remainder of his sentence. It was difficult, conversely, for a black man to escape death when he murdered a white man, even if in self defense. Under such circumstances, the black man was considered fortunate to be sentenced to life imprisonment at hard labor. An intercultural symbol emerges from these examples: it is almost all right to kill a black man.

A white man can take thousands of dollars from a black man, who automatically rationalizes that he is helpless. He can't kill the white man because he will in turn be executed. He can't seek legal redress because he perceives the white lawyers, white police, white courts of law, white judicial system, and white penal institutions as friends of the white man, and hence enemies of the black man. In short, to a black man, the blacks symbolize powerlessness while the white man is a symbol of omnipotence.

Generally, the image of the blackman as projected by the white man, through his face-to-face interactions as well as through the mass media, is that he tends to be inferior. The image of the black man is invariably one of passivity, powerlessness, ignorance, and lack of social status. The white man associates a Chinese, whether he is a banker, professor, doctor, lawyer or even a senator, with menial types of employment. The same is true of the images the white man has of brown- and red-skinned persons. On the contrary, when an American white man sees a German, he associates him with the professions such as science, industry and the academics. A Frenchman would be associated with the fine arts and culture.

The image of the American as promulgated by the white American abroad will have a profound impact on foreigners. When a Nepalese visits the American embassy in Khatmandu, he expects to see a white man as the American ambassador, not a black man, Mexican, or Japanese. To foreigners, Americans are all white and are masters, administrators, university professors and such. Some of them know there are black Americans, but they associate them with menial jobs and certainly not with the diplomatic corps.

Another area in which the white man's image is heightened is in the manner in which foreigners interact with American minorities. In support of this statement, we offer the following examples. While the American black wishes to relate to African peoples, the Africans will shy away from such contact because of their negative image of black Americans. When an African student goes to an American university, in his everyday life he would rather associate with white students. Japanese tourists in Hawaii prefer to live with whites rather than Japanese islanders.

Despite the fact we have used the American white man as a classic example, we should point out in all fairness to him that the ruling classes in other countries are promulgating similar images. The image we have of a German is that he is Aryan with blonde hair, blue eyes and white skin, while in fact there are Turkish, Italian, and even black Germans. Similarly, in Great Britain there are a considerable number of Indian, Chinese, Arabs and black Britons, but our image of a Briton is that of a white man.

Violent and Nonviolent Behavior as Symbols of Communication

We have mentioned that aggressiveness is a positive value in Western, particularly the American, cultures. Violent behavior is an off-shoot of that value. Such behavior is promoted to a great extent by the mass media. We do not mean to say that media operators deliberately promote that behavior, but the way in which their programs, particularly on television, are presented stimulate it. Sitaram defines the violent television show as

the use of unreasonable and unjustifiable force to cause damage to persons and property, the force could be physical or psychological![6]

The viewer who already believes in the value of aggressiveness is stimulated by the violent show. In his mind, he bears the image of violent characters, as has been confirmed by research.[7] The violent character becomes an ideal for the viewer, and he tries to imitate that character. The research done by Sitaram has shown that reckless automobile drivers always remember the images of violent television characters. Such images do affect the viewers' behavior in the sense that they try to imitate the characters. To these viewers, driving like the violent characters is a symbol of aggressiveness and prowess. Thus violence has become a symbol of communication in some Western cultures.

Conversely, in the non-Western cultures nonviolence has become a symbol of ideal behavior. Although the nations comprising those cultures tend to be violent at times, the people at the cultural level still remain non-violent and consider it to be a positive value. A study done in many violent and nonviolent cultures has shown that the majority of nonviolent cultures exist in Asia and Africa.

A people who believe in nonviolence as a value also believe that it needs great courage to be nonviolent in the face of violent people. They worship nonviolent personalities such as Mahatma Gandhi and Martin Luther King. However, the violent ones do not respect such personalities or those who worship them. Communication is not easy between two peoples who do not respect each other. Again, each of them judges the other on the basis of their own values. Ethnocentrism plays its role in such instances of intercultural communication. If the interacting members apply instead, the theory of cultural relativism, the violent or nonviolent method of communication, as the case may be, makes sense. In aggressive cultures such as the American, violent communication probably is more effective than nonviolent. It is possible that nonviolence is mistaken for cowardice and violence for courage. On the contrary, in the Asian cultures nonviolent methods of communication are greatly respected. In Japan, for example, people shy away from a show of power in business negotiations; they even hesitate to say "no" to the negotiators. They have other ways of saying "no" when they disagree. Refraining from answering a question is one such way. When an inexperienced American business executive tries to communicate in Japanese business circles, he might try to bear in mind the image of the Japanese as nonaggressive. But when trying to show his superiority, he may act out his own image of an aggressive business executive.

SUMMARY

Retention is defined as the activity of processing and storing information received through perception. Like perception, retention is also influenced by the retainer's culture. Information that supports his cultural values is selected for retention while other information is rejected. The individual's expression of ideas is based on his repertoire of stored information. Retention is also related to one's thought and intuition.

Ancient cultures placed great importance on retention. In Hindu, Buddhist and Islamic cultures, great value is assigned to memorizing stanzas from sacred books such as the *Vedas, Sutras* and the *Koran.* Information is retained in the form of symbols, stereotypes, images, sounds, etc.

Ancient theories of retention are related to cultural values. Modern theories of development and retention of concepts such as those by Piaget tend to ignore the influence of culture on retention.

Communication between members of different cultures is affected by the stereotypes and images retained by the members of each culture.

NOTES

1. J. F. Staal, *Word Order in Sanskrit and Universal Grammar* (Holland: D. Riedel Publishing Company, 1967).

2. Erik H. Erikson, *Dimensions of a New Identity* (New York: Norton, 1974), pp. 63-64.

3. Ibid.

4. Yasunosuke Fukukita, *Tea Cult of Japan* (Tokyo: Japan Travel Bureau, 1961), p. 17.

5. Percy H. Tannenbaum, "The Indexing in Communication," in *Communication and Culture,* ed. Alfred G. Smith (New York: Holt, Rinehart and Winston, 1966), p. 481.

6. K. S. Sitaram, "Violent Television and Aggressive Behavior," *Newsletter* of International Communication Association, Austin, Texas, 1973, and Associated Press release, April 1972.

7. Ibid.

5

Expression of Ideas:
Verbal Communication

Theoretically, expression of ideas could be compared with the output of information by a computer. The computer puts out information in response to an input. The output is sorted and selected from a storage, or memory, of information in the computer. A person's expression of ideas is the output from a vast storage of information that he emits voluntarily or in response to a stimulus.

Basically, expression is in the form of symbols, which can be verbal and nonverbal. The situation in which the symbols are used can be interpersonal or mass media. In the next three chapters we shall discuss expression of ideas in three parts: (1) verbal communication; (2) nonverbal communication; and (3) mass media communication.

The Study of Verbal Communication

Verbal communication is studied in schools and colleges in the United States and other countries under different course titles such as Speech, Speech-Communication, Linguistics, and so forth. Both at the undergraduate and high school levels, students are taught how to speak in different situations. In most schools and universities, they are taught how to speak their own language the right way. The discipline of speech is divided into subjects such as: semantics, phonology, rhetoric, public speaking, oral interpretation, and storytelling. The general trend is to teach student how to speak the "right way."

Some American universities have established departments to teach English as a second language (TESL). The purpose of TESL is to educate teachers for teaching English to those students whose mother tongues are languages other than English. Some TESLs also have programs for students who learn English as a second language. Foreign students are required to take courses in TESL departments. Another effort in teaching the English language to non-English speaking peoples is the British Broadcasting Corporation's (BBC) English language programs. We will be discussing the BBC and other broadcasting agencies' efforts to teach their language to foreigners later on.

At this point, we would like to emphasize that native teachers teach their language to their own and other students in the way they think is right. They also use expressions that are meaningful in their own cultures. For example, when a school teacher teaches the English alphabet to foreign children, he uses the expression "A is for apple," but in many cultures the children will have never seen an apple.

Origins of Language

Primitive man's urge to express himself resulted in his origination of verbal and nonverbal symbols. He used them to interact with other members of his community. As life became more complicated, he originated new symbols and refined old ones. So we might say that speech, or verbal communication, is the earliest symbolic system developed and perfected by humans. Written communication is thus recent. Writing, we might say, again, is symbolic of spoken communication. So, writing is a symbol of a symbol. The oldest effort to systematize writing and develop a grammar is about four thousand years old. It is an ancient Sumerian grammar. In any case, man's know-how in communication was limited to his own geographic area and his own community. His purpose was to express ideas related to life in his community. As symbols of communication became integral parts of his culture, man developed the hardware and software of communication. By hardware we mean the mechanical and technological developments used to communicate. Thus, use of smoke by American Indian tribes, drums in Africa, and electromagnetic television signals, are hardware, while the ideas communicated by those means are software.

Neither hardware nor software is perfect at any one time. Human life and culture are continuously evolving phenomena. That is why even today man is originating and refining techniques of communication. The attempt to refine Swahili for use as a world language is one example; the development of Esperanto as a new world language is another. A recent example in this context is the attempt by businessmen to develop an international sign language to facilitate communication in international business. When business was restricted to one community or city it was not necessary to develop an elaborate symbol system, but business enterprises now have transcended national boundaries. Businessmen around the world are finding it increasingly difficult to communicate with their employees and clients. They believe an international sign language might reduce that hardship. With the coming of such hardware as communication satellites and cable television, businessmen think such a sign language might overcome existing language barriers. Even the international sign language that is being developed in America, however, will add to the thousands of languages and will probably become sort of a dialect of American English since the expressions are basically American.

Sometimes symbols are developed to express ideas which cannot be legally expressed in spoken symbols. For example, in some Asian countries the federal film censor offices do not approve scenes of intimate relationships between men and women such as kissing on the screen. Movie makers have gotten around such regulations. They show scenes such as mixing of clouds, leaves coming closer, or rivers merging with each other to express the idea of intimacy. Asian audiences consider such scenes highly artistic. The quality of art of a movie director depends upon how creative he is in depicting ideas symbolically.

That is how modern hardware is adapted to express ideas that are approved by traditional cultural institutions and national governments. Although governments can control modern hardware, it is more difficult to control the usage of the one old and traditional software: spoken language.

Language Family

Spoken language consists of basic sound units which by themselves have no meaning but are necessary to produce a set of sounds that does have meaning. The basic units of sound are called *phonemes*. Phonemes have no meaning, but are building blocks in the development of sounds that have meaning. The group of phonemes that has meaning is called *morpheme*. Although linguists have tabulated and man can utter many phonemes, in each language only a certain number of phonemes are used to produce morphemes. Some of the phonemes may not be in use at all in other languages. For example, in many south Asian languages the sounds "f" and "z" are not used. When the south Asians need to use sounds "f" and "z" they use phonemes that come close to those of English phonemes. Thus they sometimes utter "p" for "f" and "j" for "z." They might say "pool" for "fool" and "joo" for "zoo."

Members of a group who speak the same language and dialect and can understand each other are referred to as a *language family*. They all agree on a definite meaning for an expression. For example, in the so-called hippie culture in the United States, the word "grass" usually means marijuana. The expression "grass" does not need any elaboration in that community since all members know what the speaker is talking about. In the same community, the word "cool" means "all right" or "fine." The expression "he is cool" means he is all right. The hippie community, then, is a small language family. Outside that language family, "cool" may refer to temperature. Another example of a language family is the Spanish immigrants in the U. S. who may reside in a town in California but who speak Spanish. Although their English-speaking neighbors may not understand them, they can understand each other.

Members of each language family have developed their own methods of communication to express ideas relating to life in their own culture. The main purpose of such communication seems to be to inform, to motivate, to entertain, and to enlighten. The first three are the reasons we communicate with others in our own culture. The purpose of the last is to understand the meaning of life. This sublime objective seemed to be most important for the ancient Hindus, Greeks, and Buddhists. Although Greek philosophers such as Plato and Socrates set enlightenment as the ultimate purpose of acquiring knowledge, rhetoricians such as Aristotle emphasized the importance of scientific and logical methods of studying interaction between humans. The Hindus said communication techniques should be devoted to understanding the Self and the Absolute Truth. The Hindus devoted most of their time to developing theories explaining the nature of communication within the individual rather than between individuals.

Hindu and Buddhist Theories of Verbal Communication

An explanation of ancient Hindu theories of language helps us understand why Hindu and other similar cultures pay little attention to so-called progressive ideas of materialistic development. Hindus have always shown a tendency to relate the seen to the unseen and to speculate on the nature of unseen on the basis of the seen. The Hindus said the knowledge derived from sensory perception is not the same as that derived from verbal communication; perception and verbalization are not one and the same. There are three different methods of acquiring knowledge: perception, comparison, and verbal testimony. But another Hindu school, the Mimamsa system, said that verbal communication as a source of valid information depends upon how the speaker understands the meaning of a sentence.

The Hindus believed there could be two kinds of sounds: inarticulate (Dhvani) and articulate (Varna). Dhvani is the meaningless sound produced by birds, animals and man. Dhvani has no particular linguistic meaning. Even the sounds made by newborn babies are inarticulate. Varna is the sound produced by man's "speech organs." Varna is the sound system developed by the members of a culture. Words are examples of articulate sound. "Words are symbolic sounds constituted by letters arranged in a definite order. A word is not a mere collection of letters, but a definite whole of letters and syllables which have a fixed order in the whole. It is a unity of the parts in so far as it is the object of a single cognition."[1]

The Hindus discussed the origin and structure of language as early as 1000 B.C., when the Vedas were first composed. Panini (800 B.C.) wrote the first grammar in the world. Then Patanjali (200 B.C.) wrote a commentary on the grammar. Although the Panini grammar and Patanjali commentary are in the Sanskrit language, the rules of Sanskrit grammar have been adopted by other languages in and outside of India.

Verbal testimony or information given by the spoken word is considered more important than the other two elements, perception or comparison. A trustworthy person's spoken words should be believed since such a person speaks from vast experience. A person whose character is proven and his expertise recognized should be trusted and what he says accepted, although even the information given by a trustworthy person may be in error and disputed later on. The only authority are the *Vedas*. The *Vedas* are most trustworthy:

> The Veda is eternal and authorless. It is not the work of any person, human or divine. The sages are only 'seers' not the authors of the Veda. The Veda is not composed or spoken even by God. The Veda deals with Dharma (duties of the individual) and the objects denoted by it cannot be known by perception, inference, comparison or by any other means. Hence the Vedic injunction can never be contradicted by any subsequent knowledge.[2]

Although the *Veda* is a literary work consisting of sounds and symbols, it is trustworthy since it is authorless. Other books and works are creations of their authors. Therefore, such works are prone to error of humans, while the *Vedas* are eternal.

As mentioned earlier, Hindus tend to explain the unseen on the basis of the seen. The mystical way in which they attribute validity to the *Vedas* explains why it is not easy for an American to communicate with a Hindu who trusts the unseen and unknown more than the seen and the known.

Concept of Meaning

One aspect of communication that is difficult to explain is the concept of meaning. Modern communicologists have developed devices such as the semantic differential to explain the concept. Ancient Hindus, including linguists such as Panini (800 B.C.) and Bharthrhari (tenth century A.D.), have also tried to explain the meaning of of meaning. They believed the meaning of a word depends upon what the word excludes. According to the Exclusion Theory, what is expressible can reasonably explain our everyday life. What is excluded is understood by intuition. That is how man understands the ultimate reality. According to another view, the meaning of a word is derived by associating it with a concept. For example, when we utter the word "cow," the image that appears in the mind of one hearer is different from that of another, but the "cowness" is the same. The hearer associates the word "cow" with cowness.

In order to explain the relationship between word and meaning, the Hindus developed what they called the *Explosion Theory* or *Sphota Vada*. According to this theory, the meaning of the word occurs like a sudden explosion when the speaker utters a certain phoneme or sound of the word. For example, the meaning of the word "mount" does not occur until the speaker says the last sound, "t." The utterance "moun" does not make any sense, but when the "t" is uttered, the image of a mountain appears in the mind of the hearer. Also, an addition to the word such as "eer" to make it "mountaineer" is understood and in the same order the word develops. First, the word "mountain" is understood and then a person on the mountain. Therefore, the concept of mountaineer includes first a mountain and then a person trying to climb it. This happens only if the hearer knows what "mountain" means; otherwise, he understands it by association. Hindus explain the concept of association by the example of an utterance such as "wild cow." When they say "wild cow," the phrase is first associated with a cow and then with wildness. There are two common factors in the utterance: cowness and wildness.

The concept and measurement of the meaning of words and gestures also differ from culture to culture. The Hindus said:

> It follows from this that there are three aspects in the meaning of a word, namely, a pictorial, a denotative and a connotative. A word calls up the form, denotes the individual and connotes the genus or the universal. Every word will therefore be connotative in so far as it means the generic properties of the individuals denoted by it.[3]

Hindus and Buddhists in the pre-Christian era did not explain anything as an individual and independent unit. They believed that everything in the universe is related and each depends upon the others. When explaining the meaning of words the scholar should consider the fact that the meaning of a word is relative to the speaker's experience, as is also the case with the words preceding and following the particular word whose meaning is under consideration. The unity of sounds and words in a sentence shape the meaning of a word. The first letter of a word does not make up the meaning of the entire word. The sound of each preceding letter is remembered by the hearer. When he comes to the last letter the sounds of all the preceding letters are remembered. The last sound of a word is primarily responsible for the word's conventional meaning. Even here there are other viewpoints. One particular school says it is not the unity of the words but the synthetic activity of the intellect that is responsible for the meaning. Since the hearer has some experience related to the object of the word, the separate experiences of the letters which constitute the word are remembered and all the different experiences are synthesized into a certain perception which is the object or the meaning of the word. The meaning of an entire sentence is also a synthetic function of the separate words and the order in which they are arranged.

It is not the purpose of this chapter to discuss all the linguistic theories of East and West, but to mention that the concern of early philosophers and logicians was to discuss whether the spoken and written languages could transmit the real meaning of the speaker and writer and whether the languages were adequate to explain the absolute reality. All of them have concluded that the existing languages cannot explain the world of the inner man or the self.

While the language of the outer world can be taught, that of the inner world cannot be taught. The language of the inner world depends upon the innate ability of the individual. Obviously an individual's communicative technique is shaped not only by learned behaviors and innate abilities, but also by cultural values and geographical situations.

Denotative and Connotative Meanings

A word's denotative meaning is defined as its commonly accepted or dictionary meaning. Connotative meaning is the hidden or implied or, for our purpose, cultural meaning of a word. In all cultures, certain words have special meaning. In some cases, the meaning of a word might be different in different cultures. The word "cow" in Hindu cultures is synonymous with sacredness. In western cultures, the expression "computer" is associated with accuracy. The concept of "propaganda" differs from culture to culture. In America it is associated with unethical methods of publicity, while such is not the case in other cultures. In intercultural communication the connotative rather than the denotative meaning is important since it is that meaning which brings about understanding or the lack thereof.

Concepts and Expressions

According to the ancient Hindus, concepts are developed in a child even before it learns to speak a language. The child cannot express such concepts since it has no common language at its command, but those concepts stay in the child's memory. Memory is either acquired by the child in this incarnation or transformed from its previous birth. When the child grows to adulthood, his conceptualization of the world around him is wider than the one he can construct with his language. As a result, the meanings or the concepts inside the person are not completely revealed in his speech.

The theory of one Hindu linguist, Bharthrhari (tenth century A.D.), comes close to the theories of modern linguists. He said that the form and shape of cognitive states comes from our language. Our categorization of the world is determined by the structure of our language. Bharthrhari also believed, however, that the child has both acquired and transformed memories.

Word Order in Speech

Added to the differences in beliefs regarding the validity of knowledge and acquisition of language, differences in arrangement of words in speeches make intercultural communication difficult. For example, in some Asian languages the expression "Yesterday John went to New York" could be made in several ways:

John to New York went yesterday.
Yesterday John went to New York.
John yesterday went to New York.
To New York John went yesterday.

When uttered, all four ways make sense to the hearer in those cultures. If those speakers go to Western countries, they tend to use the same word order even when speaking English or other Western languages.

In many Asian languages the sentence consists of subject, object and predicate instead of subject, predicate, and object. In Hindi, for example, instead of saying "Johnny drank milk" it would be "Johnny milk drank." Consequently, when a Hindi speaker goes to Great Britain or the United States and speaks English, his word order might be somewhat confusing to the British or American audience.

The Problem of Pronouns

In many non-Western cultures, the hierarchical system of society has given rise to a system of language that makes communication in that society easy. In the Thai language there are several pronouns, "you" for example, to identify persons of several social positions in the Thai hierarchy. In the fourteen or so languages of India, there are at least two equivalents of the pronoun "you." In Hindi, "thoom" is used to identify persons of a lower status while "aap" indentifies those of higher status. Even in old English "you.' and "thou" were used according to the social status of the person addressed. When a person from Thailand comes to the United States he feels uncomfortable using the same "you" for everybody. Sometimes he balances his concept of social status through nonverbal expressions of respect. Even when an American professor tells his students to call him Bob instead of Dr. Robert Smith, his Thai students have a hard time getting used to calling him by his first name. They would never call their Thai professor by his first name, nor would he permit such informality.

Philosophy and Language

A culture's language has been developed as a tool for explaining the philosophy of that culture. In the Hindu and Buddhist cultures, their languages include two words to indicate the English equivalent of happiness. One type of happiness explains physical pleasures such as sex, for example. Such happiness is, in Sanskrit, "sukha." The other type of happiness is intellectual, what one derives when he understands the Truth by self-realization or by reading the holy books. Such happiness is "ananda." When a Hindu speaks the English language, he feels uncomfortable using the word happiness to express the concept of ananda.

The Hindu concepts of language and meaning are somewhat similar to Whorf's findings about the language of Hopi Indians in the United States. Whorf found that the Hopis believe man is a part of the universe and not its master; the Hopi language, therefore, is full of expressions that facilitate explanation and reinforcement of such a belief.

Aims of Communication Arts

There are four Hindu schools of poetics which specify the aims of poetry and drama. These schools maintain different views on the essentials of poetry; some poets believe in more than one. These schools are the Alankara (figure) school, the Riti (style) school, the Rasa (aesthetic pleasure and emotion) school, and the Dhvani (suggestion) school.

The Alankara school maintains that the figure of the word and its import are esential. The Riti school maintains that the style of drama and literature is important. Stylists such as Dandin, well-known for the beauty of his wordings, are champions of this school. These people place more importance on the word element than on the sense element.

The third school believes in the importance of feelings and the emotions roused in the audience by the aesthetic pleasures they experience. Abhinava Gupta and Bhatta Nayaka, who base their opinions on the works of Bharata, recognize two powers of the word: the power of generalization, by which the meaning is made intelligible to the audience; and the power by which they are enabled to relish the poetry. The fourth school holds that the suggestion of the word is the essence of poetry. A word is endowed with powers of denotation, implication and suggestion. Through suggestion the subject is made clear and the sentiment aroused. The suggestion of the subject or of the figure may ultimately be reduced to that of sentiment.

Emotions

Most of the later dramatists have given importance to the aesthetic pleasures and feelings that arouse emotions and sentiments. They have recognized nine emotions and their corresponding sentiments.

> The most original and interesting part of dramatic theory is the gradual definition of the nature of the sentiment which it is the aim of the performance to evoke in the mind of the audience. The statement of the *Natyasastra* by Bharata is simple. Sentiment is produced from the union of the determinants, the consequents and the transitory feelings . . . .[4]

The objective is, therefore, to rouse emotions during the play which will later be converted into sentiments. Thus the emotions aroused in the theater are only a series of color washes before the audience's eye. The memory of emotions leads to the creation of sentiments, which is the ultimate aim of the play.

> The predominance of sentiment in Sanskrit drama has been responsible for the creation of typical characters rather than individualized figures. It is said that the characters are often conventional and not original . . . Though the best of Sanskrit dramas glow with occasional touches of realism, still the fact cannot be denied that poetic value has never been sacrificed for direct delineation of action of character . . . Further, Sanskrit dramatists have laid it down as a rule that there should be perfect fusion of sentiments and theme of plot in a drama. Overdelineation of sentiment at the cost of gradual and systematic development of plot and too much elaboration of details in the plot hampering the flow of sentiment must be carefully avoided.[5]

> An emotion is recognized as a *rasa* if it is a sufficiently permanent major instinct of man, if it is capable of being developed and delineated to its climax with its attendant and accessory feelings and if there are men of that temperament to feel imaginative emotional sympathy at the presentation of that rasa . . . Rasa is ideal beauty, a tincture, essence, flavour, aesthetic experience being described as the tasting flavour. It is a complex of determinants, consequents, moods and involuntary emotions . . . . The underlying assump-

tion of the theory of rasas is that the human mind shows eight or nine dominant moods related to fairly stable sentiments which could be developed into
works of literature . . . . The purpose of art is to give delight and aesthetic experience, is a transformation not merely of feeling, but equally of under-
taking . . . .[6]

The nine emotions, or "rasas," are eroticism caused by either separation or union of lovers; mirth caused by laughter or farcical delight; anger
caused by ill treatment, etc.; sorrow or sadness; enthusiasm caused by
pride, energy, bravery, charity or forgiveness; fear caused by a sense of at-
tack, etc; disgust caused by aversion or loathsomeness; astonishment or
wonder; and calmness or serenity or tranquility. The Hindu concept of
emotion—rasa—is somewhat similar to the modern Western concept of
kinesthetic effect discussed earlier.

The nine sentiments resulting from these emotions are love, wit or com-
icality, fury, pity or compassion or affection, heroism or patriotism or
forgiveness, terror, horror, wonder, and peace. Some dramatists believe
that peace or tranquility is the result of the other eight emotions and not a
separate sentiment in itself, but Buddhist dramatists like Asvaghosha included peace as an important sentiment. Great dramatists like Bhasa and
Kalidasa aim at one dominant emotion and its relative sentiment. The
other emotions aroused during the play are only accessories to the main
emotion. The "rasa" theory may be applied to any great play in any language; love is the sentiment in *Romeo and Juliet*, compassion in *Hamlet*.

Greek Theories of Verbal Communication

Among other Greeks, Aristotle is one name students cannot forget, since
most of the rhetorical theories taught by western scholars are those proposed by this great Greek philosopher. As Alexander the Great's tutor, he
not only had the intellectual ability but also the political power to make
his voice heard around the world. Aristotle discusses the nature of speech
in his book *Rhetorica*. Rhetoric is the study of the art of persuasion by
verbal methods. According to Aristotle, three factors contribute to a
speaker's success: Ethos, Pathos, and Logos.

Ethos is the character of a speaker. A speaker of good character can
communicate and persuade more effectively than one of bad character. A
speaker's personal character makes him credible. People tend to believe a
person of good character over a person of undesirable character. The good
character should be indicated in the subject matter of what the speaker
says. According to Aristotle, personal character is probably the single
factor responsible for persuading an audience. One way ethos will affect
communication is by *emulation*. It is the feeling a communicator creates

in his audience to aspire for things of high value. Such a feeling is created by making the audience realize it does not possess the valued objects.

Pathos is the emotions stirred in the audience by the speaker. Aristotle distinguishes clearly between stirring emotions of friendliness and pleasantness or those of anger and hostility. While a person of good character may stir good emotions, one of bad character may stir bad emotions. Good emotions should be evoked by nice language, and bad emotions by harsh language. It is not possible to evoke good emotions using harsh language, and vice versa.

Logos is the reasoning used by a speaker in order to persuade his audience. The speaker uses persuasive arguments in order to prove a truth or an apparent truth.

Aristotle says that a persuasive speaker should himself be able to perceive the three qualities. He should be able to understand human character, particularly good character. He should be able to understand the emotions and distinguish one from another. Finally, he should be able to reason logically. In applying Aristotle's theory to intercultural communication, we should point out that these three factors are also cultural. A person of good character in one culture may not be considered such in another. The way people of one culture express a certain emotion can differ from the way another people express the same emotion. Methods of reasoning may also differ from culture to culture.

Aristotle's Theory of Expression

Having discussed the Hindu, Buddhist and Greek theories of verbal communication, we are now ready to discuss the theories of the ancient Greeks, which extend to other areas of communication such as dance, drama and music. These theories are applied even today by communicators in both East and West. Again, among the Greeks, Aristotle stands out as the single most important influence on Western thought. Among Easterners, Bharata is equally important since he has influenced not only the communication artists of India but also of other Asian countries.

In his *Poetics,* Aristotle discusses in detail the characteristics of communicative arts such as drama. Although drama as discussed by Aristotle is theatrical art, today his theory has been extensively applied to several methods of communication including interpersonal communication. Probably the most important part of the *Poetics* is that which explains the purpose of an actor, whom we shall call here the communicative artist. According to Aristotle, communicative artists should try to arouse emotions. A communicator can arouse two very important emotions: pity and fear. Pity is the emotion aroused by a communicator when he depicts to his audience the tragic death of a person, a rather good person who dies a tragic death because of a wrong he did. The audience should show pity for the tragic figure. Fear is aroused when the actor indicates to his audience that they too will suffer such a tragedy if they commit such a wrong. Applying the Aristotelian theory to communication, the purpose of a communicator should be to arouse emotions of pity and fear. Aristotle discusses only these two emotions, but we know there are more than two emotions that a communicator can arouse. The ancient Hindu theorist Bharata discusses nine emotions in his treatise on the art of drama *(N Shashtra).*

Modern Theories of Verbal Communication

The Nature and Nurture Controversy

As in genetics, linguistics also has theories supporting arguments that language is either a learned behavior or an innate ability. According to one school, language is nurtured, while according to another, it comes naturally to the native speaker. Sapir is probably the foremost of the Western linguists to argue that language is entirely a learned behavior. He contends that language is entirely a learned behavior. He contends that language is a purely noninstinctive method of communication, produced by means of a system of symbols. The symbols are produced by means of the organs of speech.[7]

According to Sapir, one's speech organs are developed from childhood in such a way as to facilitate his speaking his own language. It is possible to cite evidence in support of this argument. The Chinese language is more nasal than English. Therefore, when a Chinese speaks English he produces some English sounds through his nose while native English speakers do not. The Japanese confuse native English speakers by substituting the sounds "l" for "r" and "r" for "l." Native English speakers, in turn, confuse many Asians by substituting dental "l" for retroflex "l" and dental "d" for retroflex "d" and retroflex "t" for dental "t".

The other school argues that if language is a learned behavior, it should be possible to train anyone to speak any language in the world as efficiently as do the native speakers. In reality, this is not possible, since each person has a certain innate ability to speak his own language. Such ability differs from person to person, so that everyone in a language family cannot speak the native language with equal efficiency. Chomsky is probably the foremost of those who argue for innate ability. He argues that language is a natural property of the human mind. Language is an instrument of self-expression. It provides a thought world of a unique sort, which belongs to the individual speaker.[8]

Our Definition

One explanation of the process of communication is that it involves a stimulus and a response to that stimulus. In other words, communication should always take place as a result of an outside stimulus. We do not accept this explanation. Earlier we defined communication as the act of understanding and being understood by an audience. We believe that communication is a creative process involving not only the individual and his culture but his audience's as well. Since the individual has a certain freedom to create his own communication technique from the resources available in his own culture, his success in making his audience understand him depends upon his ability to use those resources. Such ability includes his own efforts to understand his audience and their culture and developing his own technique of interacting with the members of that culture.

We define language as a symbol system developed to make interaction for members of a culture easy and meaningful. The language an individual member of a culture uses is not only learned from others but also developed as a result of her own creative ability. The individual's culture provides her plenty of raw materials to create her own language of communication. We have the need to interact with the other members of our culture, to express ideas related to life in that culture. In the twentieth century that need also includes interaction with members of a foreign culture and expression of ideas related to life in one's own and the foreign culture.

Each speaker has a certain innate ability which cannot evolve into efficient speech unless the speaker undergoes training. Despite that innate ability, one speaker may fail to get the necessary training and end up as a bad communicator, while another person of limited ability may train himself to become a great speaker. We could mention many scholars in the discipline of communication who were born stutterers but trained themselves to be fine communicators.

Literate and Nonliterate Cultures

Depending upon a society's literacy, anthropologists classify cultures as nonliterate, preliterate and literate. A nonliterate culture is one in which there is no written cultural tradition. All cultural traditions are transmitted orally from generation to generation. Many African, American Indian and even old Hawaiian clans were nonliterate cultures. A preliterate culture is one which has written tradition. Cultural norms can be learned from books written by its people in ancient times. Although a majority of people in such cultures might now be illiterate, a few learned men can read the ancient books and tell the illiterate masses about their heritage. India, Egypt and Pakistan are such preliterate cultures. Literate cultures depend entirely upon written books for their heritage. Most people in the culture are literate so that each member can read the books to learn about his native customs and traditions.

Learning by written materials is not the same as learning by oral transmission. One who learns to read from left to right and remembers the written symbols perceives differently from one who learns by oral transmission. The literate remembers the concept "house" by storing in his memory the letters H O U S E read from left to right. But the illiterate remembers "house" by storing the picture of a house in the memory. In other words, the illiterate thinks visually in terms of the pictures stored in her brain. She remembers the picture with reference to her environment. To a Nepalese Hindu, Mount Everest is not just the peak of a mountain. It is snowclad, surrounded by clouds and the abode of the Lord Himself. But to a literate who has not seen either the mountain or its picture, it is remembered in the form of the letters E V E R E S T .

Verbal and nonverbal languages are employed in both personal and impersonal communication, but audiences understand only the language they know. Even when communicator and audience live in the same nation they cannot understand each other's language if they have different cultural backgrounds. An American from Alabama cannot understand another American from the island of Niihaụ because the Alabamian could be a white American and the Niihauan is Polynesian.

In a personal situation the communicator can see his audience. He can understand, to some extent, their reaction. The audience can also ask him questions and see his reactions. This gives an opportunity to test the honesty of both the communicator and the communicatees. In a face-to-face situation the communicator establishes a psycho-physical contact and can make the audience feel the same way he does about the subject of communication. He can arouse emotions, an art known as *kinesthetics*. If the aesthetic experience of the communicator and his audience are not the same, there will be *aesthetic distance*. This distance results from the failure of the communicator to make his audience feel the way he does. This distance in the level of emotional responses can also result from differing cultural experiences of the communicator and the audience.

Literate Opinion Leaders and Illiterate Village Councillors

An individual's role in his community is important in the process of communication. A community often accepts or rejects new ideas according to what certain individuals say about the idea. This social role might be bestowed on an individual as his birthright or gained on his own merit. Opinion leadership is an example of such influential roles.

Opinion leaders in literate cultures are defined as the individuals who specialize in a particular subject and then advise, in the area of their specialization, the less active sections of their community. They read more, listen more, and watch more, then inform others. The opinion leaders influence the minds of the members of their community. Opinion leaders particularly dominate in smaller communities.

There are opinion leaders also in less literate or nonliterate cultures. When the cultures are less literate or nonliterate, even the opinion leaders are less literate or illiterate. Their sources of information are usually individuals who get their information from other interpersonal sources, or from aural and visual media of communication. Transmission of information in such cultures is mostly by oral methods. Opinion leaders in the less literate communities are sometimes religious leaders, skilled farmers, or skilled handicraft workers. People in their communities listen to them. Such leaders are able to influence even politics. A government's success in introducing new farming methods, new hybrids, family planning, and other new techniques depend upon the opinions of these leaders. When a new product appears in the market place of small illiterate communities, the illiterate opinion leaders influence even the buying of that product. Studies have shown that in less literate cultures the local leaders influence the acceptance of new ideas.

Industrial and Nonindustrial Cultures

An industrial culture is one in which the economy is based on modern technology rather than ancient techniques. A nonindustrial culture is one in which life is based on ancient customs—even the economy is based on ancient standards.

Industrial cultures are literate cultures. The invention of the printing press in the fifteenth century was primarily responsible for the beginning of literacy, and changed the entire system of thinking and information storing. The printing press led to the development of the typewriter, the telegraph, the teleprinter, the telex and finally, the facsimile. A scholar from a literate culture thinks very differently than one from a nonliterate culture, has more stored information, and is probably more methodical than the nonliterate.

Nonindustrial cultures are either nonliterate or preliterate. The people of nonindustrial cultures think in terms of visual images rather than written letters, making it difficult to develop typewriters and other communication techniques available in literate cultures. In nonliterate and preliterate cultures it is easier to develop audiovisual techniques for communication. In such cultures radio, the film, and television are more successful than the print media.

People of both industrial and nonindustrial cultures communicate with many symbols that are unique to their environment. For example, expressions such as *smog, pollution,* and *jet* make no sense to people from many nonindustrial societies. Most industrial cultures are also "affluent societies." Many expressions of such societies are meaningless in nonindustrial societies. To cite yet another example of the effects of industrialization on a community, mechanized farming results in a very small percentage of the community's population taking to farming as a profession. So, many expressions and cultural activities in such cultures do not develop around agriculture. But in nonindustrial societies many expressions and activities develop around agriculture and rural life. In India, where more than 80 percent of the population lives in rural agricultural communities, even movie stories center around rural life, as do radio programs.

In nonindustrial societies the concepts of time and distance differ greatly from those in industrial societies. Noon may not be exactly twelve o'clock; it might be anytime that the sun shines directly on an individual's head. Distance is also measured differently. When a Nepalese asks an American the distance between two points, the American might say "It is only a five-minute drive." But the Nepalese is used to directing people with reference to mountain peaks, lakes, trees, and so on. The automobile has become so much a part of the American's life that many American expressions and activities center around the automobile.

Opinion Leaders as Interpersonal Networks

The phenomenon of opinion leadership was first discovered in a study done by Lazarsfeld et al. in 1940. Since then there have been many such studies around the world to identify opinion leaders. Those studies have shown that opinion leadership differs from culture to culture and that one cannot generalize the characteristics of opinion leaders for each country. Some cultural variables, however, do affect opinion leadership in all cultures. Those are:

1. The color of the leader.
2. The caste of the leader.
3. The skill of the leader in the area of his leadership.
4. His contacts with other opinion leaders.
5. His character.
6. His innovativeness in his profession.
7. His religiousness.

We call them opinion leaders since they are sources not only of information but also influence in their communities. They act as media of information even when mass media are beyond the reach of their communities.

The leaders get information from mass and interpersonal sources and transmit it to the people in their own communities. Further, the level and quality of information thus transmitted depends upon the intellectual level of the individual audience.

Some Related Factors

In this section we shall discuss other variables affecting verbal, interpersonal communication between people of differing cultures. We shall begin with some speech variables such as pitch, articulation, and intelligibility.

Pitch is the frequency of sound wave repetition, similar to intonations on a musical scale. Certain languages are based on intonation. The same sound in a high pitch may have different meaning in a low pitch. In languages such as the Indo-European group, a raised voice may mean something different from a normal voice. For example, at a university town in Oregon, a foreign professor went to a bar for a drink. Since the professor looked young and was of small build, the cocktail waitress in the bar thought he was a minor. When she asked him for some identification he said he did not have any, but he swore that he was an adult. The waitress refused to serve the drink unless she could see proof of his age. Another customer in the bar who knew the professor went to the waitress and told her he knew the foreign man and that he was a senior professor at the university. When she heard this, the waitress could not believe her own ears. She almost screamed, "You mean *that* man is a university professor?" Her stress on the word "that" was intended to give a particular meaning. In each culture speakers use pitch according to the special meaning a word has in that culture. People of each culture can be characterized by their pitch. Japanese are said to be "soft spoken," while Arabs are said to have high pitch.

Articulation is defined as the ability to speak a language in such a way that all the phonemes in a word are pronounced so that the audience hears them and understands the word. But in any given culture no one pronounces all the phonemes in a word. Either some phonemes are omitted, wrongly pronounced, or some other phoneme added. In America, New Englanders add the sound "r" at the end of certain words. Midwesterners roll their tongues to say "r," and Southerners add the sound "i" to certain words. Chinese seem to be more nasal than Americans when speaking English. In certain parts of India, people use the sounds "s" for "sh" and "p" for "f." In some cases, it is easy to identify the caste or the state the speaker comes from by his articulation.

Differences in articulation give rise to the factors such as accent and dialect. *Accent* is defined as speaking a language in a way differing from the so-called standard. In America, we have heard of the so-called southern accent, which means simply that southerners do not speak English the way it is supposed to be spoken. But communicologists have been asking, what is standard speech? There is no acceptable answer to the question, but Americans have discriminated against people for their "accent" without really knowing what standard speech is.

Intelligibility is defined as the speaker's ability to make the hearer decode a message the way the speaker wants him to decode that message. In other words, it is the ability to create the intended image in the mind of the hearer. In intercultural communication it is not easy to say if intelligibility is achieved. We might cite a previous example of Gunavardhane, the student from Sri Lanka, who thought he and his American friend were really communicating when in fact each was not being understood the way the other intended. Yet both believed they had understood each other. Failure to achieve intelligibility can result from differences in connotative meaning, lack of understanding of the pitch, ethnocentric attitudes, or stereotyping.

Translation

Language is designed to express ideas related to a people's value system, their relationships to other people, the beauty of their world, and praise of their gods.

In south India there are a dozen words to describe different kinds of cooked and uncooked rice; in the Eskimo language there are a dozen words to describe different kinds of snow. In some south Indian languages there is no word for "snow," while there is no word for "rice" in the Eskimo's language. Since a people's language is designed to express the feelings and thoughts of only that people, their language is not adequate to express another people's feelings and thoughts. The Thai language is designed to express ideas related to a cultural system that integrates ancient Hindu, Buddhist, and Confucian cultures. In that language there are twelve second-person pronouns to express different relationships prevalent in that culture. That is adequate and useful to that culture, but the English language is not adequate to show all the relationships in Thai culture. Modern English is designed to express the relationships in a democratic, nonhierarchical culture, which is not useful in other cultures. When translating from one language to another it is not possible to translate the original ideas expressing relationships between individuals and their values and beliefs.

Even when persons from two cultures are talking, what they are transmitting are the audible or physical sounds and the accompanying meanings of the sound's originator, not his mental image and the accompanying experience, because the cultural experiences of values, beliefs, human relationships, and natural beauties are not the same for both parties. So even when the physical sound is transmitted the mental image is not.

The problem of translating from one language to another lies in translating from one symbol system to another. The translator first understands the meaning and then searches for a symbol. Sometimes the translator understands the original in his own symbol system and then translates it to his written or spoken system. Language is a meaning and symbol relationship in one's own culture, but in translation it is symbol-to-symbol relationship. It is the process of fitting the meaning of symbol "a" in the language "A" into a symbol "b" in the language "B." Then "a" does not mean the same as "b" since the meaning of "b" relates to something in the culture that uses the language B. Therefore, each time meaning is transmitted in the form of another language, part of the original meaning is lost. Since intercultural communication is also a relationship between source and receiver of two or more different value systems, the meanings transmitted in different symbol systems do not transmit the same values.

Ethnocentrism is another factor that causes imprecision in translation. The Western scientist shows ethnocentrism when he names hurricanes "Diana" and "Celeste." Stars are Apollo and Andromeda, a spot on the moon is the "Sea of Tranquillity," and the first words from space are "In the beginning God said. . . ." Although these ideas can be translated, the experiences of the original authors will be missing.

Dialect is the result of articulating language in a way that is entirely different from the standard way. A dialect may be written the same way but pronounced differently. In some cases certain new words are added in the subculture where the dialect is spoken. Pidgin, which is a dialect in Hawaii and other Pacific islands, has many Polynesian words. It is also spoken differently. Unless the speaker writes down what he is speaking, it is hard to tell that he is really speaking English.

Until recently, speaking dialects such as Pidgin was considered undignified. A person with "class" was not supposed to speak Pidgin. Teachers in Hawaii did not permit their students to speak Pidgin, gave them bad grades, and otherwise punished those who spoke the dialect. Now that Hawaiians are developing ethnic pride, they insist that their youngsters speak their own dialect. Pidgin has become a part of the native culture. Even scholars are now seeing beauty in Pidgin and other dialects, and some are insisting that Pidgin be taught in Hawaiian schools.

Bilingualism and Bidialectalism

Many countries have several language families. In India, for example, there are fourteen official languages, each spoken in one or more states. In such countries there is a real problem in adopting a national official language. The governments cannot arbitrarily adopt one official language since each language is an integral part of its speakers' culture. Each language is a primary value to its speaker, so it is not easy to ask them to give it up. The federal government in India tried to impose Hindi as the national official language and the non-Hindi speakers rose in rebellion against the government. Language problems divided the country into several factions until some leaders devised what they called the three-language formula. According to this formula, each student in Indian schools learns his mother tongue, Hindi and English. The Hindi speakers learn one south-Indian language, Hindi and English. Thus the modern Indian student is trained to become a multilinguist.

Bilingalism is based on the same formula. The student learns two languages. In the United States, the student learns English and his own mother tongue or the language of his forefathers. A Mexican-American child learns Spanish in addition to English. But the problem that arises in these programs is that both, or the three, languages the child learns are not given equal status. English in the United States and Hindi in India are given priority over the mother tongue. In some states the programs exist only on paper; nobody bothers to implement it.

Bidialectalism is a similar program that has been suggested for use in the United States. Under such a program, the child in grade school learns both English and his own dialect. In black communities, for example, the black child is supposed to learn his own dialect, such as Geechie. In Hawaii, the child should learn standard English in addition to Pidgin. But bidialectalism is not implemented in such a way as to help the child learn his own dialect which is so much a part of his culture. Geechie and Pidgin are taught, if at all, by teachers whose mother tongue is English. They teach the dialects in such a way that the children feel speaking their own dialect is shameful. Teachers of dialects are generally not experts in dialects, and there is no effective program to train teachers to teach dialects. Pidgin has a beautiful literature, which has been transmitted orally from generation to generation, but there are no concentrated efforts to gather such literature and use it in the classroom.

Consequently, both bilingualism and bidialectalism have failed to develop a sense of pride in the speakers' own culture and a love of the official language.

We wish to emphasize the effective use of dialects. In American politics, as in the politics of other countries, dialects, and particularly symbols, are used to convey certain messages to audiences without really saying what is meant, or without having to do a lot of writing or talking. To come out and say what one actually means would often be in poor taste. So to avoid the appearance of being an outright racist, for example, the speaker uses symbols and small, carefully selected phrases which convey a message to particular audiences. A political candidate might use the phrase, "Your home is your castle." Most people in America agree that a person's home is sacred. But by implication that phrase means more. It *means* to one candidate that if you vote for the other candidate, you are voting for minorities to move into your neighborhood. In the process, not only would you be inviting problems of various devastating descriptions but the value of your house would be reduced. In the next breath the candidate might say, "I am against busing." Aside from the racial overtones, few people want their children taken from their community schools to be bused ten or twenty miles away every day. So it was not necessary for the candidate to even mention race; race was implicitly understood by everyone to be a factor. All that needed saying was "I'm against busing."

During the 1972 elections tremendous attention was given to the poor, women, blacks, Chicanos, Indians, etc., who were extremely vociferous in their demands. So in the ensuing campaign the phrase "silent majority" was coined. Without having to define the silent majority, since everyone knew who had been making the loud demands, all that needed to be said was "I am for the silent majority." The implication was that the speaker was against the poor, women, blacks, Chicanos, Indians, etc. The message is effectively conveyed without having to state it.

During the sixties it was necessary to develop a strong, centralized federal government in Washington because it was thought that many states, especially southwestern and southern states, were abdicating their responsibilities pertaining to guaranteed civil rights and the general welfare of their citizenry. To combat this problem the federal government developed so-called "Great Society Programs," drawing heavily upon tax monies that would ordinarily have been returned to the states and thus under their control. To reverse this trend the phrases "states' rights" and "revenue sharing" were coined. The phrase "states' rights" is one held dearly in the hearts of most people. Since most people felt strongly opposed to "big federal government" and the large sums of money it was pouring into poverty programs over which the states had little control, the concepts of "revenue sharing" and "states' rights" took on new meaning without having to be explained. They were in and of themselves symbols used for righting wrongs.

Likewise the attention to domestic problems, those of clean environment, poverty, and depressed urban areas, gave way to a thrust in foreign affairs. As an appeasement and substitute for the expensive poverty programs which received broad support among the leadership in black and Chicano communities, "minority small business" was introduced. Blacks and Chicanos were led to believe they were going to become big businessmen. A recent survey revealed that most of those businesses are either defunct or on the verge. Through introduction of the Minority Small Business program via mass communication, the federal government was able to redirect minority aspiration at less expense. Whereas the government had been paying large sums of money for poverty programs, it was now able to reduce its expenditures to almost nothing by courting an alliance with the private sector to lend money for which the government guaranteed repayment.

In short, effective use of dialects and symbols can be subverted. The thrust of a whole country's public opinion and behavior can be manipulated by mass communication. The people in that culture whose thinking is on an intellectual level can understand and comprehend what is taking place. They are above the sensory contamination of the masses; yet, if they are not leaders, they too are affected adversely even though they understand and comprehend.

Even in intracultural or interethnic communication the above generalizations hold true. Recent research has shown that the Negro dialect is much different from that of the white man. It is the product of past history and of present social systems. The result is a subculture with its own dialect. A ghetto, where most black Americans are forced to live, looks something like a run-down, rat-infested, and crime-ridden place where no one else would want to live.[9]

But then, the American mass media that are owned by and cater to white men constantly and vividly tell blacks about life outside the ghettos Life in the white man's world is happy and gay. There everyone has equal opportunity, homes are large with ample air and light, people have everything they need. The young black expects such a life for himself, but cannot achieve it. The gap between expectation and realization creates frustration. The black man's life of frustrations and limitations has given rise to a dialect that is much different from the white man's. In this dialect one can notice clearly the hatred for the white man who enslaved the Negro for more than a century and has discriminated against him for another century. That dialect reveals the informality with which the privacies of life are viewed, but can be heard only by those who enjoy the confidence of blacks and can understand them.

How did black dialect evolve as it is today? According to one view, it is an offshoot of the languages spoken by ancestors of the African slaves brought to the Americas. A second view is that African slaves developed the dialects independently to communicate secretly among themselves.

The white slavemaster did not bother to learn the slaves' language, probably because it was difficult to learn. A third view integrates these two views.

Our own view is that present day black dialect is an effort on the part of blacks to distinguish themselves from the white man's culture. Even in the days of slavery such efforts were evident. The slaves probably did not learn to speak "standard English" in order to avoid being fully integrated into the white man's culture. It would not be difficult for blacks to learn the so-called standard English, but that would digest the black culture into the dominant white culture. The black man deliberately resists such attempts even today. Blacks also realize that no matter how hard they try to be white, they will not be accepted by whites because they simply are not white.

This attitude probably arises from the realization that there are some endemic characteristics over which they have no control that separate them from the dominant culture. Apparently minorities are beginning to see an analogy between their situation and that of the carrot held in front of the donkey: their strength and resilience lie in self-identity and self-sufficiency, and no matter how hard they try to be "white," they never will be. Whites, on the other hand, want to hold on to what they have by setting up impenetrable entry criteria into whitehood while trying to give the illusion that full acceptance is possible if certain preconditions are met. Worst yet, the preconditions are in a constant state of flux or are essentially unobtainable—at least one is, the change from black to white.

The dominant culture, out of concern of its own preservation, is constantly in search of new preconditions, such as bidialectalism and skill development, to market to the minorities so as to sustain their hope and aspiration. Without reasonable goals and some hope of achieving them, minorities, including poor whites, might be thrown into a coalition. Such a potential movement (however remote) of the disenfranchised could have devastating implications for the white ruling class whose obvious primary responsibility is to maintain the status quo.

The Plight of Hawaiians

Within a century, the white man as well as Oriental immigrants have successfully reduced the Hawaiians to the same position as the American Indian. Their frustration was well expressed in 1973 by a Hawaiian Christian priest, the Reverend Abraham Akaka. He said "They have taken our land from us; now they are trying to take our lives from us." This remark stemmed from a controversial statement made in 1972 by a state supreme court justice of Japanese origin. His statement was only his personal opinion, not official judgment, on the legality of the estate of Hawaiian Princess Bernice Bishop. Princess Bishop, who died in 1860, left a large estate to help Hawaiian or part-Hawaiian children obtain a modern education so they could compete with others in Hawaii. Her will was legal at the time of its writing. She wanted free education to be given to Hawaiian children and their teachers to be only Protestants. Later, the trustees of the estate established schools for Hawaiian children called King Kamehameha schools. These schools were fully supported by the Bishop estate. When real estate values rose in Hawaii, the first estate to come to everyone's notice was the Bishop estate, which owned almost ten percent of the state's available land. When foreign and mainland immigrants, mostly Caucasians and Japanese, multiplied, Hawaiians were reduced to a small, powerless minority. Pure Hawaiians, who owned the islands a hundred years ago, comprised in 1972 only one percent of the state's total population. In 1972, all the trustees of the Bishop estate were non-Hawaiians, mostly Japanese, each of whom was paid more than $40,000 a year. Hawaiians, who are generally fun-loving and friendly people have the least education of all groups in Hawaii. They are the poorest in the state, with many on welfare. But they still love their culture. They master Hawaiian dances and speak their own language in addition to Pidgin. But they are told that to speak Pidgin is shameful. They are also told they cannot have any preferential treatment; they will get the same treatment as anybody else in the state. Probably no Hawaiian knows how so many foreigners *(haolies)* came to their islands and outnumbered them in less than a century. Now they bitterly dislike the haolies, because the haolies took away their land and reduced them to abject poverty. In other words, they are the red Indians of Hawaii. Then a supreme court justice, of Japanese origin tells them that the Bishop estate, which is the only hope for Hawaiians, is unconstitutional. The Reverend Akaka's statement reflects his people's frustration at the situation.

Now the Hawaiians have their own political and cultural organizations. They take pride in learning and speaking Hawaiian and even Pidgin. They are making efforts to learn more about their origin and history as explained by their own people. There seems to be great unity for fighting the common enemy, the haolie culture. This is evident in their dialect. The word *haolie,* which a few years ago meant merely foreigner, is now a derogatory word. *Haolie,* which was probably once an affectionate term, has now become an expression of bitterness.

The Mexicans

Another minority in the U.S. is the Mexican American. Their mother tongue is Spanish. They were the first to immigrate to North America and settle in New Mexico and Texas. They came to the present United States in 1500, while the Pilgrims did not come to Plymouth until 1692. When English-speaking Americans came to New Mexico in large numbers, the original Mexican settlers became a minority. They were then forced to learn a foreign language to get ahead in the new society. The same situation that forced Hawaiians and blacks to unite forced the Mexicans to get together, to show pride in their mother tongue, and to dislike the "anglo." The term *anglo* in Mexican expresses the same bitterness as does the term *haolie* in Hawaiian. Emphasizing the need to teach Mexican-Americans their own language, a United States government report observed:

> The purpose included maintaining and improving the language to maintain the culture, bearing in mind the psychological impact on the child taught the mother tongue and the use of skills being imparted to transfer into the national language.
>
> This process was labled an attempt to make the cultural heritage, the language, an asset rather than a liability in intellectual development. Thus bilingualism would become, rather than a handicap, an enrichment.[10]

Problems of Immigrants

The problems of the three minorities discussed above, blacks, Hawaiians, and Mexicans, are unique. They have been forced to learn the culture and language of another people who happen to have political and financial power. But the case of immigrants is different. When a family migrates from one culture to another, the greatest sacrifice they must make is giving up their parent culture. The worst that can happen to an individual is to be forced to give up a language that has shaped his life for many years and to learn an entirely different language. European immigrants to the United States have faced such a situation. Although many cultural values of the Europeans and Americans are the same, languages are not the same. So when the immigrant switches to American English, he has to give up his whole way of perception and retention. What he has perceived in the world around him and retained in the form of his mother tongue must now be substituted by English.

The problem of the bilingual speaker is probably very well expressed in what the linguists call "thinking in one's own language." Thinking and expressing in one's own language can be observed when the bilinguist gets mad and cannot express his anger in the new language. He usually uses his own language, be it Norwegian, German, Spanish, Italian or Hawaiian.

American and Asian Rhetoric

We have stated that communication is highly cultural. A speech given by a learned person is a cultural event in the sense that we can identify a number of cultural variables in that speech. Audience reaction to the speech is also cultural; we can point out their cultural behavior in their re-actions. An experienced speaker knows his audience's culture and rein-forces their cultural beliefs, expectations, and customs. A speech given by such a speaker will be an educational experience to an outsider interested in understanding the cultures of that speaker and his audience. A speech by Winston Churchill was a cultural event since he personified the British traditional and national cultures at the time of World War Two. He rein-forced all his people's cultural values at that time. Mahatma Gandhi identified himself with the beliefs and expectations of the peoples of south Asia. The speeches of Churchill and Gandhi tell us a great deal about their cultures in their time.

Harmony with Nature

The Asian speaker tends to support his belief in man's harmony with nature. He looks at nature as a unifying force. He sees man as part of na-ture. He aims at oneness of his audience rather than attempting to create factions. In America, the speaker tends to look at each incident as a sepa-rate entity. He might support creation of factions if it helps him achieve his goals. The American sees humans as the masters of nature.

The Asian speaker adheres to his people's cultural expectations. He re-spects their tradition. An American speaker might deviate from tradition. He may say something new for the sake of newness. In America many things that are traditional are shunned.

Welfare of the Audience

An Asian speaker identifies the general welfare of his audience. Asian speech lacks individuality. The speaker reflects the group's welfare rather than his own view, sometimes sacrificing his own opinion. In America the individual's opinion is very important. Every day on American radio, television, and newspapers, we are flooded with individual opinions. In America a person who stands up for what he believes is respected.

Language

An Asian speaker makes a special effort to use lofty language, other-wise known as "King's language," which is figurative and high sound-ing. In America the speaker makes an effort to speak simple language. While the Asian speaker will quote lines from *Vedas, Sutras,* and *Koran,* the American supports his views with evidence from university studies and public opinion polls. The Asian speaker is restrained, dignified and always has an air of forgiving his opponent. The American speaker is emotional, down-to-earth and extremely critical of his opponent.

Respect for Audience

In Asia it is accepted fact that the speaker and his audience have equal responsibility in making the communication successful. Both are partners in the same effort. Treatises such as Bharata's *Principles of Drama (Natya Shastra)* discuss in detail the audience's responsibility. Asian audiences are accorded high respect. In some theaters the general practice is to offer flowers and bow respectfully to the audience at the beginning of the play before the curtain rises. In America such respect and responsibility are lacking. Audiences are not expected to prepare themselves to witness a play or hear a speech. Western books on speech and drama do not discuss in such detail the desirable qualities of an audience. An Asian speech tends to be long and usually uninterrupted; in fact, the longer the speech the greater the speaker.

Ancient Authority

An Asian speaker uses ancient books and philosophers as his authorities. Contemporary authorities take second place. Asian audiences appreciate hearing ancient authorities quoted rather than contemporary philosophers since they believe contemporary opinions should stand the test of time. In America, contemporary opinions and recent studies seem to be more acceptable than ancient texts and philosophers.

In Asia what a speaker says seems to be appreciated more than what he actually does. The speaker's words, particularly if they are quotable, are appreciated more than his behavior. Probably the belief in Karma, that each person suffers for whatever sin he commits, is responsible for disregarding undersirable acts of the speaker.

Importance of Silence

Silence is of utmost importance in Asia. During a speech audiences should maintain absolute silence. They believe that noise breaks the speaker's chain of thoughts and the concentration of his audience. Asians believe in meditation, which requires absolute silence. A great speech is an event which requires the same concentration as does meditation. Although in America audiences are expected to maintain silence, it is not looked at with such religiousness. In America it is common practice for the audience to applaud a speaker several times during his speech. In Asia such a practice is looked at with suspicion. Applauding during the speech is sometimes mistaken for the American booings and catcalls designed to ask the speaker to "shut up." Some Asian speakers ask audiences not to applaud even at the end of their speeches. Such a request is respected since it is an indication of the speaker's modesty, and modesty is an Asian virtue.

Superiority of the Speaker

A speaking situation in Asia assumes the superiority of the speaker. The fact that a person is asked to speak indicates that he has something to offer his audience and that they can gain some knowledge from him. Such a belief automatically puts the speaker in a position above his audience. In America, however, it is generally assumed that speaker and audience are equals. The speaker is supposed to treat them as equals and he is not forgiven if he puts on airs of superiority. In Asia a great scholar is forgiven even when he shows superiority.

Revelation of Truth

An Asian speaker is expected to reveal the "truth" rather than seek his personal goals. Selfish speakers are not trusted. Truth is always there; it is eternal; a speaker only points it out to his audience. He reinforces what is already known to be true. In his attempt to expose the truth, the Asian is not supposed to manipulate his audience. Consequently, Asians are not the world's greatest experts in public relations and advertising. Thus what is supposed to be absolute truth could be different from what the government recognizes as legally true. A great speaker is expected to defy even the legal truth of a ruling government and uphold the absolute truth. Governments come and go, but truth remains the same. The truth always wins; therefore, it should be supported. While the American speaker also is expected to uphold the truth, such truth tends to be legal and constitutional. Even if an American speaker upholds what he believes to be true, it may not be so for his Asian counterparts. For example, individual freedom and freedom of expression are upheld by any American speaker. Such freedoms are supposed to be "truths." Speakers who support those freedoms are respected. In Asia, freedom of expression takes second place to responsible expression. There, individual responsibility is "truth."

A Young Speaker

It is not easy to gain the acceptance by audiences in Asia, particularly for a young speaker. A speaker must prove his worth. Generally, new ideas from an unknown speaker are ignored and even ridiculed. He meets with greater opposition if he rejects accepted views and ideas that originate from ancient books such as the *Bhagavad Gita (Song of God)* or the *Sutras*. Mere logic and reasoning are not enough to convince the Asian audience when the speaker is trying to refute such books. Any quantity of empirical data does not convince the Asian audience, if the data are designed to oppose ancient views.

Ritualistic Speech

Asian speech is ceremonial and highly ritualistic. A speaker is expected to be respectable, and he should indicate his respectability in the way he dresses for the event. Audiences are also expected to maintain decorum in the auditorium. In south and southeast Asia it is common practice to offer a garland of flowers to a speaker before he begins to speak. A man puts the garland around the neck of a male speaker and a woman around the neck of a female speaker, not the other way. Offering the garland is a sign of respect. The speaker, in all humility, takes off the garland after it is put there. Such humility is also expected of a speaker. If he keeps the garland on throughout the speech, the audiences will laugh at him.

Ethos

Both in Asia and America ethos is probably the most important variable that accounts for a speaker's success. But good character in Asia may not be good character in America or in other Western cultures in general. Assuming responsibility rather than asserting rights is expected of a speaker. To give an example, when the Japanese prime minister visits China he is expected to apologize to the Chinese peoples for the wrongs Japan has done in the past to the Chinese. Such a gesture is highly respected in Asia. Although it is common practice in Western countries such as Great Britain for the prime minister to assume responsibility for the wrongdoings of his cabinet members, such is not the practice at the cultural level. In the West such a practice is noticed if at all only at the national governmental level.

American communicologists say that in the final analysis, only three variables account for a speaker's success or failure: trustworthiness, expertise, and dynamism. Of these variables, expertise and dynamism are the most important. An American speaker who is an expert in the subject area has better chances of being accepted by his audience than one who is not an expert. Mere trustworthiness, such as good character, may not be influential over expertise. Given a choice between an expert and an honest person, American audiences seem to accept the expert. Dynamism, as indicated by a speaker's youth and good looks, is an effective factor for acceptance. American speakers do everything possible to look young and attractive.

In Asia, however, trustworthiness such as good character takes precedence over expertise. Trustworthiness also stems from variables such as religiousness and old age. Given an expert and a trustworthy person, the audience will choose the trustworthy person. Although dynamism is an important variable, what is considered dynamic in Western cultures might not be so in Asian cultures. A good-looking person in America might not be considered good looking in Asia. For an Asian, young looks are not always good looks. Asian speakers do not try hard to look younger.

Pathos

In Asia, pathos, or arousing emotions, is not as important as developing sentiments. The emotions aroused by a speaker should lead to a good sentiment for the welfare of all. Arousing emotions for a speaker's selfish propaganda purpose is looked down upon, while attempts to develop sentiments leading to love of all peoples and peace on earth are looked upon with great respect. Asian theorists have said that developing sentiments should be the main purpose of communication. Of all the sentiments, they say, love, pity and peace are the greatest. Any communicator, whether a speaker or an actor, who creates the three sentiments is considered a great communicator.

Logos

Although logos is important for an Asian speaker, the logic should be designed to search for "truth." Use of logic should assume accepted techniques of argument and debate. As a consequence of argument and debate, truth should evolve. Argument that arouses destructive emotions is shunned.

In Asia, however religious a speaker may be, he is expected to be secular. He is not expected to dwell on the greatness of his religion, but is expected to show insight into other religious beliefs also. The more profound references he makes to other religions, the more respected he is. In multireligious countries such as India, secularism is an important factor. In the monoreligious cultures of the West, we seldom hear words of respect for religions other than the speaker's own and his audience's. Some Asians doubt whether Western speakers know anything about religions other their own.

Show of Power

Asians dislike a show of power by a speaker. The speaker does not have to show how powerful he is since his audience can determine that by other means. This attitude is probably a result of the Asian belief in nonviolence. Nonviolence should not be mistaken for cowardice, however. Words of bravery are respected in times of wars. Since wars are supposed to be fought to punish evil and establish righteousness, speakers are expected to stimulate the men fighting at the front. An individual speaker is not supposed to blow his own trumpet to show how mighty he is. In fact, a speaker who boasts of his own greatness is suspected to be a coward and his speech a coverup for his weakness.

In short, we might say that an Asian speech tends to be more idealistic and universal, while an American speech tends to be realistic and applicable only to the present situation.

Rhetoric of Rebels

National and cultural changes have been brought about, in many countries, by leaders who had not only the vision to see the future of their peoples but also the courage to say things that were unpopular. Benjamin Franklin said, "God, grant that not only the love of land but also a thorough knowledge of the rights of man may pervade this earth that any man may set his foot on any soil and say 'This is my country.'" It is hard to believe that an American made such a statement two hundred years ago.

Men such as Franklin had in mind the good of their peoples. Both also said things that were immediately relative to the lives of their peoples. They came up with such statements at a time when their cultures were in turmoil or confusion. From Aristotle to Malcolm X and from Nichiren to Gandhi we see five common factors: they were effective communicators; they were products of their times; their cultures were in turmoil of some sort; they related their messages to the cultures of their audiences; and they rebelled against powerful individuals, groups, or governments. In this section we shall discuss some rebellious speakers from selected countries of the world. The rebels we have selected have affected other societies as well as their own. Most so-called civilized societies have some form of government. More often than not, societies are self-governed, and if not, there is an almost natural propensity for the governed to at least yearn for their eventual freedom.

We can analyze most societal situations in the following combinations: (1) a local majority group which dominates a society socially, politically and economically; (2) a local minority dominating the majority in the three areas; and (3) a foreign group dominating both the local minority and majority. The foreign group could be a foreign government, business organization, or church.

The level of suppression of the people who are governed is directly related to the form, shape and urgency their quest for freedom assumes. The nature of the particular circumstances surrounding their situation and the values of the governor determine how the governed will choose to realize their freedom. Usually, out of the suppressed masses of the governed some leader emerges, and there is a naturally close affinity between the leadership and the governed such that the leadership, by virtue of that close affinity, is able to discern the real issues, articulate them, and create a will in the governed to endure even greater hardship in the quest of freedom. In order to command the attention and respect of the masses, a leader must possess certain characteristics, among which are intelligence, a historical perspective, oratorical skills and a sense of direction.

Although all these characteristics are important, for our purpose we will isolate oratorical skills or rhetoric for discussion. In most situations, the oppressed are deprived of political freedom, overworked, culturally deprived, underfed, undereducated, saturated with fear, despairing and generally hopeless. Against this background, it is difficult to arouse the masses. That there is competition for leadership is a fact which of course does not simplify matters. Invariably there are competing ideologies as well as competing approaches to the solution of the same problem. Out of the leadership pool, however, will emerge leadership which has carefully assessed the values, beliefs, expectations, customs, aspirations, and fears of both the oppressor and the oppressed. The leader will have studied the weaknesses and strengths of the oppressor. Based on such information, he will articulate a plan of action embodying strategies and tactics needed to achieve his goal for his people. He will create an opportunity to disseminate his views to the masses and the oppressors. If his plan is simple, reasoned, practical and delivered against a background which is identifiable and peculiar to the masses, then it will be accepted and given full support by the masses.

Let us briefly consider such a case. African slaves were stripped of all of their native culture, including their language, when brought to America. They were not allowed to pursue any activities in America reminiscent of their African heritage. In restrospect, the slavemaster made one unforgivable error, which at the time served his and the African slaves' purposes but later boomeranged—that was the introduction of Christianity to the slave. This religion was offered to the slave (a different one from his native faith) to control his mind. Through the white man's religion he was able most prodigiously to teach the African slave a code of morality and obedience which lended to his ultimate submission to and acceptance of his fate. The religion convinced the African slave that God was white just like the slavemaster. Imagine black slaves praying to and seeking from a white God their salvation and freedom, embracing the white man's teachings that they were little children who if they behaved and worked, sought nothing in this land, and feared God (a white man reinforcing the white slavemaster), they would certainly upon death go to heaven in the sky.[11]

On the other hand, introducing religion to the slave, even though it was white-oriented, served the slave well for two major reasons. It gave him tenacity to endure the strenuous and difficult life of a slave. It also gave legitimacy to assembling for discussion of his general welfare. It is not to be implied that religion accorded full sanctuary to blacks, because when the slavemaster learned that the church was being used for purposes other than worship, he had no compunction about bombing it in the name of Christianity. Nonetheless, religion did in a sense help the blacks at the same time it did irreparable damage.

The Nonviolent Approach

The late Martin Luther King, Jr., perhaps more than any single leader, personified the rhetoric which was capable of electrifying black people. His background was an extension of Baptist preachers who were expert in arousing emotions and feeding black aspirations. Since most blacks were once situated in the south, they could relate to what King was saying, how he said it, and his style, because chances are they were at one time affiliated with the Southern Baptist church. It may be said with a degree of certainty that the study of the success of any black leader in America correlates closely with the degree to which he embodied the characteristics exemplified by King. Correspondingly, the African brought to America a great oral tradition, the generating and sustaining powers of the spoken word rather than the written word, since as a slave he was forbidden to read or write, which forced him to be fluent and proficient in the art of rhetoric. A combination of the African oral tradition and strict antiliteracy laws during slavery forced blacks to use verbal communication as the medium of intracommunication.

The above example has universal implications for all peoples who struggle for freedom and liberation. As an inflated balloon submerged under water constantly seeks to emerge, so does man seek to overcome his condition whenever his basic freedoms, dignity, and needs are suppressed. Because the conditions vary so drastically from one culture to another, it is important to isolate each case in order to analyze it. For our purpose we have divided world leaders into two distinct groups, those who espoused violent means to an end and those who proposed nonviolent means. Suffice it to say that whether violent or nonviolent means were employed was not decided in a vacuum. Leaders in each group had to deal with their problems within the context of their particular circumstances. There is evidence, however, that they studied the philosophies of other leaders, and sometimes accepted in full or in part philosophies and approaches of those leaders, again depending upon their unique situation. We have explained elsewhere how the concepts of violence and nonviolence symbolize the actions of certain people.

Without reviewing such important considerations as political, economic and social philosophies, let us attempt to group these leaders. In the nonviolent group, the most prominent leaders would have to be Jesus Christ and Mahatma Gandhi. Another, and a disciple of Gandhi, would be Martin Luther King, Jr. These men reviewed their situations and for religious and cultural reasons sought the nonviolent path to freedom. It took an unusual amount of courage in the face of such strong physical might for these men to confront their oppressors without arms.

The Violent Approach

The other group would include these leaders: Caesar Chavez, leader of Mexican American farm workers; Malcolm X, a black leader of America; Fidel Castro, leader of Cuba; Bung Sukarno, leader of Indonesia; and Vladimir Lenin of Russia.

We notice that in societies such as America there were nonviolent speakers such as Martin Luther King as well as violent speakers such as Malcolm X. There are valid reasons for the dichotomy. Martin Luther King, like Mahatma Gandhi, perceived his people as a group unarmed and incapable of engaging in violence against their oppressors. Besides, both King and Gandhi believed that changing the hearts of the oppressors through rhetoric and civil disobedience was more important than changing their minds with bullets and bayonets. King and Gandhi also considered civil disobedience a symbol of nonviolent force.

Malcolm X, on the other hand, perceived his people as capable of taking to arms to defend themselves. He believed that it was more honorable to die in defense of self and family than to die without resistance. To him, violence was a symbol of manhood and characteristic of the American way of life. It should in all fairness be pointed out that Malcolm X did not advocate destructive violence that would cause unjustifiable damage to the personal property of the opponent. He merely said that blacks should not stand idle when their women are being raped by white men; that blacks should not turn the other cheek (Martin Luther King's philosophy) when struck; blacks should not allow the white man to burn their homes down; and blacks should not allow the white man to shoot them without shooting back. He also embraced a white man's slogan: "Your house is your castle, defend it." This type of violent philosophy is parallel with the philosophies of other leaders such as Kenyatta, Mao, Sukarno, and Castro.

In the case of leaders who embraced a violent philosophy and approach to the solution of the particular problem in their society, we notice that some were fighting foreign oppressors while others were fighting domestic ones. For example, while Sukarno of Indonesia was fighting the Dutch colonists, Lenin of Russia was up against his own czar. Whether or not they were fighting a domestic or foreign oppressor, all of them developed communicative techniques to unite their people against the common enemy. We can differentiate clearly between the languages employed by violent and nonviolent leaders.

Some Similarities

These incidents are excellent examples of intercultural communication, since the leaders and their opponents clearly belonged to different cultures, subcultures and races. They are good examples for another reason: the expressive techniques they used to unite their followers on the one hand and to oppose their enemies on the other have been obviously successful. Their rhetoric has brought about the change they advocated. Therefore, the common factors of communication we notice in both violent and nonviolent leaders are: (1) appeal to the cultural values of their own masses; (2) language that is easily communicable with their own people as well as with the enemy; and (3) actions and ideas that were timely and necessary. As a result of the communicative techniques the various leaders used, their followers strongly supported them. Although their common enemies punished them in the beginning, the enemies in the end succumbed to the demands of the leadership.

Another important factor is that the leaders were the products of their own cultures and used methods of communication that were also successful in their own cultures. A second important factor that emerges is that oppressed societies which do not utilize these techniques cannot realize their goals. An example of such a situation at the time of this writing would be that of the native Hawaiians. The Hawaiian culture has not yet produced a leader who could articulate the problems of Hawaiians and mobilize them. Another case in point might be the native American Indian. These societies need a leader who can mobilize the people and also communicate effectively with their opponents.

SUMMARY

Verbal communication is the study of human interaction through the spoken word. Each culture has developed a system of spoken words which makes sense to members of that culture only. Such a system is also called a language family.

Ancient Hindus and Buddhists said that verbal communication is one method of acquiring valid knowledge. They also said that the meaning of the word depends upon a certain syllable in the word. This theory is known as the explosion theory.

In intercultural communication, connotative rather than denotative meaning is important. Even the word order in a language is unique, and may differ from the order in another language. Both ancient Hindus and Greeks agreed on one aim of speech communication: creating emotions and sentiments. Modern linguistics is divided on the development of language and meaning. While one school of thought maintains that communication is a learned behavior, the other believes it is innate.

There is a variance in the degree of sophistication in speaking depending upon the level of the speaker's literacy. Other factors related to intercultural communication include pitch, articulation, intelligibility, dialect and bilingualism. The dialect of the audience seems to be an important factor in determining the efficiency of communicating with the audience.

Because values differ from one culture to another, the aim of verbal communication also differs. This can be seen clearly in the case of Asian and American rhetoric.

NOTES

1. Max Muller, *The Six Systems of Indian Philosophy* (London: Longman's Green Company, 1894), pp. 402-20.

2. Chandradhar Sharma, *A Critical Survey of Indian Philosophy* (London: Rider and Company, 1960), p. 220.

3. Ibid.

4. K. Krishnamoorthy, *Essays in Sanskrit Criticism* (Dharwar, India: Karnatak University, 1964).

5. Ibid.

6. Ibid.

7. Edward Sapir, *Language* (New York: Harcourt, Brace and World, 1949), p. 8.

8. Noam Chomsky, *Cartesian Linguistics* (New York: Harper and Row, 1966), p. 14.

9. Kenneth B. Clark, *Dark Ghetto* (New York: Harper and Row, 1965), pp. 12-40.

10. U.S. Commission on Civil Rights, *Mexican American Education Study* (Washington: Superintendent of Documents, 1971).

11. Roy T. Cogdell, "Abstract on Black Anger," Unpublished paper presented at the National Association of Black Psychologists, Nashville, Tennessee, 1972, p. 6.

6

Expression of Ideas:
Nonverbal Communication

Human interaction by means other than speech is studied under headings such as paralinguistics, kinesics and nonverbal communication. In this chapter we shall use the term *nonverbal communication* for such interaction. Ancients such as the Greeks, Hindus, Chinese and Japanese have discussed nonverbal communication, and Asians have discussed such communication in explaining the nature of communicative arts such as dance, drama and even music.

Communication by nonverbal means seems to occur more often than by verbal means. A person communicates his real intentions nonverbally. Even while one is expressing an idea in speech, he can express exactly the contrary idea by his nonverbal methods. It is common in Asian and American cultures for politicians to go to their constituencies and ask voters to support them. Although a voter may not plan to vote for a particular candidate, he might still say "Certainly, I will vote for you," while his nonverbal expression may indicate the opposite. In India, religious leaders influence their followers' voting behavior. Religious swamies sometimes go to their people to tell them to vote for a certain candidate. If a candidate of another religion goes soliciting votes, the followers of that swami will say "Yes sir, we will certainly vote for you. How can we say no when you have come all the way to our door to ask for votes?" But a close look at their faces will indicate that they have no intention of voting for a person of another religion.

Some communicologists call communication of unintended information *metacommunication*. In the above instance, the people of India may indicate in their nonverbal expression, "You belong to a different religion, so we do not want to vote for you." Better understanding of metacommunication will help a person understand the real intentions of his audience. This is probably why wisemen of olden days said, "Face is the index of mind." That is, regardless of what a person says in a conversation or speech, in order to comprehend his true meaning, it is necessary to observe his nonverbal expressions. To the extent that what is said conforms to nonverbal signs exhibited by the speaker, the more precise the integration of the two sources. If the speaker, for example, says one thing but his nonverbal behavior is at variance, his audience will most likely sense the interference with negative overtones.

Habitual Use of Nonverbal Methods

Hardly anyone would argue against the importance of verbal language as a means of communication but few people fully appreciate the importance of nonverbal language as an effective means of communication. For purposes of our discussion, we will define *nonverbal language* as a system of symbols, signs and gestures which convey specific messages with a high degree of accuracy, developed and used for communication by members of a given culture.

A person learns his nonverbal symbols from four sources: (1) from his own culture through interpersonal means by observing the people in his community; (2) by observing the visual media of television, film and newspaper; (3) by developing his own idiosyncratic methods; and (4) by transferability through interaction with members of another culture. In each culture, the blinking of the eye has a certain meaning; in America, it generally means agreement or approval. It may not have the same meaning in other cultures. Even in America, blinking an eye has other meanings depending upon the situation and the accompanying facial expression. This could also be true in other cultures. A young child in America learns the American meaning of blinking by observing his parents and others in his own culture. On the other hand, an Asian child is taught not to blink at people since blinking is an undesirable habit.

Mass media, particularly television in Western cultures, have taught their audience many nonverbal expressions. Almost everyone knows the meaning of expressions from watching this medium. Although each nonverbal sign has a definite meaning in each culture, the way one person uses a sign will be different from the way another uses the same sign. When blinking, one person may position his head straight and blink, while another may tilt his head to the right and blink, still another may bend his head forward. In Asia, blinking has a derogatory meaning. But when an Asian immigrates to America and stays here for a number of years, he learns to blink to communicate the American meaning of that sign. This is essentially what we mean by transferability.

As a culture evolves, perpetuates and refines itself, so does nonverbal language modify, solidify and evolve new symbols, signs and gestures which communicate certain meanings, feelings and attitudes which are more or less limited to and unique to that given culture. Persons outside that culture will not understand the exact meaning of nonverbal language peculiar to another culture, unless by mere coincidence (or because of proximity to and sharing of the particular culture) some aspects are adopted or influenced by the neighboring culture. In the case of East and West comparisons of nonverbal language, it is quite possible that the unsophisticated communicant from one culture visiting another may presume that because a sign, symbol or gesture has the same form, identification and description, it conveys the same message in a different culture. In Western cultures it is not uncommon for a young man to blink his eye at an attractive young lady upon whom he wishes to lavish amorous attention. If there is mutual attraction, the blinking of the eye might well be received as the prelude to a fruitful relationship. On the other hand, in an Eastern culture, the male, by blinking his eyes at a young lady whom he finds attractive, would more than likely evoke the young lady's anger and indignation, and possibly cultural ostracism.

While there are obviously many theories of nonverbal communication, let us consider a few, both ancient and modern.

Hindu Theories

The Hindus and Buddhists called the ability of a word to represent a certain experience *Power of Word (Shabda Shakthi)*. This power is the relationship binding the words with the objects which they are supposed to represent and the whole experience that people have in relationship to that object. The word "cow" does not just mean an animal to Hindus. Ideas related to sacredness, motherhood and righteousness are attached to it. Similarly, the White House and the Kremlin are not just buildings. The experience of an entire people is attached to the names of these buildings.

Hindus and Buddhists also believed that knowledge is presented primarily in written or spoken words. Anything that cannot be expressed in words cannot usually be said to be knowledge. However, certain knowledge cannot be expressed in spoken or written words. It can be expressed only in gestures. Gestures are symbols that represent "words" in the minds of the speakers. Gestures are words, since they are ultimately explained in words. Some Hindu and Buddhist scholars, however, did not agree with this theory. These scholars said that gestures are not the same as words. They substitute, rather than supplement, words.

Hindu discussions of nonverbal communication center around the gestures used in dance and drama. In classical Indian dance, movement of hands synchronized with movement of eyes, neck and other parts of body is a highly developed art. Each movement, or gesture, or *mudras* in Sanskrit, is a symbol and represents a certain meaning. We find similar gestures used extensively in the dances of other Asian and Pacific cultures such as the Thai, Indonesian, Japanese and Hawaiian. We also notice similarities between gestures used by those peoples in their daily life during interpersonal communication and the gestures used by their classical dancers in concerts. Some gestures used by laymen may have evolved from those of the dances.

Although gestures were used in the classical dances of Asia and the mimes of ancient Greece, few systematic studies have been done to determine the origin of the present day nonverbal techniques of communication in those cultures.

Modern Theories

Some excellent studies done by Birdwhistell are not really intercultural in nature.[1] The study of gestures and other methods of nonverbal communication is itself in its infant stages and most such studies are intracultural in nature. A gesture that is commonly used in one culture may be associated with a meaning entirely different from its meaning in another culture. For example, the gesture of making a ring of the index finger and the thumb to say "o.k." in America does not have the same meaning in South Asia. In that part of Asia it is a very obscene gesture. Birdwhistell calls such gestures "kines." A kine that has a "good" meaning in America might have a "bad" meaning in Asia.

Personal Space

Personal space is defined as that distance which is characteristically kept between persons in various cultures. In the first chapter we discussed how a Muslim greets another Muslim by embracing him as a show of brotherhood. In the American culture, one would have to isolate many variables which would figure prominently in determining how close one would respectfully situate himself to another person without incurring discomfort. Some considerations include the level of familiarity, sex, race, subculture, and social climate. Close familiarity entitles one to some privileges beyond those with someone one barely knows. Persons who are rather familiar with each other, that is, have on more than several occasions been in each other's presence on an informal basis, would, without regard to amorous inclination, feel comfortable in being close to each other so long as their bodies did not touch for an unreasonably extended period. If the occasion arose that for some reason their bodies did touch, one could observe, particularly if the touching were an accident, a degree of discomfort and an obvious, conscious attempt to regain, on the part of both, a certain distance.

With regard to interaction between members of the opposite sex, personal space as a nonverbal behavior is predicted on consideration of familiarity and intent. It is expected that persons of the opposite sex will maintain a personal distance that allows each to be close enough to the other that they may engage in conversation without having to raise their voices loud enough to be overheard by another person nearby. Again, however, if a man and woman sit or stand unusually close to each other for an extended period of time, the conclusion likely to be drawn by observers is that a serious amorous affair is developing, especially if the two are touching each other.

Personal space maintained between members of different races depends on many variables, among which, particularly in the case of black and white and sex differences, is familiarity and the section of the country they live in. For example, in both formal and informal settings it is expected that members of the black and white race will maintain considerable personal distance from each other. This holds true especially in the case of opposite sex interaction among black and white members of American society.

Personal space, then, is a sensitive issue, and symbolic of the kind, nature and extent of the relationships between people. Many messages can be drawn from how close one sits or stands to another person. In all cultures there are accepted limits to space that a person occupies while he interacts with another person. Such space depends upon the interacting individuals and the nature of the business for which the interaction is taking place. In his studies on proxemics, Edward Hall mentions four types of personal space noticed in America. First there is intimate space, which is a foot or less left between persons who are intimate. Parents and children and husband and wife are examples of those who use intimate space during interaction. The second is social space, which is the distance between two individuals who are meeting for a social purpose. Social space would be about one-and-a-half to three feet. The third is public space, when two or more persons meet on occasions such as a public meeting or a classroom lecture. The fourth is personal space which is generally maintained by a person between him/herself and others.[2]

Studies done in American schools have shown correlation between closeness to the teacher and grades earned in that class. In other words, a student who sits close to a teacher learns better and earns better grades in that class than students who sit farther from the teacher. Other studies have shown a correlation between closeness of healthy persons to a sick person and the speed with which that person is cured. In some American cultures, leaving a person alone in his sick bed indicates his approaching death.

Personal space depends upon the culture in which it is used. In cultures with high population density, personal space shrinks on certain occasions. Social distance, which is about three feet in America, shrinks to about one foot in certain crowded Asian cultures. It is not uncommon in Asian societies to see men holding hands and walking in the street, which only indicates that the two men are good friends, not homosexuals, as such closeness would indicate in America. Perhaps such closeness in Asian societies is related to the absence of boys and girls dating as they do in Western societies. In Asian cultures, however, it is not common to see a husband and wife walking together hand in hand.

Asian and African cultures exhibit many types of personal space, not just the four Hall has observed in America. The distance depends upon the social status of the communicator and his audience and the situation in which communication is taking place. In Thailand, the king holds the supreme position in all social settings. His subjects stand at a distance when he walks in front of them. When he talks to them they stand at an equally great distance. Such a distance can be noticed even in Western countries. The president of the United States is usually at a distance from the people, surrounded by secret service men. The king or queen of Great Britain also maintains such a distance.

On religious occasions, even a king takes second place. The head of the religious institution, such as the monastery in Thailand, is higher than the king, who stands at a respectful distance. On such occasions the distance between the common people and the head of the religious institution is greater since they have to keep their distance from two superior individuals: the king and the monk.

In Asian cultures personal space also depends upon the caste of the interacting persons. Higher caste persons stand at a certain distance from lower caste persons. The distance between teachers and their pupils is greater than that in America since teachers are accorded more respect in Asian cultures than they are in American cultures. Social distance is an indicator of respect. Parents are also accorded high respect, and therefore the distance between parents and children is greater in Asian cultures than in the American cultures. In professional life also, such distance is observed in Asia. Subordinates maintain a respectful distance from their bosses. Generally, parents and children, teacher and pupils, and bosses and subordinates maintain approximately the same distance. Kings and subjects, presidents and the people, and religious heads and their followers maintain a greater distance.

The Smile

From the earliest point in children's lives, they learn from their peers and others how to communicate by gestures whether an experience is pleasurable, desirable, distasteful or repugnant. The smile, for example, is a way of saying, nonverbally, that you are feeling good, happy and contented. That same smile can be directed at someone to convey to him or her that you are feeling good about their presence, you are happy to see them and so on. A frown, which by contraction of the brow connotes displeasure and gives evidence of disapproval, can symbolize and convey bad humor, sullenness, or resentful puzzlement. It can be used to imply contempt, anger or defiance without uttering a word. It should be pointed out that unlike the nonverbal behavior of personal space, smiles and frowns can be thought of as universal in their usage, having almost the same meaning and effect on the receiver in any cultural setting. We should also point out that smiles can be used negatively as a way to symbolize contempt, ridicule, derision or scorn.

Posture

In examining posture, the relatively erect arrangement of the different parts of the body, we associate this phenomenon with a person's frame of mind and general attitude about himself. One's posture, the erectness of the body, and the manner in which one carries the body, communicates to a great extent how one feels about himself, how one feels about others, and, to a degree, how one expects others to relate to him. In America, walking with a straight body symbolizes strength, aggressiveness and confidence. To a non-American, this posture might symbolize arrogance. In other words, the posture is characteristic and symbolic of what one communicates to others about himself. His posture connotes that he believes in himself, has the respect of others, and is proud of himself. Conversely, we see the person whose posture is not erect, one which is stuporous, lethargic and stooped, as characteristic of loss of stature, dignity, and rank in a given society. This state is evidenced by—and conveyed to others with which there is social and cultural intercourse—the visible medium of nonverbal communication. The symbol conveys the message to the receiver or observer.

Habits of sitting and standing are also cultural. Postures in all cultures indicate the relationship between communicator and audience. Posture also depends upon the occasion and the sex of the communicator and his audience. In Asia, women are supposed to sit in certain positions depending upon the occasion. In India, a bride at the marriage hall is supposed to sit with her left leg flat on the ground and the right leg folded so that the knee touches her chin. While she eats, the bride is supposed to place her hands to the left of the right leg. Although this is not an easy position for an American girl even to try, such a position is considered highly feminine. The bridegroom sits with both of his legs crossed on the foor. In Japan, women are always supposed to sit with both legs folded so that their bottoms rest on their hind legs. With their legs in such a position, they sit with their hands folded on the stomach. Generally, Asian women, while standing or sitting, are not supposed to lay their hands below the waist line. It is considered obscene for a woman to bring her hands in front of her genitals. In many Eastern and Western cultures women are not supposed to stand or sit with their legs far apart. Such a woman is considered to be of loose morals. An Asian woman is supposed to hold her hands over her mouth while she laughs. This indicates that she is not emotional and does not forget that she is a decent woman, particularly when men are around.

Asian men are not supposed to sit with legs so far apart as to show their masculinity. Such men are considered indecent. While standing or sitting, men are not supposed to twirl their moustaches. In the company of women it indicates that he is trying to show his masculinity. In the company of another man, he is trying to show his power, and such show of power is not liked by other men.

Both men and women in Asia are not supposed to sit with legs stretched in the direction of other persons, particularly elders, teachers, bosses and husbands, while the practice of stretching one's legs in the direction of a teacher, or putting one's feet on chairs or desks is a common scene in American colleges. In the West, women are supposed to stand or sit in certain positions depending upon the occasion and the company. A common standing posture is to put one's right foot in front of the left. When sitting in car, a Western woman first sits on the car seat and then pulls her legs inside. The man then closes the door. In physical education classes in the West, women are taught the correct way to walk, sit and stand. Many films are shown to support the Western concept of posture for women.

The point to remember is that what is considered decent posture in one culture could be nothing, or even indecent, in another.

Smell

Although we use the term *smell,* we really allude to distinct, peculiar odors in a given culture. Odor is derived from the type of food consumed, the state of sanitation, and the kind of society, whether agricultural, industrial or modern. Odors considered offensive, strange, and repulsive to foreigners of a certain culture may in fact have high tolerance among those members of that culture who have been exposed to them for many centuries. One such case in point is that of the Koreans, whose national food staple is rice, usually served with a side dish called *kimchi.* Among the contents of kimchi are onions and hot peppers. Because these two vegetables carry strong characteristic odors, when allowed to ferment in wooden containers for three months or more, the intensity of the odor is multiplied immensely. In a culture where consumption of kimchi is widespread, the odor within that culture takes on a less conspicuous awareness level among its members than with persons external to it. When two people have just consumed a meal of rice and kimchi and are suddenly thrusted in contact with a nonkimchi consumer, there is a strong probability that the latter will detect a strange unpleasant odor.

The smell of hard-boiled eggs is very common in American homes. The odor is not offensive at all to Americans. To some Asians, however, this odor is offensive and smells like rotten fish. This is because those Asians do not eat hard-boiled eggs nor do they have occasion to smell them. To Americans, on the other hand, the smell of curry could be offensive, particularly after being kept in the refrigerator for a few days.

Eye Contact

Eye contact, or looking at the audience at the time of interaction, is considered important in Western cultures dominated by white men. If a person does not look at his audience while he is speaking to them, such a speaker is considered dishonest. The common saying is "If a man does not look at you and face you, you should not trust him." Eye contact is not necessarily a must in black cultures. When a black is speaking with a white, generally speaking, he does not look straight into the eyes of the white. The black's attitude indicates he is either acknowledging the white's superiority or ignoring the white's dictates. In Asian cultures such an attitude indicates that the person who is not looking straight into the eyes of the other speaker is showing respect to him. When a boss says something, or admonishes his subordinate, the latter looks down or sometimes just smiles indicating the superiority of the boss and his right to admonish. Asian women are not expected to look straight into the eyes of men or men into the eyes of women. This is permitted only in the case of husband and wife. Even then, the husband has the right to look straight in the face of his wife and not usually the other way. Women of loose character are supposed to look straight at men's faces. In Japan, eye contact at the time of speech is considered bad manners. It is common for a Japanese speaker to look sideways while he speaks. Obviously, an American would think the Japanese speaker was trying to hide something and was therefore a hypocrite. A Japanese would think the American who looks straight into the eye of his Japanese audience is arrogant and trying to show his superiority.

In America, sometimes, a man who looks at another man or a woman who looks at another woman is considered homosexual. Of course, this depends on how the person looks at the other person; an extended stare is suggestive.

Communication by Touch

Otherwise known as *tactile communication,* communication by touch is another relatively unexplored area. In Western cultures, where personal space is generally wider than in Eastern cultures, touching is perhaps not always an effective method of communication. Touch is, however, most effective at certain times. A man can communicate very well by touching a woman. Sometimes he can communicate plenty of information that he cannot communicate easily by verbal means. At the University of Oregon, a student was asking a secretary at the registrar's office for a correction in his old transcript. He was telling the secretary,

"I know that my professor has sent a correction of my grade last year."

"If he has sent it, your transcript should have been corrected soon after the correction came. Since there is no correction, it means your professor has not sent it in."

The student did not think any verbal exchange would help with the adamant secretary. He stretched his hand inside the window, put it on the secretary's hand and in a pleading voice said,

"I know my professor has sent it in. Probably somebody did forget to make the correction. Would you *please* take a look into my folder?"

His touch worked. She smiled, went in and brought his folder. Surely, there was the professor's note making the correction. She included the new grade and made a copy for the student. In this case the student was not an American. He was a foreign student. He just took a chance and used tactile communication as an alternative.

In Asia, touch communicates affection, a patronizing attitude, and the superiority of the person who touches. A touch at the shoulder or on the back indicates friendship. In Arab and some Eastern European countries, the touch of friendship is extended further. There, men hug each other to indicate friendship. Among Muslims, hugging shoulder to shoulder is indicative of Islamic brotherhood. In Asia, however, nobody should touch a person on the head. Touching or patting the head is an insult. In Asian authoritarian cultures, some teachers do hit their students on their heads and those students take this as a great insult.

Attire as a Communication Symbol

The style and quality of one's dress connotes much about a person. Until recently, the way a person dressed may have said more about him than it does now because of the approach toward universal styles, which may be a trend toward westernization of clothes. Despite recent developing trends, there is still a clear distinction between dressing patterns and styles of the East compared to those of the West. Since we are focusing on American culture here, suffice it to say that there is a pattern of dress in each culture which communicates to the receiver the social status of its members.

When one sees a person wearing expensive clothes in America, certain tentative conclusions can be drawn. The man who wears a suit which cost $300, especially if he has several, is not likely to be a poor man. He is not likely to be a laborer, nor is he likely to be void of the peripheral amenities associated with those who have wealth. He most often is a professional, a lawyer, doctor, accountant or businessman. There are, of course, some notable exceptions. One may be a gangster, but most people will see him as a criminal type, and will react to him differently because he will most often lack cultural refinement and upbringing. He is not likely to be educated or sophisticated enough to blend in with the genuine, legitimate person who wears the $300 suit.

Moving away from purely socioeconomic determinants of dress, consider the individual who prefers unconventional or modern clothes, which set him apart from most people. This individual has special needs. He may be short, skinny, considered ugly or whatever. The kind of dress he prefers may distinguish him from the crowd, give him a feeling of individuality and focus attention on him.

The uniformed police officer immediately evokes a series of signs and symbols, depending on the perceiver's background or field experiences. Without any overt or verbal action on the part of the uniformed police officer, his/her dress can symbolize authority, love, protection, death, blood, fear, or hate. The list is infinite, and the nonverbal language communicated to an individual will be a proliferation of all of things this person knows about police officers in addition to the behavior, proximity, intensity, and nature of his/her most recent encounter.

While there is an inexhaustible list of examples of how dress communicates signs and symbols which stimulate message encoding, we offer one more highly illustrative point. By accident or design, depending on the ideological persuasion, whiteness has come to symbolize virtue, cleaniness, purity and many other things associated with good as opposed as evil. For many centuries in the Western world, especially in the hospital setting, the white dress has been a sign of cleaniness. The doctor, nurse, orderly, and attendant generally wear partial or full white garments. The hospital's atmosphere, walls, floors, sheets, and furniture are often white. This attitude of white purity is often generalized to include all things white, including people, as being pure and good. The obvious conclusion of the antonym, black, or nonwhite, for that matter, is that of being bad, impure, or evil. We suspect the negative concept of black or nonwhite is also generalized to include people. In sum, the man dressed in a white suit invariably represents good, while the man dressed in the black suit represents, as well as communicates, bad. Death is considered bad, so we wear black garments to a funeral; a wedding is good, so we wear white.

People communicate by the way they dress up for a certain occasion or for a person. In the Western cultures both boys and girls dress up for dates. If a girl wants to impress a boy she puts on her best dress. A boy may think his date is not interested in him if she dresses sloppily. At the marriage hall, in Western cultures, the white gown is sacred for the bride. The black dress is worn only during a funeral. Giving a black dress as a gift on occasions such as marriage is considered an insult and a wish for bad luck. When a young man goes for a job interview, he is supposed to wear a suit and tie. The suit and tie indicate respect to the interviewer. People wear formal dress while going to concerts, dinners and other formal occasions. When attending receptions for dignitaries such as ambassadors, suit and tie are usually required. Not wearing the required or expected dress is considered an insult.

In some Asian cultures, red is not an auspicious color. Women are not supposed to be given red dresses. In India you are not supposed to give a red sari as a gift to a woman on occasions such as her marriage. In other Asian cultures, giving a black dress as a gift is a bad omen. Some American Peace Corps volunteers were interested in meeting with the chief minister of the Asian state where they were working. They made an appointment through the chief minister's secretary to see the chief minister one morning in his office. The secretary was there a few minutes before the meeting, as were the volunteers. The secretary was shocked to see them in such undesirable dress. Girl volunteers were wearing shorts and some of them had patches on the bottoms. Boys were also wearing shorts, some of them torn. The secretary could not believe that these were Americans, people from the land of plenty. He did not want his boss to see the American volunteers in unmannerly attire. He cancelled the meeting giving some excuse to the volunteers. The Peace Corps volunteers went back saying the chief minister had no manners since he had cancelled their appointment. The secretary told the chief minister what had happened. The chief minister thought those who trained the volunteers should have taught them better manners.

The Automobile as a Communication Symbol

In America, the automobile is not only a status symbol, but a pivot around which a great deal of the economy revolves. The year, make and model of automobile one drives communicates much about the driver, some impressions of which are real and some manufactured in order to present a front. Some people have been known to purchase expensive, large automobiles for show. Their income may be insufficient to cover little other than the automobile payments, making it necessary to skimp on necessities.

Combining dress with the automobile, we are able to discern an even stronger mode of nonverbal language permeating the American culture. Since these two signs and symbols are such profound messages about people, it is fitting to provide a single example to elucidate our point on the joint impact of both.

In the so-called underworld, there is a small, select class of men commonly referred to as "pimps." Their role is to recruit, cultivate and maintain prostitutes, who sell their sexual services. In order for a pimp to be considered successful, a prostitute-recruitment attraction, it is necessary for him to have what is generally called a "front." The front frequently consists of an expensive wardrobe, an attractive apartment ("pad"), and a late model, expensive automobile ("ride," "hog"). Together these items communicate success, despite the illicit nature of how they are acquired. In the larger community, a person possessing them through socially acceptable, legitimate means would be considered by most standards to have "arrived." These same symbols of success are generalized to other members of the community who find it difficult, if not impossible, to acquire them through legitimate sources. The idea is that these items communicate success to the perceiver without the use of verbal language to get the message across.

In other cultures, also, an automobile is a status symbol. In cultures where few possess automobiles, it symbolizes high status no matter what the size, cost, or make of the automobile. Foreign automobiles in some cultures carry higher status than domestic ones. In Japan, for example, American and European automobiles carry a higher status than Japanese-made automobiles.

These are but a few of the innumerable examples which could be cited to demonstrate the existence of a social appetite for nonverbal symbols and behavior. Whether we are dealing with personal space, gesture, posture, smell, dress, the automobile or some of the other inexhaustible store of nonverbal symbols, the drive to form signs, symbols and gestures as a means of communication is prevalent in all societies and cultures. They emerge as a derivative of the culture, as a natural outgrowth of its uniqueness and peculiarities.

Superstitions

There are superstitions in all cultures. Superstitions may be defined as beliefs or expectations of a cultural origin which are based on some supernatural phenomenon and are not susceptible to scientific investigation. Superstition can generate positive or negative response.

In America, for example, the number thirteen is a bad number. In Asia, a sneeze is considered a bad omen. When the elders negotiate important contracts, such as marriage contract, children are asked to go far away and play because they might sneeze while negotiations are going on. In most Asian cultures, the sight of a cat first thing in the morning is a bad sign. Cutting fingernails after sunset is bad luck. Sweeping the house after turning on the lights in the evening is a sign of bad luck. A woman who always cries brings bad luck to her family. The lotus flower, the cow, and golden images are signs of good luck. Guests who arrive unannounced in the evening are a sign of good luck since it is possible that the Lord himself comes in the form of such guests. A gift of flowers is good luck, and a white elephant is good luck.

A superstition which is considered bad luck should be avoided. For example, if a foreigner sneezes in an Asian home when the Asians are discussing important matters, the foreigner may be unwelcome in that home. A foreigner who gives a gift of a black dress to an American bride would well be an unwelcome guest.

Status of Women

The status of women in the American culture is evidenced by many variables, including simple things that are nonverbal yet which have a profound influence over the relationships between men and women. Consider the amount of space claimed by the male when sleeping with a female in a double bed. The amount of space he takes is far out of proportion to his relative size. He usually decides who sleeps on what side. Scholars have found that men touch others more than women do, and women are more likely to be touched, by both men and other women.

Nonverbal behavior may perpetuate sex-role stereotypes by reflecting dominance or submissiveness. Our gestures communicate either dominance or submissiveness. Women usually sit with their legs together, or cross their legs at the ankle. They also sit more erect and probably are less comfortable when sitting. Men tend to cross their legs at the thighs, are more likely to slouch, and generally take up more room. We suggest that taking up more room is a nonverbal expression of dominance, and for women to accept it is similarly an expression of submissiveness. Excessive smiling sometimes communicates submissiveness. Some people, especially women, tend to smile as an appeasing gesture. Women communicate low status, often unconsciously, through their use of nonverbal feminine cues. For example, body movement or facial expression which is considered by a male to be sexy may perpetuate society's sex role stereotypes and lower status for women. This attitude is difficult to change because so many people are not aware they emit nonverbal cues or that they interpret other people's nonverbal behavior as they do.

Women are rather expected, and have done so in the past, to use the nonverbal behavior associated with their sex. Some women have chosen between so-called feminine and assertive behavior and studies have shown that their failure to perform appropriately has resulted in their being labeled unladylike, which elicits a negative reaction from both men and women. In other cultures as well, women symbolize their roles by nonverbal means.

SUMMARY

Nonverbal communication is human interaction by means of symbols, signs, and gestures which convey specific messages in a given culture. Although the ancients talked about this area, no systematic work was done until the mid-twentieth century. Personal space seems to be one topic of intercultural communication which has been studied in some detail. The other topics include smile, posture, smell, eye contact, touch, attire and superstitions.

NOTES

1. Ray L. Birdwhistell, *Kinesics and Context* (Philadelphia: University of Pennsylvania Press, 1969).

2. Edward T. Hall, *The Hidden Dimension* (New York: Anchor Books, 1969).

7

Expression of Ideas:
Mass Media Communication

Mass communication in all cultures involves large audiences. Messages are transmitted via one or more media. We may consider mass communication under two headings: mass communication via traditional media and mass communication via the modern media of radio, television, newspapers and the film. Exhibitions, fairs and festivals could be considered under both categories since they include both traditional and modern methods of mass contact.

Our definition of mass communication is simply that process of communication involving one or more communicators and large numbers of audiences. Compared with verbal and nonverbal methods, mass communication tends to be one-way, in the sense that the audience has little opportunity to interact with those sending the messages. It would therefore be possible for an effective intercultural communicator to affect the behavior of his audience using mass media more than in the other two situations. It would also be possible for the mass audience to at least see the communicators who use traditional media face-to-face, while even this is not possible in the modern media situations.

Traditional Media

The traditional methods of mass communication include all interpersonal techniques. These are primarily oral, but many other traditional skills are used independently to supplement word-of-mouth. These skills differ from culture to culture. In fact, some of them are specialties of each culture. Religious storytelling is a specialty of India. In Indonesia, the specialty is puppetry and shadow play. In Mexico, the folk dances, and in the

Philippines, the fiestas are the specialties. Public meetings, however, seem to be the most common method of mass contact in all preliterate and illiterate cultures.

Public meetings became popular during the colonial days. The native leaders who were trying to mobilize their people against the colonial rulers developed highly sophisticated styles to rouse nationalist feelings and reinstate cultural pride in their audiences. When Mahatma Gandhi spoke, hundreds of thousands of people in Africa and India came to listen to him. Sukarno of Indonesia could stir the minds of thousands of Indonesians and rouse them against the Dutch colonialists. Jomo Kenyata of Kenya could hold the attention of several thousands of his people in public speeches. Large masses of people were inspirations to their leaders. One common factor in all these leaders' speeches was their emphasis on cultural values. Wearing the simple white dhoti and spinning the wheel, Gandhi reminded his people of the humility that was an essential attribute of a great man and of the handicrafts that were considered sacred in Indian cultures.

Today, speakers use public address systems, but they also rely heavily on their own speaking abilities. Speakers who are known for their rhetoric are popular in their cultures. Popular speakers appeal to hearts rather than minds; they rouse emotions rather than appeal to reason. During election campaigns, political parties recruit local leaders who are reputed to be good speakers. They organize meetings in public parks that can hold several thousand persons. In rural areas, meetings are held in the centers of villages. In some villages, they are held in temples, churches or mosques. Evening is the time when men are at home and women have finished the day's work. All adults, and some children, attend the meetings. In villages without electricity, kerosene lamps or oil torches are used to light the meetings. Most speeches are not reported by radio or the newspapers, but candidates do visit all villages and actively campaign. If a candidate personally visits a village, he can be sure of more votes.

During the general elections of 1972 in India, leaders of Indira Gandhi's party visited the villages in their constituencies. In addition to speaking to the voters, they used a very effective technique. Their election symbol was a cow and a calf. The cow, which is sacred to Indians, had an additional appeal: a cow nursing its calf was a symbol of motherhood. There was also a picture of Indira Gandhi who reminded the Indians of a goddess who came to save them. When the voters went to the polls, they remembered the cow and the calf more than any other symbol. The voice of their candidate, "vote for cow and calf, vote for Indira," was still ringing in their ears. A majority of the Indians voted for the cow and calf.

Businessmen who try to popularize new products use the same technique. They organize public speeches, participate in exhibitions and visit the people's homes.

Storytelling can be entirely oral or through a medium such as puppetry. It is not only a means of informing people but also an opportunity for them to get together and gossip. Although the stories have been told many times before, audiences sit for hours to hear them once again. Each time a story is told, the storyteller uses new skills. Each one has his or her own speciality. He adapts an ancient story to modern-day life. Rama, a mythological prince, is presented as an ideal to modern man. Rama's rule is upheld as the ideal and is subtly compared with the present-day rule of heavy taxes and unethical politics. While listening to the story, women whisper among themselves about the neighbor's daughter who ran away with a young man of another religion. Storytelling meetings are something to which the entire community looks forward. They are informative, educational and entertaining.

Speaking about the importance of oral communication and particularly storytelling, John Morris, former head of BBC's Third Program, has said:

> In addressing listeners in the Far East, the broadcaster has one great advantage in that he is speaking to peoples who are still, to a large extent, dominated by oral tradition. Even in these days of widespread education, ideas on current affairs, politics, philosophy and religion or what have you, are mostly passed around by word of mouth. The professional storyteller (and what a broadcaster he would make) is still the most popular figure.
>
> The practical effect of all this is that in preparing scripts for the Far East we are able to use much material that in other circumstances would be considered unsuitable for broadcasting. Social custom and long formed habit make it possible for Orientals to absorb by ear much of what Westerners cannot fully comprehend without resort to the printed page.[1]

Storytellers have become integral parts of the mass communication systems of many traditional cultures. They are respected because they incorporate traditional values in the messages they give. The storyteller is more of an artist than a technologist. While he is telling a story orally, or through a medium such as puppetry, he feels the "pulse" of his audience. He knows when they accept or reject his message. He knows what makes them angry, sad or happy. He can change the emphasis of his message depending upon the emotions they express during his performance.

The storyteller works within the framework of his cultural tradition. He knows the values of his culture. He is highly knowledgeable in the

mythology and folklore of his people. He knows the various schools of
dance, drama, and music that are his audience's heritage. He can tell
which are the values of his own culture and which have come from outside. The audiences know the merits of their storyteller. He tells them
what they would like to hear. Because of his popularity, he is always in
great demand. During times of community festivals, such as Rama's
birthday, he receives invitations from several communities. Some of them
invite him to tell stories for a few hours or to inaugurate a year-long storytelling festival. The entire story of Lord Rama is told every day for a
year. Each day thousands of persons listen. Sometimes the stories are in
English to attract college students and professors.

Because storytelling is an integral part of traditional culture and the
storyteller's message is from ancient books, governments dare not impose
legal restrictions on this method of mass communication, although they
do have regulations to control media such as newspapers. On the other
hand, many Asian governments are encouraging the traditional arts of
mass communication. Under the five-year plans of India, annual awards
are given to the best puppet players, folk singers and storytellers. In Japan, the Japanese Broadcasting Corporation also gives awards to the best
folk singers.

Exhibitions

A modern version of the ancient fairs and festivals is the so-called exhibition. Exhibitions include both ancient and modern aural and visual
methods of mass communication. Government as well as private organizations use this medium extensively. They construct large and attractive
pavilions, put up pictures, show films, and have volunteers talk to the audiences in local languages. Illiterate audiences can easily understand the
pictures, see the films and talk with the volunteers. Many governments
have established departments to organize exhibitions. Although comparative effects of exhibitions and other traditional media have not been
empirically studied, some surveys conducted by government institutions
in India have shown that exhibitions organized by the Indian government
have been quite popular. One report says:

> The Exhibition Division and its 31 field units along with the mobile vans
> organized 742 exhibitions during 1969-70. These included exhibitions on dif-
> ferent themes such as "Our India," "Family Planning," "Science in Every-
> day Life," "Glimpses of India," etc. About 10 million visitors saw the exhibi-
> tions during the year.
>
> ... Traditional media like song, drama, Harikatha, etc., are also used ...
>
> In 1969 the field publicity units of the Directorate visited 28,489 places all
> over the country, organized 27,353 public meetings, held 35,021 group dis-
> cussions, arranged 34,216 film shows and 8,373 song and drama programs.

During 1969 the Song and Drama Division organized 6,043 performances
of various types such as ballet, drama poetic symposia, folk recital, puppet
shows, composite programs, etc.[2]

The use of exhibitions as a mass medium is unique to the less industrialized and preliterate cultures such as India and China. This medium
uses traditional media such as puppetry and modern media such as the
film.

Mass Media and Cultural Reinforcement

In this chapter we shall discuss in brief how members of each culture have
developed their own media systems and techniques to reinforce their own
values. We notice that all mass media systems of the world fall under five
categories. These are: (1) media systems which are entirely owned and operated by private commercial or noncommercial agencies such as in the
United States; (2) systems which are entirely owned and operated by governments such as those in the Soviet Union, China and India; (3) systems
which are owned and operated by both private agencies and the government departments such as those in Japan, Canada and Australia; (4) systems which are controlled by government-sponsored corporations as in
Great Britain and France; and (5) systems which are entirely cooperative
enterprises of the people, such as that in Switzerland.

Privately owned and operated systems have little government interference, although the electronic media (radio and television) are under a
certain degree of government control based on the belief that the airwaves
belong to the peoples of the country and no private person or organization
has the right to own the waves. In these countries newspapers are freer
than the broadcast media. Films are private enterprises. In order to insure
freedom of expression and freedom of information, the United States
Congress has passed several acts. The First Amendment to the Constitution says that Congress shall pass no acts to curtail an individual's freedom of expression. As mentioned elsewhere, the U.S. Communications
Act of 1934 provides for fairness to all peoples in radio and television
broadcasts. The Supreme Court of the United States has ruled that each
community should decide whether or not a film should be shown or
whether or not a book or magazine should be sold in that community.
These efforts are designed to protect cultural values such as individual
freedom of expression. The laws do not curtail freedom of expression and
creativity; they place the responsibility on the individual to demand his
freedom from mass communicators, or such communicators might take
away the freedoms. A good example is that of a school teacher who wrote
a postcard to the Federal Communications Commission protesting cigarette commercials on American television. His contention was that the

commercials showed only positive aspects of cigarette smoking without showing negative aspects, such as the possibility of contracting cancer as a result of cigarette smoking. The postcard originated a series of debates in Congress, the mass media, and in the public sector. Finally Congress passed a bill banning cigarette commercials from television. It also required cigarette advertisers to mention in their advertisements that cigarette smoking might cause cancer. Until the ban on cigarette advertising was passed, cigarette commercials on American television projected the image of a person who smokes as one with status and good looks. Attractive closeups of smokers in beautiful environments were shown on the screen. American audiences have been trained to believe that anything that is projected with a closeup is very important.

Another technique applied by American broadcasters is the appeal to fear, such as informing the audience that if they do not use a particular shampoo, they might get dandruff. Dandruff is an ugly disease which might turn people away from the person suffering from it. A successful person should get rid of dandruff and the only way to do so is to use a particular brand of shampoo. The mild fear appeal seems to work. Psychologists who work for radio and television networks and advertising agencies specialize in appeals to sell the products of the companies sponsoring the commercials.

Clearly, the American system is based on the philosophy that mass communication is a free enterprise where a number of ideas are available for the people. Each person can pick up whatever idea he likes. In such a marketplace of ideas, both communicators and audiences have freedom of choice. Communicators develop techniques of communication which help them sell their ideas to their audiences. Consequently, it is possible that the few businessmen who own and operate the media also control the messages on the media. The United States is probably the only country in the world where the government does not control the hands of media communicators while they develop their messages. Once they have developed their messages and transmit them to the public, it is their responsibility to prove that the messages are conducive to the public interest. The messages should stand the test of acts such as the Communications Act 1934, community standards, and constitutional amendments such as the First Amendment.

Government-owned Systems

Most countries have various forms of government-owned and operated media systems, of which there are three types. In countries such as the Soviet Union and China, the media are entirely controlled by the Communist party. In Communist countries, all mass media messages are controlled by the party and reflect their ideology. Whether radio, television, or newspaper, the messages are all similar and often the same message goes on all the media. An important feature of mass communication in Communist countries is the wired radio systems. Such radios are placed in public places, such as a cultural center, workers associations, and farms. The party and the government broadcast their messages to the people through wired radios, often emphasizing government programs.

A second type of government-owned system is that found in kingdoms and dictatorships. In countries ruled by dictators and kings, radio and television are often directly controlled by the government. Messages on these media support the rulers. Generally, these media do not meddle with traditional cultures, unless they oppose the king or the dictator. The other media in such countries are generally owned and operated by private businessmen, although strict government laws are enforced to support the regime. Newspaper editors who do not support the dictator or the king are put in jail, and in extreme cases are even executed.

A third type of government-owned and operated system is the one such as that in India. In India, radio and television are owned and operated by the central (federal) government. Government bureaucrats decide what messages go on the air. Since India has fourteen regional languages, radio and television messages directed to the peoples of those regions are in the regional languages. At the national level, Hindi and English messages are broadcast. Although India is a democratic country with several political parties, the government-controlled media tend to support the ruling party's programs. The news and commentaries tend to support the ruling party, or are sometimes "nonaligned." The broadcasters have developed the art of giving messages that are secular and moderate; secular because the country's population consist of Hindus, Sikhs, Muslims, Christians and others, and moderate because the country has several political parties and messages can be neither entirely socialistic nor capitalistic.

In this third type of government system, the newspaper and the film industries are owned and operated by private business. In fact, India has the largest film industry in the world. Even these media, however, are controlled by government regulations. As mentioned in chapter 9, such regulations are designed not only to insure the support of government programs, but also to make sure that cultural values are at least not insulted, if not always supported. Consequently, media communicators have developed symbolism techniques to a very high level. Media messages are not as exciting as they are in Western countries where freedom of expression is guaranteed by a constitution. In government-controlled systems, media messages are usually dull and emphasize the responsibilities of both communicators and audiences.

If a foreigner tries to use the media, he will find it extremely hard to develop messages to fit the government-controlled media. He has to work not only within the framework of government regulations but also in conformity with cultural values. On the other hand, when a person comes to the United States from a country such as China, the Soviet Union, or India, he finds it hard to understand the freedom and sometimes irresponsibility with which American communicators broadcast or publish their messages.

The Mixed Systems

In a mixed system, government-owned media exist along with privately-owned media. In Japan, for example, the government-sponsored broadcast network Ninon Hoso Kyokai (NHK) owns cultural and educational radio and television stations. Since they are owned by NHK, a publicly-supported corporation, the messages are supposed to be nonpartisan, educational and cultural. NHK is also a noncommercial organization supported by the taxpayer. Broadcasters therefore have two alternatives: to give secular, nonpartisan, "objective," and, consequently, dull programs, such as those in India, or to raise the programs to a high cultural and artistic level. In Japan, the NHK has chosen the second alternative. Its radio and television programs are of a high level. An advantage the Japanese have is that their country is monocultural. They do not have the problems of multicultural countries where the broadcasting institution supported by the taxpayer has to please peoples of all cultures. NHK can concentrate on the quality of radio and television programs directed toward just one culture. In addition, NHK can take advantage of the high quality of electronic equipment such as color television cameras produced in the country.

Japan has a colorful history. With its stories of samurai, Buddhist and religious histories, and a line of emperors who have ruled the country for over two millenia, Japanese culture offers as many stories as the media can handle. Since the government-owned media offer programs of such high quality, the privately-owned and operated media must compete in quality. The private media owners have to maintain high quality and still direct their programs to the audience who will buy the products of the programs' sponsors. The result is a popular culture developed by the electronic media. The owners of the media support traditional arts such as folk music, Kabuki drama and the Japanese version of rock-and-roll. Series of samurai stories are as popular as soap operas are on American television. The Japanese film industry is a private enterprise, the second largest in the world. Movies are as popular as television. Some Japanese movie directors place among the world's greatest.

Newspapers in Japan are among the world's most highly advanced, both in terms of quality and circulation. Even production techniques are highly advanced, as in the case of the electronic media.

An important point to note is that in mixed systems, the quality of the messages on mass media tend to be high, since both government and private organizations compete for the attention of the same audience. We see evidence of this in all mixed systems including those of Canada and Australia. Even the quality of educational broadcasting is high in these systems since such broadcasting is handled in the public interest by the government. The entire effort of government broadcasting is educational and cultural. In a free enterprise system, as seen in the United States, the dominant effort is to commercialize the system. Consequently, educational and cultural broadcasts recede to an unimportant position.

Government-sponsored Corporations

Some countries believe the public interest can be best served if radio and television broadcasting is entrusted to an autonomous corporation. In Great Britain and France, for example, broadcasting is handled by corporations sponsored by the respective governments.

Great Britain has an interesting history of corporate ownership in broadcasting. The British Broadcasting Corporation (BBC) began in the 1920s as a radio broadcasting corporation sponsored by the government. Now with its four radio networks, BBC fulfills the needs of all audiences: intellectuals, young people, and others. Television broadcasting began as a noncommercial enterprise. Under BBC it was entirely educational and cultural, with plenty of news broadcasts, particulary during Parliamentary sessions. But the Britains felt broadcasts that are entirely educational and cultural tended to be dull. Some of them thought the broadcasts in a free enterprise system, such as that in America, were more exciting. In 1964, the British Parliament approved the formation of a commercial network under government sponsorship. The new network was called the Independent Television Authority (ITA). As in America, the British ITA is based on the concept that airwaves belong to the people. Unlike the American system, however, the British Parliament thought government was a better trustee, rather than private businessmen, for what belongs to the people. ITA therefore owns the broadcasting facilities in the country. Private businessmen are granted contracts to use the facilities to produce and broadcast commercial television programs. Under government regulations similar to the United States Communications Act of 1934, ITA controls commercial broadcasting in Great Britain, and is free from everyday supervision by government bureaucrats and party bosses.

France has a corporation called Radio Television France (RTF). RTF is similar to BBC in many respects except in a few details of organizational structure and procedural matters, yet RTF has retained its unique French character.

In these systems, newspapers and the film are privately-owned operations. Sometimes newspapers such as the English *Manchester Guardian* and the French *Le Monde* guide governmental and public opinion. Being independent, these newspapers have gained respect for their opinions on educational, cultural, political and other matters.

The film industry in such systems is well-developed and noted for its quality. Filmmakers express their opinions, sometimes independently of their governments. They may even incur the displeasure of their own and foreign governments. A case in point is a series of films made in 1970 by a French movie director named Louie Mall, who made a series called "The Phantom India." The purpose of the film was to depict the life and culture of India's peoples. The BBC considered the film a piece of good art, and broadcast it. The Indian government, however, thought the film did not depict India's cultures as well as a director of Louie Malls' calibre could, and even thought the film insulted Indian cultures. The Indian government asked the BBC to withdraw the series from its network. The BBC rejected the Indian's request. Then, as a protest, the Indian government asked BBC to close its offices in New Delhi.

This incident is another example of bad intercultural communication. The film is the perception of a person who did not understand the foreign culture very well. As mentioned in chapter 8, ethnocentrism is practiced unconsciously and habitually. Usually an ethnocentric person does not intend to insult another culture. Sometimes he is even unaware that he is insulting another people. A mass media communicator born and raised in a monocultural country such as France or Japan does not have the opportunity to understand other cultures as does one in a multicultural country. In addition, if one does not make an effort to understand and respect other cultures, a mass media communicator can create breakdowns in intercultural communication. In fact, what the Mall film showed does exist in India. For example, he shows for several minutes a dog eating the hind parts of a dead buffalo. Buffalos do die in India and are eaten by dogs and vultures. There is nothing special about it. What is so Indian about a dead buffalo being eaten by a dog? Each people feels their culture is the greatest in the world. Indians are not exceptions to this. They think theirs is an ancient and great culture, and expect the world to recognize it as such. As mentioned earlier, each people has its own auto-stereotype. They reinforce such stereotypes in their media messages. When somebody fails to reinforce, they react violently. That is what the Indians did. Auto-stereotyping is an outcome of ethnocentrism. When two ethnocentric persons try to interact, misunderstanding occurs.

Incidents such as this could happen even in systems that have autonomous corporations like those in Great Britain and France. The corporations are independent of both the government and the public. Although Louie Mall was an independent movie director, his series was shown by BBC, which was not answerable to the British government or its public. The situation would probably have been different in a free enterprise system such as in America, or government-owned, as in India. In those systems either the public or the government keeps an eye on everyday functions of the broadcasters. In a free system the public would have protested when the film was shown. In a government system the bureaucrats would have feared protest from the other government.

Cooperative System

This is probably the best mass media system in the sense that the system will have input from all members of the public. In a cooperative system, the local radio and television stations' program policies are shaped by officials elected by the local people. The local stations elect representatives to the national corporation. The national corporation decides the nature of broadcasts at the national and international level. The facilities are owned by the government and operated by the locally- and nationally-elected representatives of the peoples. This system is clearly derived from the other systems, but has many advantages of its own. An important advantage is that this system serves the cultures and subcultures at grassroots levels. It insures variety in cultures at the local level. A cooperative system exists in Switzerland. Since the Swiss peoples belong to several European cultures, such a system serves those cultures quite well.

Mass Media in Education and Culture

Mass media in all countries have played an important role in their audiences' cultural development. In chapter 9 we have cited examples of countries in both East and West where the media have been instrumental in reinforcing existing cultural values and introducing those from other cultures.

Recently, the mass media have taken over the function of schools, also. They not only give information of an educational nature but also teach lessons and award degrees. The Open University in Great Britain broadcasts lessons and sends out printed information to students at home who are working for degrees from bachelor's to doctoral levels. Radio Television France has radio broadcasts "to reach not only the French public but listeners from all countries in Europe and from all over the world."[3]

These broadcasts are made by Université Radiophonique Internationale. Broadcasting schools and universities are increasing under all the five systems. In some countries, newspapers also print lessons and award credit. The lessons are usually written by university professors, and that university awards credit to students who learn by reading the newspaper lessons.

A drawback of education by television might be the way in which the students of television interact with those who are educated in interpersonal situations such as traditional classrooms. The television students think in images they have seen on the screen; they do not think in terms of sounds or other means that are available to the students of interpersonal education. Although we do not have much research evidence at this time on the effects of television education on the thinking processes of its students, it is possible such students will be unable to interact with people in interpersonal situations, since they are not trained to interact on a face-to-face basis.

In countries where mass media have made deep inroads into the lives of their peoples, the media have created a new subculture called *mass culture* or *popular culture*. The subculture consists of beliefs, customs, and arts created by the media that are commonly noticed around the country. Such beliefs, however, are not longlasting. They change quite often.

Communication Satellites in Education and Culture

In chapter 2 we mentioned that organization and administration of communication satellites are national and international in nature. It takes special efforts to make them intercultural, since to bring about intercultural understanding we have to establish two-way communication between communicator and audience. Although technically it would be possible to establish channels between the communicator and his audience via satellites, it is not practical for the following reasons. Take, for example, Intelsat Four series, which was launched in 1973. These are satellites owned by International Telecommunications Satellites Consortium, an international business enterprise. The stocks are owned by the countries that use the intelsats. The United States uses the satellites most heavily. The traffic between Europe and America is heavier than between any other continents. The American Comsat Corporation manages Intelsats on the Atlantic Ocean than on the Pacific or Indian oceans. The latest satellites were first launched and used on the Atlantic and then on the other oceans. An organization that is involved in business, even if it is latest satellites were first launched and used on the Atlantic and then on the other oceans. An orization that is involved in business, even if it is communication, would be more interested in making profits than in achieving intercultural understanding.

Communication satellites are only relay stations situated in synchronous orbit at about 22,500 miles above the earth's surface. Since they orbit the earth at the same speed that the earth rotates, they are also called *geostationary satellites.* Each satellite can cover about 40 percent of the earth's surface. Three satellites are therefore sufficient to cover the entire earth. The three satellites can relay the same message to countries around the earth in less than one minute, because the electromagnetic waves that carry the radio-television messages travel at 186,000 miles per second. These satellites can relay four types of messages: voice, picture, data and facsimile. In the latest intelsats, there are 12,000 telephone, or twelve television channels. Business organizations and broadcasting networks use the intelsats for all four purposes, although most traffic seems to be for telephone and television relay.

So far we have talked of satellite communication between countries. There is also a great need for satellites within the same country such as the United States, the Soviet Union and Canada. These are large countries where people use telephones heavily, and broadcasting networks relay programs across the country. The three broadcasting networks in the United States, National Broadcasting Company, American Broadcasting Corporation and Columbia Broadcasting System, relay programs from their stations in New York, Washington, D.C., and Los Angeles to affiliate stations in all the fifty states. Some of the programs are live. The telephone companies use satellites for long distance calls. Technically, it is not possible for all the 216 million persons in the United States to communicate with each other using the satellites since the telephone lines and television channels are limited in number. Broadcasting communication via satellites is one-way, from the broadcaster to the masses.

Not all satellites are used for communication. Certain types of satellites are used to study weather conditions to predict tomorrow's weather. Only the rich countries can afford them. If Pakistan could have used a weather satellite in 1970, it would have been easy to predict the movement of the cyclone that hit East Bengal and thus to have saved a million lives. The United States uses earth resources technology satellites (ERTS) to take pictures of the earth. The ERTS photos are very sharp. ERTS can take detailed photos of every inch of the land below it, so it can be used to take pictures of any country, including those the American government considers unfriendly. The applications technology satellites (ATS) are used for testing. The ATS-6, launched by NASA in 1974, is used to study the effects of educational broadcasts. It enables classrooms in distant states such as Alaska and New Mexico to communicate with each other. ATS-6 can relay the voices and pictures of the classroom participants. Since there is not enough money to spend on satellites for education, however, the results of the ATS-6 experiment will remain matters of academic discussion in communication journals and textbooks, but will not be applied in everyday education either in the United States or other countries.

Communication satellites could be very useful in countries such as India which are struggling to catch up with the rest of the world in introducing modern agricultural technology and family planning techniques. Satellites could be an excellent means of educating the illiterate. Some of those countries also have another formidable problem: language. In India there are fourteen languages with histories going back to the second century B.C. Sending modern messages to the more than a half billion Indians who speak so many languages and dialects is a problem to national planners. Communication satellites have come as boons to those planners. A satellite with fourteen channels can relay one video, synchronized with thirteen audios of different languages. Synchronizing the same picture with different voices in India would be technically easy since all the Indian languages have been influenced by Sanskrit and therefore have similar phonemes. There might be a problem in the cases of languages that are less influenced by Sanskrit, but this problem could be solved by using morphemes that sound alike.

In the United States, which has one national language, there is now a new ethnic awareness. Each ethnic group would like to speak its own language or dialect. Programs such as bidialectalism also stimulate such awareness. It should be possible to use the same video on the satellite but different languages or dialects depending upon the audience.

In the multicultural countries of the United States and India, cultural differences could become a problem for satellite communication. Even when the same video is synchronized with the language or dialect of the audience, that audience might not like to see persons of a different ethnic group speaking their language or dialect. If the broadcasts were in the Geechie dialect of the southern blacks, for example, it would be ridiculous to show a group of white actors speaking that dialect. On an agricultural program that comes from a satellite in India, it would be funny to see a Punjabi speak Tamil or a Tamilian speak Punjabi. Such programs look ridiculous since a white man cannot speak a black man's accent or a Tamilian a Punjabi's accent.

In addition to the problem of cultural differences, there are some political problems. As mentioned earlier, only the United States and the Soviet Union have, at this time, the capability to launch satellites. They can also launch a number of communication satellites, ATSs and ERTSs. It is possible for the two countries to send messages to the peoples of other countries without even obtaining the permission of the governments of those peoples. In other words, the two superpowers can violate the sovereignty of less powerful countries. It is also possible for the two powers to intercept messages being relayed between two foreign countries or to stop such relays.

Although communication satellites are capable of bringing about inter-cultural and international understanding, the way those satellites are owned and operated now makes it impossible to achieve such understanding. This is true because although mass media do not have minds of their own, the men behind them do. If those men ignore the need to achieve intercultural and international understanding, any number of communication satellites cannot bring the peoples of the world closer. Whether the satellite used is an American ATS or the Russian Molniya, if it allowed free flow of cultural information between peoples of different parts of the world, it would be possible for those peoples to know each other.

We have shown that communication by satellite tends to be one-way. Even so, it would be possible to achieve some understanding of other cultures by relaying programs such as foreign language lessons given by the native speakers, seminars of foreign cultures conducted in the land of those cultures, fairs and festivals from other cultures, etc.

Some Effects of the Media

The mass media in each culture have developed their own dialects and conditioned their audiences to those dialects. They have also developed their own symbols in order to make communication easy and vivid. As a result, the language of mass media in each culture is different from that of oral communication. Because time is money on radio and television, the broadcasters in each culture have come to use few words and give more information. On the other hand, in newspapers space is money. Newspaper editors also have developed techniques of saying more in less space. One important technique is stereotyping.

Stereotyping

Stereotypes are symbols intended to identify ethnic groups or races. They are usually standardized mental pictures used to oversimplify the characteristics of members of a large ethnic group, race, subculture or culture. These oversimplifications stem from opinions and observations of a broadcaster or a reporter in just one or two situations. Although stereotyping makes it easy for media men to communicate with their audiences, they create misunderstanding about the people that are stereotyped.

Ethnocentrism

Mass communicators tend to be ethnocentric. They judge other value systems by their own values. The audiences that receive ethnocentric information tend to look at other people as inferiors. For example, the way kings, sheiks, and gurus are represented in American mass media is not designed to create the same respect those men are accorded in their own cultures. As a result, when we look at a crown like the one we have seen in a funny television commercial we tend to laugh at the thing that probably symbolizes the sovereignty of another people. Ethnocentric communication makes the audience behave arrogantly toward other people.

Cultural Values

Any communication that does not reinforce the values of its audience fails to affect that audience. A study done in rural India has shown that the rural Indian audience remembered radio broadcasts on religion and culture more than those on farming and family planning.[4]

Cognitive Skills

Visual media such as the film, television and comic books inform by means of images. The images have connotative meanings that differ from denotative meanings. Visual media in each culture use symbolic images. Children learn the meanings of images and each time they see them they associate the images with the learned meanings. They also learn to relate several images in a sequence in order to make them meaningful. The image-meaning association is cultural. Studies done in Japan have shown that children learn such cognitive skills at grade-school level.[5]

Social Change

The most important effect of mass media is social change. This is brought about by increasing awareness of social problems. Problems related to untouchability were brought to the notice of the people in India by the media, several years before Mahatma Gandhi appeared on the social scene. Movies and television in America have shown that the black man is as talented as the white man. Television is credited with bringing about the awareness of the role of the black man in American society. In less developed countries, the mass media are used extensively to bring about awareness that will lead the peoples to modernization. Some communication specialists believe the mass media not only inform their audiences but also motivate them. These specialists recommend certain media techniques to develop messages that will motivate their audiences in order to bring about social change.

Motivation

Hovland, Janis and Kelly have done several studies on the effects of fear appeals as motivating factors. These studies have shown that films using moderate fear appeals are more successful in motivating their audiences than high fear appeals.[6] In India, family planning communicators are using fear appeals as motivating factors. They show films that tell of the horrors of life in families with too many children as compared to the happiness in families with two or three children.

A communication-action study done in India has shown that even illiterate persons can be motivated to adopt family planning practices provided the content of communication includes motivating factors. After exposure to certain types of communication, the audience purchased contraceptives or went to family planning clinics for sterilization.

SUMMARY

Mass communication in intercultural settings is both traditional and modern. Traditional techniques include public meetings, storytelling, exhibitions, fairs and festivals. These techniques seem to be most effective in less industrialized cultures. Modern methods include communication by radio, television, newspapers and the film. The nature of organization of modern media in each culture depends upon the political structure in which the culture is situated. We have identified five major systems and five major functions of the media in the world today.

The mass media play an important role in developing education and culture. Recently, communication satellites began contributing a great deal to intercultural understanding.

NOTES

1. John Morris (op cit), Rex Keating, "The Third Programme Problems in Certain Underdeveloped Areas," *Cultural Radio Broadcasts* (Reports and Papers on Mass Communication, Paris, UNESCO, 1956, p. 33).

2. *India 1973* (New Delhi: Publication Division, Government of India, 1973).

3. UNESCO, *Cultural Radio Broadcasts,* Paris, 1953.

4. K. S. Sitaram, "Some Effects of Radio Broadcasts on Rural Indian Audiences," Doctoral dissertation, University of Oregon, 1969.

5. Tosi fumi Tada, *Image Cognition* (Tokyo: NHK Radio-TV Culture Research Institute, 1969).

6. Carl I. Hovland, Irving L. Janis, and Harold H. Kelly, *Communication and Persuasion* (New Haven, Conn.: Yale University Press, 1953).

8

Value Systems

The history of the United States probably begins with the American's fight for freedom of expression. Benjamin Franklin said that if he were asked to choose between a government without the press and the press without a government, he would choose the latter. He believed the press insured freedom of expression and a country whose people were free to express their opinions could organize a good government. Since Franklin, many Americans have gone to jail for defying any government regulations that curtailed their freedom of expression.

The concept of free expression originates in the American belief that an individual should speak for what he believes in. The individual's opinion is important to the maintenance of healthy democracy. The individual also has the right to speak and to be heard. This right was guaranteed to the white American in 1776 when the new nation was born and its Bill of Rights approved. In 1864, the Emancipation Act granted certain freedoms to the black man. In 1964, the Civil Rights Act gave the black man the same legal freedoms enjoyed by the white man. Nonetheless, even today young and old, men and women, white and black, are fighting for some kind of freedom. Individuality has become the most important value in the American cultures.

When Americans fight for freedom of one kind or another they generally do not tend to take seriously the opposing views of other people. They firmly believe that the individual should stand up for what he believes. This would surprise members of Asian cultures since Asians do not fight so hard for individual freedoms.

In Japan, where student demonstrations are everyday occurrences, the agitations are more for social reforms than individual freedoms. To the Asian, individuality is not as important as his peer's opinion. Even if his peer's or community's opinion is different from his own, he tends to sacrifice his own views and adhere to his community's views. A Pakistani believes he is a part of his Muslim community. His living is communal, not individual. That the community is superior to the individual is a belief that has originated from his religious value of Islamic brotherhood. In Islamic cultures, several beliefs, hundreds of expectations and thousands of customs have all branched out of just one value: Islamic brotherhood.

In any culture there exists a complex of values, beliefs, expectations and customs. Each value gives rise to many beliefs, expectations and customs, which we call value systems.

Values

Anthropologists and psychologists classify values on the basis of religious and emotional factors. Anthropologist Shibutani classifies values as positive and negative. Psychologist Rokeach classifies them as terminal and instrumental. Depending upon their importance to a culture, we classify values as primary, secondary and tertiary, each of which is either positive or negative. Shibutani defines *values* as follows:

> Valuations may be viewed behavioristically as preferences—what one covets, wishes to avoid or seeks to destroy. An object may be said to have value when one has special interest in it.[1]

Rokeach defines *values* on somewhat the same lines:

> I consider value to be a type of belief, centrally located within one's total belief system, about how one ought or ought not to behave, or about some end-state of existence worth or not worth attaining.[2]

Value seems to us to be a person's basis of decision. It tells him how something ought to be and for what his life is worth living, worth fighting and even worth dying. Since value is so important, it is also necessary to influence others to accept it as the only end state of life. Value thus becomes the standard for a person to judge his own and others' actions.

Values are guiding lights that show a person which way he should go. They are standards by which the individual decides his relationship with: (1) himself; (2) the other men with whom he interacts; (3) machines that produce the commodities he needs; (4) nature around him; and (5) God, who is supposed to help him attain salvation.

Value System and Human Nature

We often tend to confuse cultural values with human nature. Biological instincts drive a person to seek food, money, and sex. These loves are aspects of human nature, not parts of a value system. In fact, values are sometimes imposed by cultures to suppress human nature that upsets peaceful living in the society.

While attraction to the opposite sex is human nature, some cultures prohibit any show of affection between the opposite sexes in public places. Other cultures do not impose total prohibition on shows of affection. In Western cultures, for example, it is not uncommon to see unmarried boys and girls kissing each other on sidewalks and in moving cars. In those cultures it is customary for boys and girls to have some limited relationship in order to know each other before they get married. Knowing each other before marriage and making their own decisions is another way of reinforcing the value of individual freedom that is so much cherished in Western cultures.

Three Types of Values

Some values are most important and worth guarding at the cost of the individual life. Others are important, but not worth dying for. Some Americans believe democracy is worth preserving. If a weak country is being taken over by communism, it is necessary to save that country and preserve its democracy. If necessary, arms should be used to fight communism. In such an operation, a few Americans might have to give their lives; but it is worth their lives to those who believe that democracy is of primary value.

Although individual freedom and preservation of democracy are primary values to Americans, they are not so important to the peoples of Asia and Africa. In some cases, these are not even secondary values. Those people consider individuality and democracy a tertiary value. There are numerous examples of peoples giving up easily their individual freedom and democratic way of life to dictators and autocratic regimes.

Americans also believe it necessary to help the farmers of underdeveloped countries modernize their agricultural technology. They believe those farmers should use tractors in place of oxen and fertilizers instead of cow dung. But Americans might not wage a war to make those farmers substitute fertilizer for cow dung. Tractors and fertilizer are not as important as democracy and freedom. Modernization of agriculture is a secondary value.

In medieval England the most worthy recognition a young man could attain was knighthood. He could attain such recognition in several ways. He could fight in combat in the arena, kill the antagonist and win the hand of the king's daughter, or, he could fight bravely against the king's enemy and save the kingdom. In any case, the youth had to fight. He might even get killed in such a venture. But recognition was so important it was worth dying for. To the medieval Englishmen, such recognition was a primary value. History is full of such heroism, not only in England, but in other parts of the world. The *samurai* of Japan, the Mongol warriors of Persia, and the Hindu heroes of India are other examples. To all of them, recognition as heroes was a primary value.

Negative and Positive Values

Values can be either positive, negative or neutral. Preserving democracy and freedom is a positive value to Americans; not preserving them is negative. Fighting communism is positive, not doing so is negative. Positive values are given credit and negative ones are discredited. A person who fights for democracy and freedom is accorded highest recognition; one who does not fight for such values is discredited and even punished. Those who fought on the American side in Vietnam were recognized and honored; those that did not want to fight had to run away to other countries such as Canada or go underground. Even after the war ended and peace was declared, the President said those who ran away from their duties to their country should not receive amnesty. Many Americans supported him and said that amnesty should not be given to the runaways. Even in medieval Europe and Asia those who did not fight for their king were disgraced and called traitors; when so-called traitors were captured they were beheaded.

Positive values in one culture can be negative in another culture. Those who fight for positive values are acclaimed as heroes and stories are told about them. Legends and songs are composed and sung in that culture. Those who do not fight are ridiculed. Stories are written to show how bad they were. The good ones are used as examples for the young to follow. The bad ones are ridiculed in order to insure that the young do not follow their footsteps. In Russia, those who fought for communism are acclaimed as people's heroes. Lenin, the father of the Russian Revolution, is acclaimed a model for young Russians. In China, Mao Tse-tung is an ideal person and young Chinese say that hard work is good because Chairman Mao says so. On the other hand, hundreds of thousands of men and women did not fight on the side of Lenin in Russia and Mao in China. These men and women, ridiculed as enemies of the people, were then used as bad examples to the young. While saving democracy and freedom are positive values in America, saving communism is a positive value in Russia and China.

Degrees of Positiveness and Negativeness

Values are not always at the two extremes. A value could be extremely positive in one culture, extremely negative in another, and neutral in a third. Let us consider a value such as democracy, where decisions are made by the majority after a free discussion of issues by all interested parties. Democracy could be extremely positive in Culture A, extremely negative in Culture C, and neutral in Culture B.

Value: Democracy where decisions are made by the majority after a free and impartial discussion of issues by all interested parties.

1 ____ 2 ____ 3 ____ 4 ____ 5 ____ 6 ____ 7 ____

Positive: Neutral: Negative:
Culture A   Culture B   Culture C

Similarly, values can be primary in one culture, secondary in another, and neutral in a third. It is possible that democracy as defined above does not make sense to peoples of some cultures. In such cases the value would be placed on the neutral point. It is also possible that sometime people will change either to left or right, to positive or negative sides of the scale. Women's Liberation and all the freedoms attached to such liberation is a positive and primary value to many women in the United States. It might also be positive to women in another culture, but not at point "1" on the above scale; it could be somewhere between points "1" and "3" on the scale. To the same women it could be a secondary value.

Until recently, no scientific effort was made to locate cultural values of either Eastern or Western peoples. We have heard young people say, "our values are much different from those of our parents," or "our values are different from those of the . . . people." But nobody says what definitely *their* values are. It seems that values are hidden away beneath the complex of beliefs, expectations and customs of the world's cultures. Probably, the ancients who originated the values meant it to be that way. They wanted values to be mysterious secrets. People should talk about them, but should not know what they really are. It is something like the talk about Absolute Reality. We talk about it, but we do not know what it really is. Scientific studies in each culture to discover primary values will show they are the roots from which the thousands of beliefs, expectations and customs have stemmed. In the final analysis, we might find out that there are just a few, perhaps two or three, primary values in each culture which distinguish that culture from others.

Values and Communication

A people's values do not easily change. Although national and personal values change quite often, those that are learned as tradition are hard to change. Even when changes occur, those that change are secondary, not primary values. Changes that do take place happen as a result of extremely efficient communicative techniques. When younger people say their "values" are different from those of their parents, they are really talking about beliefs rather than values. Even changes in beliefs or secondary values come about by effective communication. A close look at the history of both Eastern and Western peoples shows that their primary values have not changed in many centuries. Traditional values of even the so-called progressive peoples have remained intact for many centuries.

Social scientists often give the example of Japan as a culture that has changed as a result of its contact with American culture, but any Japanese social scientist would laugh at such observations since he knows the so-called progressive tendency is inherent to the Japanese culture. They also give the example of India, which became democratic as a result of the British influence. Even this is not true. The Indian style of democracy has been in existence in that country's villages for several thousand years. Indian epics such as *Ramayana,* written about the eighth century B.C., has several stanzas to show that the king considered the popular opinion. China is supposed to have shaken off its old tradition and embraced communism. This is also far from true. The old Confucian system had already paved the way for an authoritarian society. In fact, the Chinese people always submitted themselves to authority. One authoritative culture gave way to another.

Efficient communicative techniques, economic needs, and existing political systems have all worked to industrialize China and India. The Indian's determination to use modern weaponry and warfare to defeat Pakistan in the 1971 war was a result of cultural differences between the two countries. Although many political and military strategies have been given as the reasons for India's decision to fight it out with her neighbor, historically the basis for most of these lie in cultural differences. Whatever changes have been brought about in the political, industrial and other structures of India and China, the leaders of the two countries used effective communicative techniques to make the changes possible.

Mahatma Gandhi always worked within the framework of India's cultures. His emphasis on nonviolence originated from Buddhist and Jain values. His goal of independence was part of Hindu tradition. His concept of rural industries was Aryan in origin. His belief in brotherhood of all Indians came from the Islamic Koran. Mao Tse-tung's concepts of a modern China and peoples' revolution had their origins in Confucian and Buddhist philosophies. We have discussed this aspect of cultural communication in the chapter on perception.

It seems that the changes brought about by Gandhi or Mao were really changes from secondary to primary values. They did not help bring about any change from negative to positive. Changes that seemed to be from the negative were only skillful reinterpretations of what seemed to be negative but was not really so. To give just one example, the two leaders are credited with elevating the position of women to that of men. Equality of women was never a negative value in either Indian or Chinese cultures. Philosophies of both cultures have always indicated that men and women have equal status, each with definite responsibilities. The two leaders reinterpreted the old philosophies to suit the changing times. In other words, the leaders were highly efficient communicators and could affect the behaviors of their peoples in their respective cultural settings.

Old Values, New Meanings

We are not trying to say that a leader who is also an effective communicator in his own culture cannot bring about any drastic changes. With the advantage of his effective communication, a leader can find out how to use the existing values to change a negative value to positive or vice versa. A people's changing needs can force them to give up old values. In many Asian cultures a high value was placed on offspring. They believed that children were given by God and so were sacred. Some of them placed a higher premium on male children. The male child was supposed to be responsible for performing the rites after the death of his parents in order to send them to heaven. He was also responsible for guarding the honor of his family. Then came the modern leaders in those cultures who stressed the need for population control. In India there are large signs in all parts of the country in all languages saying "children by choice, not by chance." Those signs show happy parents with only two children. A federal government minister picked a stanza from the *Vedas* that says:

> Four sons are as useful as a lake, four lakes are as useful as a tree; therefore, why not raise a tree instead of producing a son?[3]

Sometimes, cultural values that seem to have changed are really old ones that have new meanings as a result of changing needs and times. In the United States the old Jeffersonian concept of freedom of expression has taken on several different forms. Elderly Americans believe it is the responsibility of their country to fight communism anywhere in the world in order to save the freedom of those who are under the threat of communist domination. Opposition to communism is equated with support of free enterprise. Communism is a negative value and free enterprise a positive value. But the younger generation believes that Americans have no business interfering with the affairs of peoples of other cultures. They believe that peoples of other cultures have the freedom to embrace communism if they want to. Young people believe the American style of free enterprise is not free since it is dominated by a few rich persons.

Both young and old Americans believe in individual freedom. But the younger people look at it differently, and complain that their freedom is being infringed upon by the elders by not allowing them to express their opposition to the present system of free enterprise.

Different Cultures, Similar Values

A culture's values, beliefs, expectations and customs are designed to support each other. Even in two different cultural complexes, we occasionally come across values and beliefs that are similar. In those instances, it would be possible for the different cultures to influence each other in the areas covered by similar values, beliefs, expectations and customs.

Although the English and Indian cultures are entirely different, the value attached to royalty was similar in both. The literatures of both countries influenced each other. Shakespearian plays were eagerly received by audiences of different linguistic regions in India. Plays written by ancient playwrights such as Kalidasa and modern ones such as Tagore became popular in England. Sir Monier Williams translated Kalidasa's *Shakuntala* in the eighteenth century. Some of the most well-known plays translated into Indian languages are *Hamlet, A Midsummer Night's Dream,* and *Othello.* The undecided nature of Hamlet is easily understood by the Indian mind since Indian philosophers also make statements such as the ones made by Hamlet. Indian philosophers are known for their seemingly ambiguous statements.

Violence has become a part of American culture. The violent beating of the African drum and the Indian *tabla* became quite popular in America.

Sexual freedom, which is important to the lives of Western peoples, is well described in the fourth century Hindu book *Kama Sutra.* The book became more popular in the West than in India. Although the book is rarely read and discussed by the peoples of India, it has found its way into many paperback editions in Europe and America. An Indian dare not make a movie based on that book, but there have been several such movies in America.

Sometimes during the course of their life history a people may become disappointed in their values. In crucial times their own values fail. They then look for value systems which seem to have withstood the test of time. Members of the younger generation in the West, disillusioned by their own value systems, are now trying to understand Eastern values. Some of them have been studying the African cultures. Consequently, many American young people know more about African and Eastern cultures than do African and Eastern youngsters.

On the other hand, Eastern peoples, particularly the younger ones, are disappointed with their own failures in achieving material happiness. They blame their value systems for the failures, and have begun adopting Western values. The values of East and West that have influenced each other are the similar ones that are easily adoptable without upsetting too much of the existing systems. A young American might not accept the Hindu value of giving up beef and drinking, but he will eat more vegetables and read *Kama Sutra.* The Hindu might not accept the American habit of eating beef, but he will certainly have no objection to eating "vegetarian egg" and reading *Playboy.*

Because leisure-time activities such as entertainment and games are becoming important in Japan, the Japanese are turning toward the West where such activities are dominant. Until recently, the Japanese did not consider taking a vacation once a year as their right. Now Japanese business organizations and the mass media are encouraging vacations and other leisure-time activities. In addition, rock-and-roll theaters are popular in all Japanese cities.

European and American cultures have influenced each other for centuries. Asian and Pacific cultures have more than two thousand years of cultural contact.

Dating: East and West

Let us consider an example. Lucy has been dating Fred, whom she has known for several years. He is well behaved, and Lucy's friends and relatives like him. Her parents certainly like him. Whenever Lucy goes out with Fred she gets the impression that he also likes her, although he does not say it in so many words. The softness of his few words, the warmth in his embraces and the touch of his lips all tell her that he likes her.

One morning he unexpectedly calls her and asks if she will be free that evening. He says "I have something very important to tell you!" Lucy says she will be free. She believes he is going to propose to her. Their friends and relatives know that someday Fred and Lucy are going to get married. What Lucy and Fred have done is nothing surprising. Like all young boys and girls in that culture, they have gone steady and lately have seen a lot of each other. This behavior conforms with the cultural values of their people. They have tried to understand each other and to find out if each is suited to the other. That is what they are supposed to do. By doing so they have given the impression that they are going to get married. The decision of the individuals who are going to marry, not an arrangement by their elders, is the accepted behavior. Everybody in Lucy's culture believes in that kind of decision. Individuality is valued. Suppose somebody asks Lucy if her parents also decided to marry the same way. She would say: of course, yes. Her parents might not have told her everything they did before they decided to get married. But she believes that is what they did. Lucy knows she has the right to choose Fred as her life partner. Lucy is doing exactly the same thing she believes her parents did. Her experience in that culture has made her believe that choosing the partner is her own right.

But instead of Fred, suppose Lucy is going with a student from Thailand. His name is Bhoomipal. Since it is not easy to say his full name, she calls him Paul. Paul is a fine young man. He is probably the most brilliant man Lucy has met. He is decent. She likes his looks, his dark hair, brown eyes and soft voice. She met him when she was a sophomore. At that time he was working on his master's. Now she is a senior and he is finishing his doctorate. They have gone steady for more than three years. He likes her very much, probably even loves her. She certainly loves him.

But would her friends, relatives and parents like Paul the same way they would Fred? Would they believe that Paul is going to marry her? Is that what Lucy is supposed to do? Is that what everyone in her culture is doing? Is that what her parents did? Has everybody in her community given her the impression that she has the right to go steady with a boy from Thailand? Going one step further, have all her cultural colleagues given her the impression that they know Lucy is going to marry Paul? Do her cultural values promote the kind of individuality that permits her to marry a member of an entirely different culture? The answer to all these questions is: probably no!

Suppose one morning Paul calls Lucy and says: "Lucy, I have something very important to tell you!" Does she automatically believe that he is going to put an engagement ring on her finger? He might have given her the impression that he is madly in love with her, but has he given her the impression that he is going to marry her? The answer to all these questions also is: probably, no.

These examples show there is a great deal of difference between human nature and cultural values. It is human nature for a girl to fall in love with a boy who she thinks is the best in the world. But it is not likely that they are going to get married. What is humanly possible may not be culturally probable. The cultural values and beliefs decide the probability. Something that is believed to be probable in one culture might not be so in another culture.

Beliefs

Values are the basis of most human behaviors. They are deep-rooted, hidden somewhere beneath the whole complex of a people's value system. A value system consists of a few values, many beliefs, expectations and customs. Values are not easily changeable, but beliefs are. While it is not easy to pinpoint a person's values, it would be possible to know his beliefs. Values are like the roots of a tree; beliefs are like its stems.

Many Americans or Europeans believe that God is white. Angels are white. They are all pure. Cinderella, the ideal of purity and innocence, is also white. The value attached to whiteness is the root of these beliefs. Few churches have an image of Jesus or picture of angels in black or yellow. It is not even conceivable for an "anglo" to think that God is black. He believes that God created man in his own image. He blessed him, too; the blessed ones are white. All these beliefs stem from the value that white man is the beloved of God. It is not easy to change this value.

White Man, the Leader

A young university professor who had originally come from Boston to teach in Hawaii, became the leader of some younger professors and liberal students who were demonstrating against the establishment. The young professor overnight became a celebrity among the younger ones. He grew a long beard. He thought he had he right to lead and to be followed. Then came along several local young men. He patronized them as long as they followed him and accepted his leadership. This continued until one of the local young men became a threat to his leadership. The local had the same liberal ideas and probably was equally capable, but the professor thought only he should lead and all the locals should follow him. The local leader accused him of being a racist and of trying to dominate the locals. When the locals took over the leadership, the young white professor left the liberals, shaved off his beard, married a white girl from Boston and joined the old conservatives. Even there he was not happy since the old conservatives had already established their hierarchy. But he felt more comfortable in accepting the leadership of his own people rather than working under a group of locals. His wanderings from group to group resulted from his belief that only a white man could lead, even in areas such as liberalism.

Some Japanese believe they are the highest people in the world since they came directly from the Sun Goddess. The Brahmins of India believe they are the highest class in the world since God created them first.

The belief that each people is pure and superior has given rise to several ugly attitudes. Some white men believe they have the right to master nature and dominate people who are not white. We have heard of the early white settlers in Tasmania, America, and other parts of the world trying to massacre the native peoples that looked "ugly" and different and so had no right to live on this earth.

Same Value, Different Beliefs

Earlier in this chapter we showed how the value of individual freedom has given rise to different beliefs. Older Americans believe that support of free enterprise insures such freedom while younger people believe such a system takes away freedom and places it in the hands of a few entrepreneurs. Although both think they are fighting for different values, they are only fighting to establish different beliefs. We also pointed out how the leaders of India, China and Japan tried to change the beliefs of their peoples by giving a new interpretation to their old values.

In the United States, liberal-minded people are trying to convince others that the black man and the Chicano are equal to the whites. Although both young and old whites value equality, some of them believe nonwhites are not equal to whites. The liberals are trying to change that belief and have been successful to some extent, since it is a task of changing only a belief, not a value.

Expectations

Because a people have accepted certain values and beliefs, they expect things around them to go a certain way. The young liberal white professor in Hawaii believed he was the one to lead the local liberals, and expected the others to follow him. Since many whites sincerely believe they are superior, they expect the blacks, Chicanos and other minorities to behave as inferiors. They expect the minorities to know exactly where they belong. They are not expected to act like the whites. Even growing long hair is the monopoly of the whites, according to some white teachers in Chicano schools. Miss Talvara, a Mexican teacher in a Chicano school, says of a boy whose long hair was cut by a white teacher:

> Shamefaced and almost in tears, Mexico-born John Garcia took his seat in class. His head was bald in spots. He tried to hide the black tufts of hair that stuck out all over. There was an awkward silence. Garcia's humiliation was to serve as a warning to the other boys. [4]

Blacks in America are expected not to compete with whites. As mentioned earlier, some whites honestly believe blacks cannot compete with them because of the blacks' "low achievements." Others do not want them to be equals. In the final analysis the expectation is the same. Baseball player Hank Aaron received several hundred letters threatening him not to exceed a white man's record in hitting home runs. The letters berated him because he was a black. In 1973, when Aaron was just about to break the record of Babe Ruth, the following statement, attributed to Aaron, appeared in all the major newspapers.

> If I were a white man all America would be proud of me. But I am black. You have to be black in America to know how sick some people are. I've always though racism a problem, even with as much progress as America has made. [5]

Those who wrote the hate mail did not expect, nor did they want, Aaron to beat Babe Ruth's record of 714 home runs.

When a Harijan in India achieves a high position, the upper class members say patronizingly: He is a Harijan, but he is very capable. It does not matter what caste he is, as long as he is good. . . But beneath the patronizing, the upper-class man is shaken at the achievement of the untouchable. He is shaken because the Harijan's achievement is inconsistent with the upper-class members' expectations of a Harijan. In Japan, the Aettas and the Burakumins, who are also untouchables, are moving higher in social status. They get from the upper-class Japanese the same treatment the Harijans in India get from the upper-class Indians.

When a person does not behave as expected, the perceiver suffers cultural shock, as in the case of an Asian student who came to do graduate work at an American university. He rented a room in a businessman's home. The businessman's secretary, a pretty divorcee, used to come once in a while to see her boss. She would say hello to the foreign student. One day the student asked if she would help him find a store to buy some shirts. She did. In a few months they became good friends. One weekend she came to see her boss. She was ravishingly attractive. Her tight dress, partly-exposed breasts, attractive lipstick, and blond hair beautifully falling on her shoulder drove the foreign student crazy. While still in his country he had read about the free love in America. He had even had a few chances to peep into the pages of *Playboy* magazine at the university bookstore. He expected the secretary to be free like the women he had heard of and those that he had seen in the magazine. While she was waiting for her boss and nobody was around, he went close to her and without saying a word, tried to embrace her. The secretary was shocked. She had thought all foreign students were meek and did not know a thing. She already had a boyfriend. She was not interested in anybody else, certainly not a naive student like the one who was clumsily trying to embrace and kiss her. She chided him, and scared him by saying, "If you don't go back to your room, I'll call my boss."

The student was shocked to see the American woman so "promiscuously" dressed and not interested in a man. The secretary was equally shocked at the unexpected behavior of the alien student. Obviously, their expectations about the behavior of the members of each other's cultures were wrong.

An American Peace Corps volunteer was made to believe that the farmers in his host country were backward, that they obediently listened to any American and did whatever he asked them to do. He went to an Asian country to work in villages and help farmers raise poultry. Within a few days after he settled down in one village, he began ordering the village folks to do things his way. None of them listened. They thought they knew better. One day he was invited to dinner by a farmer. Although the farmer was the richest in the village he did not show off and appeared to be simple and naive. The volunteer did not know he was rich. At the farmer's home he saw a big teakwood cot, the most beautiful he had seen in his life. When he went back to his home he sent word to the farmer that he would like to have that cot for himself. He expected the simple farmer to give away the cot with due respect to the American volunteer. The farmer's family had a great sentimental attachment to the cot since it was given to them by the farmer's parents. Since it had been passed down by the elders, it was considered sacred. They expected the intelligent-looking American to know this. Besides, the village people were told that the American was given adequate instruction in the culture of that Asian people. The farmer was shocked when his expectations were wrong. He complained to the higher officials of the Peace Corps. The volunteer was transferred to another village. After a few days in the new village, he also found that most of his expectations were wrong. He suffered a terrible cultural shock and returned to America.

Expectations are future-oriented cultural beliefs. Each person believes another person will behave in a particular way as a result of a certain stimulus from him. He expects the people of other cultures to react to him in a certain way. When the other member in his own or alien culture does not reinforce the expectation, the individual suffers a shock.

Expectations are probably second in importance to values in affecting intercultural communication. Ignorance of another's cultural values, beliefs and customs leads a person to wrong expectations. Finally, all lead to a breakdown in communication between the members of the two cultures.

Customs

In each culture its members have been taught to do things a particular way. There may be no logic for doing things that way, but if it is not done that way, it is bad manners. Is there any logic for placing silver on the left side of the dinner plate, as is done in American homes? Is there any logic for eating noisily just to show that the food is delicious, as is done in some Asian homes?

At the United Nations, an Asian diplomat broke a European record for the longest speech given by a diplomat. One day the European had spoken for three hours, thus setting the record for the longest speech at the UN. Then the Asian, who was originally supposed to speak for a few minutes, stood up to speak. He spoke for more than seven hours. Because of his long speech, the activities of the world body had to be put off by one day. In his country, all newspapers proudly acclaimed the Asian as a record-maker. They said he elevated the honor of his country by setting the record for the longest speech. But he was considered unmannerly by Americans, for no one speaks so long as to upset the schedule of so many important persons. Customarily, punctuality and promptness are given high importance in Western cultures; it is good manners to respect other's time. But these are not the customs in many Asian cultures.

An American student wrote a letter to the nearest Japanese consulate general asking for information on studies of interest to him in Japanese universities. The consulate general did not answer. Instead, one day a secretary in the consulate general called the student on the telephone and told him there were no opportunities in Japan for the kind of study he was interested in. The American asked why no one had answered his inquiry. The Japanese secretary said that was the official answer. He also said that they would not answer letters written by individuals. Only if the head of his university wrote would he receive an official answer from the consulate general. The American was surprised. Later, he was informed that the Japanese will customarily not commit themselves in writing, but it was considered respectful to call a person and give him the information he had asked for. That way the Japanese have shown respect and at the same time not have committed themselves.

Cultural customs are important aspects of communication and anyone who fails to know the customs automatically closes the door between himself and his audience. There are stories of how westernized Asian men have insulted their own cultural colleagues and have been unable to talk with them. A young Indian who had a doctorate from an American university and stayed in America for a long time met an elderly Indian lady. She was wearing a beautiful sari and he remarked on it. The Indian lady did not like it. Indian men do not express their admiration of the dress of girls or women in public. Even if the woman is his wife, a man does so only in private. A young Japanese man who had stayed in America for many years was introduced to a senior businessman from Tokyo. When the businessman tried to bow, the young man tried to shake his hand. The young Japanese thereby insulted the senior.

Nobody knows exactly what the values are in most cultures. It is not easy to find the values that are the basis for most beliefs, expectations and customs. But it should be easy to learn customs. The popular intercultural communicators are those who almost blindly follow the customs of their audience's culture.

Ethnocentrism

Ethnocentrism is probably a major barrier to intercultural understanding. Most individuals judge other peoples' cultural values using their own values as the standard. This type of value judgment is called *ethnocentrism*. Ethnocentric communicators do not realize that each culture is developed by a people to make *their* own life meaningful and to establish order in their own societies. The hierarchical system of the Orient or the caste system of south Asia were developed in those cultures more than two thousand years ago to establish order in those societies. Those systems worked well in those days to those people. But to a foreigner, the caste system and the hierarchical system seem terrible.

Similarly, the horizontal system of Western cultures seems incredible to Asians. Asians still believe there is no such thing as absolute equality. They look scornfully at the so-called equality in Western cultures. Because of this attitude, a Western-educated girl is a threat to Asian boys. The boys believe such a girl would not be a good wife since her mind is polluted by the concept of equality. A Japanese girl educated in America cannot easily find a husband in Japan. If she does, her marriage will not be happy if she judges her husband's attitudes according to her American ideas.

Types of Ethnocentrism

Herkowitz identifies two types of ethnocentrism. One is benevolent ethnocentrism, which is the act of judging the value system of another culture using one's own values as the standard, but tolerating the cultural difference. The second type, militant ethnocentrism, is the act of not only judging another value system using one's own values as the standard but also forcefully imposing one's own values on the others. Religious missionaries and some conquerors of early days were militantly ethnocentric. Even today many individuals practice militant ethnocentrism.

Herkowitz suggests that cultural relativism[6] may be the answer to the problem created by ethnocentrism. It is the method of studying a value of another culture in relation to that overall value system. We then find that each value, belief and expectation makes sense.

Cultural Change

Depending upon their political, economic, and social needs, all cultures change. There is no one culture in the world that has not changed. Change is the response to inside and outside stimuli.

Cultural change is a result of effective communication. An effective communicator is also a change agent. He studies a society's needs and tries to bring about social change to fulfill those needs. In order to bring about change he develops his own art of communication.

Cultural Distance

In intercultural situations audiences see the symbols used by the communicator as they would see those symbols in their own culture, and understand his language as they would understand it according to their own cultural standards. Members of one culture judge another culture on the basis of their own cultural standards.

Even scholars are sometimes ethnocentric. Many Western rhetoricians judge all speech techniques by Aristotelian standards. Western philosophers judge all systems of philosophy from the Platonic viewpoint. Many Western musicians judge the music systems of other cultures from the Beethovian standards. When, in the United Nations, a great classical Indian musican sang an English song in the Indian style, many ethnocentric Indian musicians scorned the Indian musician. In 1968, the Japanese ambassador to Brazil was fired because he wrote a book in which he said that Japanese women are not the most beautiful in the world, thereby insulting the Japanese culture.

Even before the process of communication begins, ethnocentrism creates a distance between the communicator and his audience. This distance could be called *cultural distance.* Awareness of cultural differences, ethnocentrism, or some other variable causes the cultural distance.

Ethnocentrism is not the problem of the communicator of any one culture. Peoples of all cultures suffer from it. Consequently, the ethnocentric person fails to see the worth of other cultures and fails to communicate in intercultural situations.

Immigration and the Third Culture

The Third Culture is an entity that evolves as a result of a person's emigrating from his first (or parent) culture to a second (or adopted) culture in which he integrates the value systems of both. According to some scholars, members of the Third Culture face several problems. Cultural estrangement and alienation exist between persons in highly industrialized and pluralistic societies such as the United States. These estrangements and alienations also cause intra- and intercultural misunderstandings and hatreds. Some of these problems are self-alienation, objectivation, rootlessness and dehumanization,[7] expectations and realizations.

Self-alienation

A person may become separated from his original culture because of professional or social reasons. He might take a job in an industrial community that is different from his parent cultural setting. An older person might go to live in a senior citizens home. The behavioral patterns in the new industrial community or citizens home are much different. The individual is forced to adopt an entirely new behavior pattern.

A possible result of separation is self-alienation. The individual lives two lives. Within himself he lives the life of his original culture, while in the new environment, he lives another life. He alienates himself by cherishing his old culture while living in the new culture.

Objectivation

In the world of objectivity where the "I" part of the individual is transformed into a "non-I," the "I" part becomes less important. What the individual thinks, within himself, becomes less important than what he says to people outside. Everything he does is objective. What he says and does belong to his society, not to himself. The result is a conflict within the individual. This conflict, the agony of the "I," is something he cannot tell anybody. As time passes, the individual adopts the external form as his own. In other words, what is objective is forced to become subjective. He is forced to cherish what he did not want to cherish—a mental state of dissonance. The resultant conflict creates hatred against his own society.

Rootlessness and Dehumanization

These two factors are sometimes interrelated. Changing political and economic situations may make the individual move from his home to a place that is entirely new. The refugees of south Asia and the Jewish immigrants from Asia to Israel are examples of rootlessness. Sometimes the immigrants are forced to move to a new culture, as in the case of the blacks who were brought from Africa to America. New opportunities might bring them to a strange culture, as in the case of the Filipinos of Hawaii. Many years later the members of the minority groups realize they are not members of the main culture of their adopted land. They feel rootless; they do not have a cultural identity. The identity crisis creates hatred of the main culture. In addition, the members of the main culture may not accept the immigrants as a part of their culture. The rejection may add to the hatred, which makes the hatred reciprocal.

If the individual works in a factory, he further loses his identity. Life in front of a machine all day dehumanizes him. The individual should adjust himself to the system. It is possible that as a result of continous association with the machine, a person may begin to love the machine more than his fellow men. He may even hate his fellow men while he loves and lives with the machine.

Expectations and Realization

Where mass media are important cultural institutions, the media tell their audience what their social values, beliefs and expectations are. For example, the mass media in one culture might keep saying that absolute individual freedom is a fact of life. The audiences listen to and watch the media messages and come to believe that it is true. All they see on the television screen and hear on radio raise their expectations. When they do not realize those expectations in real life, they rebel against society. This gap between expectations and realizations is one reason for the problems of many advanced societies.

Another effect of the mass media is their ability to build images. According to the American mass media, the American is the richest, strongest and most generous person in the world. He is achievement-oriented. He is the champion of democracy and supporter of individual freedom. This "Perfect American" image has at least two negative effects. The young American, believing he is such a person, will suffer a terrible shock when he goes to other cultures and realizes he is not that perfect. Members of other cultures who believe in the Perfect American image will be greatly disappointed when they discover the image is not correct. They may not be disappointed in a Chinese because they have no "Perfect Chinese" image, but they do have a Perfect American image.

We have tried to discuss in detail the importance of values, beliefs, expectations and customs because these variables shape a people's communicative behaviors. The reason an individual uses one word instead of another to express an idea has much to do with his value system. The reason a person bows instead of shaking hands is guided by his culture. The several cultural institutions insure that their people respect and follow their value system.

Values

We have tried to classify several concepts that are considered values in five major cultures of the world, the Western, Eastern, African, Muslim and American black. We are not saying that other cultures do not exist, but there is adequate information on these five cultures enabling us to classify them. The members of these five major cultures also constitute almost 90 percent of the world's population.

The five cultures include many subcultures. By Western culture, we mean the culture of the white man who lives in the Americas, Europe and elsewhere. By Eastern, we mean the cultures of Hindus and Buddhists. Although there are many subcultures of the Hindus and Buddhists, we have tried to include values common to all those subcultures. Although Muslims live in many Asian countries, including India, their culture is distinct and cannot be classified as part of either Hindu or Buddhist culture. We have also treated African culture as a separate entity since scholars have tended to ignore that culture or have tried to include it in Eastern culture. Recent studies and African opinion indicate, however, that African culture is not a part of either Eastern or Western culture and is distinct. Although we do not yet have complete information on all African subcultures, we have classified the African culture as one entity on the basis of books written by African scholars and newspaper accounts published in the West. There is possibly more than one culture in Africa, but we have taken common factors from the available data on the subcultures. In fact, this is what we have done in classifying all the five major cultures. It is also sometimes said that the American black people's culture is part of the overall American culture. It should be made clear that there is no such thing as one American culture. In America we notice several cultures. The black culture is one such, and blacks consider their culture separate from the white man's culture.

We have identified some values as common to more than one culture. However, applying the theory of cultural relativism, we find that the reason a certain concept is a value in several cultures is not always the same. Our explanation of each value indicates this.

Values are not always of primary importance. One value could be of less importance than another. We have thus classified them as primary, secondary and tertiary. We have also noted that what is of great value to one people could be of negligible value to another. We have deliberately avoided saying that a value of one people may mean nothing to another, since it is possible there are a few persons in one culture who believe in the value of another culture.

Human Dignity

Human dignity is a belief that includes respect for another person and high regard for his personal rights. It also means that the other person should not be treated as an inferior. This value is observed by members of a culture among themselves. An extension of this value is observed in the kind of job a person is asked to do. In Western cultures, servitude is rarely seen. Even if one is rich, he generally does his own job and does not hire servants from among the members of his culture. It is not common practice to hire many servants or to have people clean lavatories. Another simple situation where we can observe this value is in answering letters and questions. Americans generally answer letters coming from strangers. Even when the answer to a question is negative or unpleasant, the American does not hesitate to answer. He respects the right of the other person to have an answer. In Asian cultures, however, if the writer of a letter happens to be a stranger or a person of a lower status, the recipient does not answer. In some cases, he might ask his secretary to answer.

Efficiency

This is certainly a Western value. By efficiency, we mean doing the job the way it ought to be done, systematically and on time. Meeting deadlines is a part of efficiency. Americans reached the moon according to their plans. They developed computers and other devices to improve the quality and accuracy of work.

Frankness

Westerners, particularly Americans, seem to be frank when dealing with people of another culture. They do not hesitate to criticize when criticism is needed. In Asian cultures, frankness is not practiced, particularly when the frankness happens to be unpleasant criticism. In the Japanese culture, the practice is not to answer at all if the answer happens to be negative.

Patriotism

Sometimes this is also called *nationalism*. It is a primary value in most African-Asian cultures. To fight and die for one's own country or king is highly regarded by Asians and Africans. In the West, patriotism is not blind. One is expected to decide whether or not his country or leader is right in dealing with another country. A person does not have to go and fight for his country if his country is wrong. Americans rising against their leaders' decision to go to war in Vietnam in the 1960s is one example. Young Americans question the policies of their government, while this is not generally done in the Asian-African cultures.

Religion

Everyone loves his own religion or denomination. Whether a person is a Brahmin, Catholic, Hinayana Buddhist, or a Sunnie Muslim, each has a great love for his own religion. Sometimes, in order to love his own, he might hate other religions. Many beliefs are generated from this value. The Christian belief that Jesus is the son of God and the Hindu belief that Krishna is a reincarnation of the Lord are just two examples. Any doubts of religious beliefs are not tolerated. When a person ridicules the beliefs of another religious group, he should be prepared to face violence from the others.

Authoritarianism

This is the value attached to a center of authority, which can be an individual or group of individuals. Those who value authoritarianism believe that law and order can be assured only if authority is placed in the hands of one person or group of persons. Once a person is given authority he should be obeyed. Obedience to authority is sanctioned even by religious books such as **Bhagavad Gita, Sayings of Confucius,** and **Koran.** Authoritarianism is a primary value in Asian-African cultures.

Education

Education is a valued factor in many cultures, particularly the Western. Parents spend much of their earnings to give their children a good education. In Eastern cultures, education is a prestige factor. The teaching profession ranks at the top of prestigious jobs. A Sanskrit saying goes: teacher is God. Education is a valued factor for certain segments of Asian cultures. The Japanese culture is an exception to this rule; all Japanese value education. In the West, everyone values education. In America, education means money and well paying jobs. Therefore, whites, blacks and others alike value education. Education is often equated with intelligence. It is generally believed that an educated person can communicate better.

Gratefulness/Loyalty

Gratefulness or loyalty to someone who helps in an hour of need is an Eastern value. An Asian tends to be grateful to one who helps him find a job or saves his life. Duration of gratitude is lifelong. Many American university professors have misunderstood their Asian students when they have shown unusual loyalty. The Asian students were loyal to their professors for giving them assistantships or scholarships and thus helping them get a good education, but the Americans have suspected the Asians of ulterior motives.

Peace

To live peacefully among neighbors is an Eastern value. Even when his right is infringed upon by his neighbor, an Asian tends to overlook it in the interest of peaceful living. This value extends to the cultural and national levels also. Easterners believe in peaceful living even when they are subjected to aggression by warlike neighbors. History shows that Asians have been conquered repeatedly by Western warriors. They have either refused to fight or have given up after initial resistance in the interest of peace and to prevent bloodshed. The famous five principles of peaceful coexistence pronounced by Nehru of India, Sukarno of Indonesia, Tito of Yugoslavia and Chou-En-lai of China in the 1950s are outgrowths of the value of peace. Those who are familiar with T.S. Eliot's poetry know that he says: *Shanthi, Shanthi, Shanthi* which means "peace" in Sanskrit. Hindus, before eating their meals, offer prayers for peace.

Modesty

Modesty is a virtue for an Easterner. Scholars and rich men are expected to be modest and not to show off. Easterners believe that a fragrant flower does not have to announce its existence to the world. Even if it is hiding behind a leaf, the world will know it by its fragrance. A bronze jar filled with water does not spill, it is only the half-filled jar that spills and makes noise. Scholars and rich men are expected to be like fragrant flowers behind a leaf and jars filled with water. On the other hand, it is common practice for a Westerner to assert himself and announce his achievements. These days it is common practice to appear on television and tell how much a person donated to a charity. In Asia, they say that your left hand should not know what your right hand gave away. Many Americans of Chinese and Japanese ancestry have been deprived of equal consideration for jobs since they do not boast of their achievements as do their white counterparts.

Karma

Hindus and Buddhists believe a person suffers or enjoys in his life depending upon what he did in his past. If a person is happy, it is because he has earned it. If he is suffering, he is paying for his past deeds. Hindus and Buddhists generally do not go to the assistance of another Hindu or Buddhist if that person is suffering. Since a person must suffer for his past deeds, why should anyone help him? Even if one tries to help, how can anybody save him? This value is almost the opposite of the Western value of saviorism.

Collective Responsibility

This is probably the most important value for Easterners, primarily Hindus and Buddhists. In contrast to Western individuality, Easterners believe a person is a member of his family, society, country, or whatever group he belongs to and works for. His primary responsibility is to the groups to which he belongs. In order to be responsible, he must sometimes give up his own rights. For example, in order to be a responsible father or mother, a person should give up his or her own happiness. Even if the parents do not get along well, they should tolerate each other in the interest of their children. This value is expected to be followed even by Easterners who immigrate to Western cultures, where they are expected to uphold the honor of their parent cultures. On the other hand, parent cultures are also expected to support their people who have immigrated to other cultures. Japan for example, is extending financial assistance to Americans of Japanese origin to study Japanese culture in Japan.

Respect for Elders

Ancestor worship is standard practice in many Asian-African cultures. Asians conduct death anniversaries of their ancestors in grandeur. Respect for living elders is expected of youngters. When an Asian young man talks with older persons he is unusually polite and respectful. It is common for older people in Asia to live with their children, and a son is expected to take care of his parents when they grow old. If he neglects his parents his people consider him a villain. In Asian cultures, senior citizen homes are not heard of.

Hospitality to Guests

Eastern religious books say "guest is God." Serving excellent food to guests even when the host's children are starving is standard practice in Asia. The Hindu feasts, Japanese dinners, and the Filipino fiestas are similar examples. A person who does not treat guests with special foods is considered a bad person. History is full of Asian kings who were extremely hospitable to European businessmen. In India in the sixteenth century, English businessmen were accorded great hospitality by Mogul emperors, and were given free lands to build forts to store merchandise.

Inherited Property

Property passed down from parents to children is considered sacred in Hindu cultures. Children generally do not sell inherited property. Even if such property is junk, they tend to keep it. This value is probably related to ancestor worship. Since ancestors are supposed to become angels and watch their children from heaven, children do not want to sell the property and anger the heavenly parents.

Respect for Environment

In Eastern cultures, humans are considered a part of nature. Hindus consider nature the creation of God. The spirit of God exists in the running waters, high mountains, green trees and living animals. Therefore nature and all living beings are sacred. No one has the right to destroy them, nor can anyone be the master of nature.

Sacredness of Farmland

Farmland gives food to the farmer. The farmer owes his living to the farmland. In other words, farmland is like God extending his generous hand to the farmer. Like a mother gives food to her children, a farm gives food to its cultivator. Similarly, Hindus consider the cow as sacred since that animal gives milk. Man owes his life to the cow since he grew up drinking its milk. The cow is also like the mother who nurses her children.

Individuality

This phenomenon is paramount in American culture. It is rooted in the spirit of success and winning. Individuality coincides closely with the whole notion of capitalism, which presupposes that if one works harder than his strongest competitor his reward is a direct reflection of his worth and recognition. Unlike in many Eastern cultures and in a limited number of Western cultures, such as Russia, where actions are focused on group welfare, in American culture individuals from birth, especially the male child, are taught the value of excelling in all their endeavors. Often this may be at the expense of the needs of members of the family and friends. Americans value strength, toughness, and aggressiveness. The individual is important. His opinion should be heard. A person should stand up for what he believes. When such a person communicates with members of another culture, he may give the impression that he is arrogant and inconsiderate of others' feelings and values.

Respect for Youth

Since capitalism is the foundation of free enterprise, its basic aim is to identify those segments of society to which it can market its merchandise. Through exploitation of mass media, youth are given great importance, catered to, and even made to feel that through mass consumption of material goods their status in society is enhanced. Youth, for example, prior to the mid-sixties, were saturated with expensive clothes. On recognizing this, the media then made it popular to wear faded blue denims, causing youth to flood stores in search of clothes which give the appearance of being old. Because of the preferential treatment accorded to youth, whose membership constitutes more than half the American culture, the impact of mass media in the shaping of public opinion can also be observed in older people who attempt to effect a youthful appearance as well as engage in activity normally associated with youth. Conversely, in Eastern cultures older people tend to be revered and cared for because of the knowledge and wisdom gained through more living experience. Their children do not cast them aside when they are old as the Americans do.

Motherhood

As noted earlier, older people in American culture are not held in high esteem as compared with those in Eastern cultures. For example, in the Hindu culture a child would not consider bringing a lawsuit against his mother, but in the Western culture such a situation might easily arise, particularly where money is involved. Exceptions in Western culture can be observed in the manner in which Mexican-Americans and blacks behave toward their mothers. Blacks, for example, will not tolerate insulting, demeaning remarks by anyone against their mother. It is common knowledge that the best way to start a fight with a black person is to say something derogatory about his mother. Hence, respect for motherhood is a deeply-rooted black value. Additionally, in the Eastern culture the concept and practice of the extended family presupposes that when people become old, younger members of the family will keep them in their homes and care for them. In the American culture, when a person becomes too old to care for himself, he is likely to be placed in either a public or private home for the elderly because of the probable burden it would otherwise cause the youth.

Hierarchical System

The structure of a culture can be observed in several forms. In America there is a separation between church and state. Within each of these structures is a hierarchy that delineates authority and responsibility. Some cultures, both Eastern and Western, combine the activities of church and state, making the two systems integral in conducting affairs of state. While in America the hierarchy is clearly defined, there is prevalent feeling that if one is industrious he can move freely from one level to another, depending upon his own merit—individuality. Eastern cultures seem to be somewhat static in that birth tends to predict status, and there is tremendous respect for those in high positions. Since most civilized and even some so-called primitive cultures are highly structured, the major difference we are trying to elucidate is the freedom of movement, up and down, within any given culture. This difference does not appear to be prominent between cultures as they tend to be hierarchical in nature.

Hierarchical society is approved by ancient books and prophets of the East. The Koran clearly separates men and their duties. Confucianism advocates stern authoritarianism. *Bhagavad Gita* says God created the four castes. Hierarchy can be noticed in all aspects of Asian-African societies. Even the modern leaders that boast of bringing about change have not been able to abolish the hierarchical systems of Asia and Africa. This does not mean the hierarchical system is not a Western value. Even there, different levels of jobs and persons exist. A hierarchical system seems to be common to all cultures. There is a caste system in Hindu cultures, while the color bar still exists in Western cultures.

Masculinity

The traditional role of the male in most cultures has been that of a provider and protector of his immediate and extended family as well as of the society in which he resides. This role has undergone moderate to massive change in nature and description as various cultures move from hunting and gathering to agricultural to industrialized existences. The element of masculinity is generally built into the male role. These general principles hold true in most cultures found in the East as well as the West. It has been noted by many distinguished scholars, however, that deliberate attempts have been made by colonizers to emasculate male natives or imported male slaves. The process calls for a radical reversal of traditional roles formerly held by the males: a transition from the provider-protector functions which reinforce manhood to that of the subhuman beast with no power or dignity. The act is intended to strip the person of his masculinity. While masculinity is a priori in most cultures vis-à-vis the definitive role of the man as compared to that of the woman, it should be noted that the black male in America considers his masculinity under constant threat. Masculinity is a value not only for men but also for women. In all cultures women like their men to be masculine. Although the traits of masculinity vary from culture to culture, a man who is considered masculine in his culture is likely to communicate better with women than one who is not considered masculine.

Color of Skin

Every culture seems to have its own "niggers." These "niggers" do not necessarily have to be black. Germany used the Jews as scapegoats for most of the ills of that society. Hitler, Germany's leader at the time, persuaded his people, through the mass media, that it was all right to murder Jews for the good of that culture. It is significant to observe that throughout history, major powers have conquered minor powers, enslaving their captives. The captives are not always of darker complexions. This phenomenon is more recent with the Western peoples since their empires have been mostly established in Eastern cultures made up of darker-skinned peoples. The probability that those conquered will have a lot to do with the color of skin is much older than the prowess of Western military strength. For instance, in 3000 B.C. in India, the Aryans slaughtered millions of Dasyus whose skin color was dark. Although they were a peaceful, nonagressive people, the Aryans killed off most of them, and prohibited intermarriage on the basis of skin color. The West has, however, used the color of skin as a unique means to establishing order of importance in their cultures. As mentioned in chapter 2, there are distinct gradations of importance within America based on the color of one's skin. This practice clearly places the color of skin as a value in American culture. To members of each culture, the color of one's own skin is a primary value.

Money

There is perhaps no value in America so ingrained as purchasing and holding power. In a capitalistic culture where there is an absence of the extended family concept, possession of money is virtually an end in itself.

Money takes on a special significance because without it one cannot eat, obtain shelter or clothing, or commute from one place to another. The possession of money is so valued in America that it is not uncommon at all to read where someone has murdered a close relative or friend over a dispute involving a small amount of money. A person's status is basically determined in America by amount of money and holdings. Although money is important to non-Western peoples, it is not of primary value to them. Because money is of primary importance to existence in America, the minorities also believe in its primary value.

Punctuality

The work ethic in America is so mechanized that it is imperative to be on time. Although during the agricultural era in America people worked a ten- to twelve-hour day, the industrial movement in the thirties and forties, even for a shorter work day of eight hours, began to emphasize the need for punctuality. The machines and assembly lines could not operate until the worker appeared on the scene. It was therefore critical that the worker arrive on time so the work could start on time. Punctuality also ties in with the term *efficiency*. If punctuality and efficiency can be controlled, then quality and production can be controlled, which results in higher profits. Since profits are the root of capitalism, punctuality is an important value in America. People lose their jobs for not being punctual. In cultures where the profit motive is less significant, the need to be punctual is also less important. Consider Mexico, for example, where each day before noon practically everything closes down for the two-hour siesta. When an American talks with a Mexican, he expects him to respect punctuality, while the Mexican may not take it seriously because it is not of primary importance to him. In the Mexican culture punctuality is not always important and therefore a worker might not lose his job for not being punctual.

Saviorism

The best example of saviorism as a value can be seen via two major thrusts. One is the church. The Western church is known for its propensity to spread Christianity to non-Christian cultures via missionaries. They are so fanatic that they tend to ignore the religion of the host culture, bent on converting the natives to Christianity and to their way of life. The second thrust of the saviorism mentality is to choose cultures which are incapable of defending themselves militarily against aggression. Underlying saviorism is the zeal to halt the spread of communism, and the acquisition of territory and raw materials. The president is sometimes the titular head advancing the cause of industrialists under some popular heading and slogan. The one used for Vietnam was "To Defend the Right of Self-Determination of the Vietnamese People."

Firstness

The need to be first in Western cultures is closely akin to individuality, aggression, masculinity, money and many other values deeply entrenched in Western culture. Americans pride themselves for having been "first to land on the moon," first to make the automobile, first to make the train, first to discover electricity, etc. Being the first to lay claim to an invention or creation can have many manifestations, not the least of which is the acquisition of large sums of money. Hence, firstness is built into other values held dearly by Americans. Europeans as well as Americans believe in being first. Two cases in point are that Columbus *discovered* America and that Vasco-da-Gama, the Portuguese, discovered India.

Aggressiveness

While in Western cultures there are rules defining the parameters of aggressiveness, success at the expense of breaking a few rules is often overlooked. Certain kinds and intensity of aggressiveness are the result of training and preparation given to most Western children early in their development. They are trained to be persistent; they are taught the value of not giving up in the face of mounting odds. They are taught how to "use" others in order to achieve their goals. Young people are given leadership training in the Boy Scouts, in the military, and in schools, particularly in sports. In the American culture, football and boxing are relatively dangerous sports, yet young men are encouraged as well as paid to injure each other to win. Aggressiveness is basic to the Western way of life, while in Eastern cultures passive behavior, the opposite of aggressiveness, is favored. When a Westerner tries to interact with Easterners, he will be appalled by their passiveness, while they may equate his aggressiveness with arrogance and ignorance. A classic example is the Western and the Eastern perceptions of conquest. Western historians continue to write that Alexander the Great conquered Asia, while Asians even today believe they educated the Greek barbarian in the arts of warfare. The Greek had never seen an elephant before being introduied to them by Asians, who used them in warfare. Later, Alexander learned from the Asians how to use the huge animals in war with maximum effect. While Western historians fervently believe that Alexander conquered Asia, Asians have never thought so.

Earlier we mentioned that a value is not of the same importance to all peoples. It can be of primary importance to one people and of secondary or no importance at all to another. We have tried to classify the twenty-eight values we discussed. According to this system of classification, values are either primary, secondary, tertiary, or negligible to the peoples of the major cultures of the world.

Value Classification System

Value	Primary	Secondary	Tertiary	Negligible
Individuality	W	B	E	M
Motherhood	BE	MW	—	—
Hierarchy	WEMA	B	—	—
Masculinity	BMEWA	—	—	—
Gratefulness	EA	MB	W	—
Peace	E	B	WA	M
Money	WAB	M	E	—
Modesty	E	BAM	—	W
Punctuality	W	B	ME	A
Saviorism	W	M	—	EBM
Karma	E	—	—	MWBA
Firstness	W	B	—	EAM
Aggressiveness	WB	M	AE	—
Collective Responsibility	EAM	B	—	W
Respect for Elders	EAM	B	—	W
Respect for Youth	W	MABE	—	—
Hospitality to Guests	EA	B	MW	—
Inherited Property	E	—	MWAB	—
Preservation of Environment	E	BA	W	M
Color of Skin	EWB	M	—	A
Sacredness of Farm Land	E	A	—	BMW
Equality of Women	W	EB	A	M
Human Dignity	WB	EAM	—	—
Efficiency	W	B	EM	—
Patriotism	BMAE	W	—	—
Religion	WBMAE	—	—	—
Authoritarianism	EMA	WB	—	—
Education	WB	EAM	—	—
Frankness	W	BEMA	—	—

Legend—W = Western cultures
      E = Eastern cultures
      B = Black cultures
      A = African cultures
      M = Muslim cultures

After reading this long list of values cherished by peoples around the world, the reader might ask what all these values have to do with communication. We have tried to answer this question several times before. Again we emphasize the point that values have much to do with communication. They give rise to beliefs and expectations. Expectations play a dominant role in intercultural communication. In each culture, people communicate expecting something to happen. Usualy expectations are fulfilled and understanding takes place if the communicator and his audience are from the same culture. When members of different cultures interact, if they do not know each other's expectations, understanding does not take place. Take the case of an Asian student in an American university. He meets an American girl and they start talking. The girl indicates that she would like to go out with him. He asks her out. The dating continues for some time. Then one day the girl suddenly says she has other things to do. She does not go out with him anymore. He thinks he has done something wrong, that perhaps he is ugly and dumb. His disappointment leads to shock. It affects his grades at the university. Sometimes he thinks the American girl exploited him, since he had spent a considerable amount of money on her. However, the girl does not know anything about the Asian boy's state of mind. The Asian boy, when he started going out with the girl, began establishing his right over her. He began thinking that she was his, the way he would think of a girl in his own culture if she were going out with him. He was shocked because it was a blow to his masculinity. Being rejected by a girl is a great insult in his culture. There, such an incident would generally not occur. A girl is expected to go out whenever the man or boy asks her out. On the other hand, if the boy were American, he would not have suffered such a shock. To him such occurrences are normal. He expects the girl to go out with many other boys before she decides on one. The American expectation is that if the girl does not go out with many boys, there is something wrong with her. A girl who has many dates is the envy of other girls. A boy who succeeds in taking her out is proud of himself.

Similarities and differences in expectations are responsible for success or failure in communication. Knowledge of the audience's values and expectations will pave the way for a communicator's success. Also, knowing one's own values and expectations will help one realize why he communicates the way he does. A value system is not one's own making, but the work of one's cultural institutions. One ought to know in which valu system he/she is trying to communicate, for such knowledge enable him/her to achieve good results.

SUMMARY

A value system consists of values, beliefs, expectations, customs and attitudes of a people. A value is defined as the guiding light which directs the actions of a people. Cultural values are developed to direct human nature. We have identified three types of values: primary, secondary, and tertiary. A value that is positive in one culture could be negative in another. Values are basic and seldom change. Beliefs and expectations based on a value may change.

Cultural values are often confused with national values. Cultural values do not change as often as national values do. Values play an important role in intercultural communication. Ignorance of values can cause intercultural misunderstandings.

Of the twenty-eight values listed, some seem to be common to all cultures while others are unique to a culture. Blind belief in one's own values can result in ethnocentrism and stereotyping. Cultural relativism seems preferable to ethnocentrism. Immigration from one culture to another is one cause of culture change. Some adverse effects of such a change are self-alienation, exteriorization and rootlessness.

NOTES

1. Tomotsu Shibutani, *Society and Personality* (Englewood Cliffs, N.J.: Prentice-Hall, Inc., 1961), p. 105.

2. Milton Rokeach, *The Nature of Human Values* (New York: Lee Press, 1973).

3. *Padma Purana* (Original in Sanskrit; translated by K.S. Sitaram).

4. Ronald Arias, "We're Supposed to Believe We're Inferior," *The Chicanos,* ed. Ed Ludwig and James Santibanez (Baltimore: Penguin Books, 1971), p. 173.

5. *Honolulu Advertiser,* Honolulu, Hawaii, August 1973.

6. Melville J. Herskowits, *Cultural Relativism: Perspectives in Cultural Pluralism* (New York: Random House, 1973).

7. Deric Regin, *Sources of Cultural Estrangement* (The Hague: Mouton and Co., 1969).

9

Cultural Institutions

Certain societies have survived for many centuries. Common among all are tightly-knit structures of cultural values, beliefs, expectations and customs. Social order in those societies is predicated on the assumption that each member respects the structure and knows that all others will do likewise. Because members of a society cooperate with each other in answering each other's expectations, communication has been easy and predictable.

Cultural institutions direct members of a society as to what to expect and what not to expect. They are responsible for originating new values, reinforcing old ones and accepting or rejecting those that come from outside. They develop norms and customs to control human instincts and aggressive behaviors that adversely affect peace and harmony in their societies. In order to support their own, they accept or reject the values and beliefs that come from outside. The individuals who conform to and support society's values are rewarded by the institutions. They are accorded social status and elected to high offices. When a member fights and dies for those values, he is made a hero. Those who do not support them are ridiculed and even punished.

A classic example is that of the recipients of the medal of honor awarded by the British queen. When the queen awarded the same honor to the Beatles, the long-haired singers of Great Britain, some former recipients became angry because the honor was given to a group of young men who had so clearly deviated from their parent culture. The old awardees in protest returned their medals to the queen.

In the United States, conservatives believed that in order to preserve individual freedom it was their duty to fight on the American side in Vietnam. Many conservative institutions supported the war. Those that neither fought nor supported the war were ridiculed.

In each culture there are several institutions that serve their own cultural traditions. To show their role in intercultural communication, we shall briefly study four of them: the family, the church, the school and mass media.

The Family

When a child comes into this world he shows only his hereditary and racial characteristics. Most cultural traits are acquired as he grows up. Some geneticists believe there is a relationship between a child's genetic characteristics and his intellectual performance. We do not yet have any scientific data to support such a belief. It is true that certain families in all cultures have consistently produced highly intelligent people. We can cite examples of such families from almost all cultures. Although such occurrences do not prove that intelligence is inherited, we cannot dispute the fact that the families do reinforce the value of intellectual achievement in their younger members.

Intellectual Abilities

The hypothesis that the human genes carry intellectual characteristics is acceptable to one group of geneticists. It is common knowledge now that many genes in humans are not always active, but are passed down from parent to child. They become active only when they come in contact with another particular type of gene or are exposed to a particular environment. The genes responsible for intellectual abilities seem to become active in the right environment. Some of the intellectual abilities with which we are concerned are the individual's ability to perceive the world, retain information, express ideas, solve problems, be logical, and conceptualize the relationship between what one perceives and what one retains. These abilities are shaped by not only the individual's hereditary characteristics but are also taught by the people around him, primarily his family members. They teach him how to see things and express ideas.

"Proper Behavior"

In the family, the child is taught to behave "properly." How to hold a fork or chopsticks or to use fingers while eating become part of his cultural training. In some cultures the child soon learns the only way to express affection is to kiss. When beloved ones see him, he can expect a kiss. Until recently, children in the Japanese culture were unaware of kissing as an expression of affection, but they are accustomed to taking baths with their parents in the same bathtub.

Concept of the Family

The concept of family and friends becomes familiar at a very early age. To the Asian child, family means not only brothers, sisters and parents but also grandparents, uncles, aunts, and several other relatives. By growing up with them, hearing from them and talking about them he develops a sense of responsibility toward them. Responsibility to his family is an important value to the Asian. Some families in each community set examples for others by ardently following their cultural values and customs. The others in the community look to the ideal families for cultural information. The child who grows up in such a family has more responsibilities to his culture and community than anybody else there. The first son of the chief priest in Japanese temples is just one example. In Western cultures, families such as the Kennedys of the United States become ideals to the entire country. Members of such families automatically become opinion leaders and inform and influence the people of their community.

The Child's Own Values

The important thing to remember is that the child learns the values, customs and communicative techniques of his own culture. He is trained to believe his values are the right ones. He judges those of others from the standpoint of his own values. He is also rewarded for upholding his value system. In nineteenth-century America the Negro slave was not supposed to learn how to read and write. Those that taught him to read and write were cultural offenders. Outstanding men such as Thomas Jefferson did not believe in Negro slavery, but at the same time they had slaves in their homes. They respected all the beliefs related to slavery.

One slave boy was taught how to read and write just a few letters in the English alphabet by a young white woman. The woman was stopped by her husband. In the slave's own words:

> He said, "If you give a nigger an inch, he will take an ell. A nigger should know nothing but obey his master—to do as he is told to do. Learning will spoil the best nigger in the world." "Now," he said, "if you teach that nigger (speaking of myself) how to read, there would be no keeping him." [1]

All families in all cultures teach their own values and customs to the child. The child is told who he is and how he should treat others. The upper classes in Asia, the Brahmins of India, for example, teach their children how to talk to others, how to address upper and lower class people. The child is even taught the "right" accent of his language.

The Family Dinner Table

Teaching and reinforcing values are probably done most effectively at the family dinner table. Family prayers and table manners are taught there. The children's daily activities are reviewed, admired and admonished. A neighbor's behavior is criticized. The children are told what are positive and negative values, what is right and wrong, and what to expect and what not to expect.

Watching the Elders

Children learn by watching their parents. When American parents criticize government regulations, children believe everybody has freedom of expression and the right to criticize their government. But in China, the child grows up believing he cannot criticize the government because under Chairman Mao's guidance it does everything right. In most authoritarian cultures, the child grows up believing that his freedom to criticize is limited. In certain authoritarian cultures, such freedom is a negative value. A youngster who opposes authority is a "lost" child. The entire neighborhood talks about the child. This is one reason Asian students in American universities are shy about expressing their opinions.

On the other hand, the Asian child learns he is responsible for many things. He learns his responsibilities more than he does his rights. He thinks more in terms of his duty to others than of his rights over them.

Showing affection in public is a positive value in Western cultures, and a negative value in Asian cultures. The Asian child grows up not knowing how to express intimate feelings. When he grows up and gets married, he has to wait until he and his wife retire to their bedroom to express his love for her. During the day their expression is mostly nonverbal. When there are elders around, they steal a look or two to express their intimate feelings.

"Generation Gap"

When the child grows up and no longer has to depend upon his parents, he learns to adopt the communication techniques and cultural values of his peers. If the peers' values are different and if communication in the family is not very effective, he begins to adopt peer values more than family values. In cultures that are rapidly changing, new beliefs and customs are being introduced to the youngster by his peers. Some of the beliefs are strange to the parents. They complain that they cannot understand their own children. Thus a generation gap is created and widened.

In each culture there are occasions, such as Christmas in Western cultures, when family members get together and reinforce their cultural values. The Christmas tree, the gifts, and the family dinner are occasions to look forward to and remember. The kinds of gifts a youngster receives and the things that are said on the Christmas card tell him a lot about his cultural values. The Diwali of India and the children's day of Japan are also such occasions. These are opportunities to teach those from other cultures about the cultural values of the host families.

Playing the Role

A young member of the family learns the role he should play when he grows to be an adult. Even when the members of one culture immigrate to another culture, they tend to adopt the values of the parent culture. In Asian cultures, the father is the head of the family. That authority is implicitly and explicitly accepted by everybody in the family. The Japanese of Hawaii still value parts of their original tradition:

> In a Japanese family, the father is the ultimate authority, and there is a strict subservience to his wishes by all members of the family. The father as head of the family is served first at meals, goes first into bath, and receives with a nod deep bows of the family.[2]

The male child learns this authoritarianism and acts the way his father does. He learns to play the role of father by communicating as such with other members of the family. In his community he receives the respect that the head of a family should receive. The child knows how his father behaves in his community and learns to behave that way.

In Mexico as in Japan, the father is the authority. First generation Mexicans in the United States value the same custom. The father of the family is the boss of the house. He manages most family affairs. He represents his family in the outside world.

Contrary to the subservient-wife image that many Westerners have of Asian and Mexican women, these women command great respect in their families and communities. Children accord great respect to their parents. A reason why the mother is respected is that she sacrifices her own needs for the welfare of the family.

Firm Foundation

Caste and class prejudices socially separate members of all cultures. The child learns from his parents that he is superior, or inferior, to others because he is black, brown or untouchable. When the child learns that such a classification is not right, he may fight such an attitude. Sometimes parents begin the fight by telling the child that all are equal. The attitude toward accepting or rejecting caste systems also begins in the family. A firm foundation for class prejudice, or opposition to it, is laid in the family and shapes the outlook of the young child. It affects his communicative behavior in his adult life. The child's family trains him to the type of role he plays and the way he communicates in adulthood.

Bearing in mind the available resources in that culture, the family helps the child develop his expectations. The child's achievement orientation or fatalistic attitude takes its roots when family members tell him what he can or cannot do. The so-called "American Dream" of the American child or the four goals of life of the Hindu youngster originate in his family. Church and school then help him in building up that dream or seeking the goals.

The Church

Church is used here to represent all religious institutions, such as the Christian church, the Hindu matt, the Buddhist temple and the Islamic majid.

Values and customs that are taught the child by his family are closely associated with the teachings of the Bible, the Vedas, the Koran, the Sutras, and Confucius and Taoist teachings. Religion as taught by the church, directly and indirectly, affects one's values. Religious values penetrate activities not only of individuals and households but also of business organizations and political parties.

Business and Politics

Churchgoing enhances one's prestige. It helps one in business or politics by projecting the image of one who has high ethical standards. Businessmen support their own religion or those of their employees. They have funds to help their church or religious organization.

Some countries have declared a particular religion as that of the state. Islam is the religion of Pakistan, Catholicism the religion of Ireland. The King of England is the guardian of the Protestant church. The state's policies are shaped by the teachings of its adopted religion. Secular governments do their best to respect all the religions of their peoples.

Festivals such as Christmas, Diwali, or Buddha's birthday are excellent occasions for the church to reinforce its influence. Huge images of Santa Claus or Rama or Buddha are put up in public places and business centers. Christmas trees, banana stems or other plants are used for decoration. Each sign or image or plant symbolizes something religious.

Even in modern and secular societies such as America and England, church influence can be clearly seen. In so-called traditional societies church influence penetrates almost every aspect of daily life. In small communities and rural villages, communal festivals are organized by churches. The fiestas, fairs and festivals of Asia and Latin America are held in churchyards. African communal dances are held in front of tribal temples in the presence of the tribal priest. Even foreign-student dinners in the United States are held in churches. During such gatherings, religious values are reinforced or introduced.

The political influence of the church is a historical fact. Pope Paul's opinions on international affairs are quoted by mass media. The Vatican's

views on birth control influence the population programs of many governments. Vehement opposition to the American involvement in Vietnam or
strong support of the British policy in Ireland or the Indian government's
attitude on cow slaughter have come from the church.

Social Behavior

The Buddhist temple is still the center of cultural affairs in rural Japan.
The head priest or his wife keeps birth, death and marriage records of
his/her devotees to remind them of the rituals they have to perform at
times. The priest's wife or a member of the temple teaches flower arrangement, tea ceremony and kimono-making to young ladies. Just
before they get married, the young ladies are also trained in housekeep-
ing and good behavior. The presence of the priest is necessary at times
of birth, marriage and death. When ground is broken for a new home or
a new ship is launched, the priest will be present to bless the home or the
ship.

In India, swamies or heads of temples are also opinion leaders. They
teach the people for whom to vote, what product to buy and what values
and customs to accept or reject. They have even organized mass rallies
against cow slaughter.

In the United States, the role of some churches in fighting racism is
well known. The Reverend Martin Luther King and the Reverend Ralph
Abernathy have been known for their activities for social causes.

Temple Bells

The church reminds its followers of its presence through various means,
one of which is the church bell. Muslim priests pray loudly from the top of
their majid towers so that everybody around the majid can hear them.
Some majids use public address systems to reach a larger audience. Sunday morning services are heard by everybody around the church. Hindu
temples have hundreds of bells that ring constantly. Dozens of priests
chant Vedic hymns in chorus. Buddhist temples also ring bells and chant
Sutras. African tribal drums and songs can be heard for several miles.
The assemblies and loud prayers help to reinforce religious beliefs and remind the members of their cultural customs.

The church serves as an important center of cultural information.
Church libraries and scholars are great sources of such information.
Sometimes the only references for cultural studies are in the church. In
some cultures, the church has helped preserve classical schools of dance,
drama and music. The ancient temples of Asia are sometimes the only
sources of information on ancient culture. The carvings on temple walls
and paintings on murals are most valued ancient and cultural monu-
ments. Some churches have established schools and universities. By sup-

porting the educational institutions they remind the young people of their presence.

The School

An old Sanskrit saying goes thus: Guru is Brahma, guru is Vishnu and guru is Shiva; salutations to guru. That shows the value attached to the teacher in Hindu and Buddhist cultures. While parents and priests *prescribe* to the child his cultural values and customs, the teacher *describes* them to him. Prescriptive teaching gives no alternative. It tells the youngster what to do, not why he should do it. But descriptive teaching shows many alternatives, and tells the youngster why he should do as he has been taught. Parents and priests tell the youngster that their way is the right one. The teacher discusses several ways while the student can decide what he wants. The teacher guides the student rather than commanding him to do things in just one way.

Perception of Others

At school, the youngster is exposed to several cultures. Particularly in pluralistic societies, he comes in contact with colleagues and instructors of several colors and creeds. The values the child has learned at home are tested in the school. A grade-school teacher in the United States wanted to test how far learned behaviors change the child's perception of other races. She asked the children in her grade to do an experiment. For one week all the blue-eyed children pretended to be inferior to the dark-eyed ones in that grade. The blue-eyed children showed all respect to the dark-eyed ones. They let them drink first from the fountain, get their lunches first, and always stood at a respectable distance from them. The next week the dark-eyed children were considered inferior. By conducting this experiment the teacher showed that superiority and inferiority complexes are learned behaviors, not natural phenomena.

The Child's Own Values

Individual freedom and social responsibility or equality and authoritarianism are the values introduced at the family level, but they take firm roots at the school level. When the majority of students and teachers believe in the same values, they are reinforced. Group discussions and student criticisms are common in Western schools. The students who participate in such exercises develop a sense of free criticism and independent thinking. They grow up thinking that everybody has the right to criticize and to think as individuals. On the other hand, Eastern cultures discourage such attitudes. The concepts that everybody is not qualified to criticize and that all are not equal are reinforced by teachers who do not conduct seminars and critiques. Instead of free criticism, responsible criticism is taught; rather than individual freedom, social responsibility is emphasized.

The belief in free thinking takes several behavior forms. In the West, students and teachers like being informal. They dress informally and grow long hair. They even bring their dogs to classes. On the other hand, in Eastern cultures formality is encouraged. Some governments have even ordered students not to wear tight pants and or to grow long hair.

Ethnocentrism

Self-criticism of values and resultant social change is more possible at the college level than at the grade-school level. This is probably due to careful curriculum planning at the grade-school level. At that level, the country's own history and its majority peoples' culture are emphasized. Because students up to the high-school level are under parental control, their teachers give due consideration to parents' opinion. Parents would like their children to learn their own history and culture. This does not mean that the attitude automatically changes at the college level. Even then only a few students and instructors seek cultural change. Communication professors in America still teach Aristotle as the only rhetorician and Plato as the only philosopher. Even when they teach behaviorist-oriented communication, their guide is a Western scientist. Most of the time, the ethnocentrism that begins at the family and church levels is reinforced at the college level. The following blind reverence to Aristotle supports the point: "To this day no complete non-Aristotle rhetoric has been written, or is it likely to be." [3]

In order to reinforce the same old ideas, books written by authors belonging to the same culture are used as texts. A look at the bibliography of most American text books show the ethnocentrism of even intellectuals. Books in communication are one example. The reader seldom sees quotations from European or Canadian authors. Those who are quoted have either published in the United States or have won Nobel prizes. Other top-ranking foreign authors are totally ignored, probably because their books are not translated into English. We mention only Canadian and European writers. In Western cultures, most Asian authors are unheard of. Those who are known have either taught at Western universities or have published in that part of the world. These ethnocentric attitudes of Western intellectuals reinforce the same attitude in their students.

Can-Do Attitude

One consequence of ethnocentrism at the college level is the belief that a communicator *can* change the attitude of his audience. In order to do so, all he has to do is to encode the message in the right form. If the communicator, or message sender, is efficient, his audience will automatically change. In the hands of the communicator, the mind of the audience is like clay. He can shape it into any form he likes. Communication begins with the sender of the message and ends in the attitude change of his audience. Communication techniques to change audience attitude have become specialities of many professors.

At the University of Hawaii, an American graduate student went to see a visiting professor from an Asian country. The student wanted to do a study of satellite communication broadcasting in the Asian country from which the visiting professor came. He told the visitor he wanted to chat with him about broadcasting in his country. The Asian politely asked him if he knew anything about the cultures of the Asian country where he wanted to do the research.

"Not really," said the young American.

"Do you know anything about broadcasting in my country?"

"No."

"Do you know anything about satellite communications?"

"No."

"Now, have you taken any courses in broadcasting in any American university?"

"No."

"Then, what can I do for you?"

"I wanted to chat with you and learn something about culture and communication in your country."

"I don't think you can learn much by chatting with me for a few minutes. You have to take at least one course from me and read several books. I would be glad to get some books for you from my home."

"That is an excellent idea. I will see you again," said the young American, and left.

As the Asian professor expected, the young man did not go back to take the course. The Asian professor knew the young man was never advised by the American professor to take such a course. He would probably have given that advice only if the course was taught by an American. At the bottom of such an attitude was probably the fear the young American would learn something from the Asian professor that no American professor would be able to teach.

Educational institutions in general have failed to teach students how to interact with members of other cultures. Awareness of other cultures has probably come from mass media, not from family, church, or school.

Mass Media

The media, like the church of the old days, originate new values, support the existing ones and accept or reject those that come from other cultures. Governments and leaders think it necessary to regulate the media since they not only inform the masses but have also become a powerful means of influencing them.

In industrialized and urbanized cultures they have even taken over the jobs of schools and colleges. In the United States, radio and television regularly broadcast Sunday sermons. Some evangelists have become popular for their blessings on the screen. Awarding degrees on open universities is becoming fashionable. New trends in the arts, technology, fashions and home living are popularized by the media. Who had heard of the Nehru jacket in America until it was made popular by television? How many had seen long hair and beards until they were shown on television? Not too many Americans knew of chopsticks and Japanese flower arranging until they were shown on television and movie screens. Yoga, meditation, karate, and vegetarian foods are now well known in Western cultures as a result of information given by the media. Expressions such as pundit, guro and hara-kiri are used extensively by the American media. In Japan, rock and roll is popular on television. English words such as bucket and hamburger are popularized by mass media in Japan. These words are made Japanese by adding the sound "u" and saying "buckethsu" and "hambagu!" These examples suggest two very important cultural activities of mass media: reinforcing old values and introducing new ones.

Cultural activities of the media are insured in two ways: by government regulations, and by popular pressures. Charles Wright lists four functions of mass media: (1) surveillance; (2) correlation; (3) heritage transmission; and (4) entertainment.[4] Surveillance deals with the mass communicators' gathering information related to an event. Correlation is the adding of editorial comments to gathered information. Heritage transmission is the inclusion of the audience's cultural values in the information transmitted to them. Lastly, entertainment is to amuse and hold the audience's attention. In all four functions the mass communicator reinforces his people's existing cultural values and supports certain values of other peoples. Outside values are supported only if they can enrich the audience culture without upsetting it in any way.

Government Regulations

The organization of each country's mass media depends upon the political system in that country. In democracies such as the United States, the media are generally free; in communist countries they are controlled by the party. In some countries, such as Japan and Canada, they are both government controlled and privately owned. Whatever the nature of organization of the media, the government of each country regulates them in such a way as to insure that they do not adversely affect the existing cultures. Since we are concerned with traditional cultures, we will not go into a discussion of how the country's national culture is guarded by government regulation.

Traditional cultures are promoted in several ways. In some countries, government regulations state clearly that the country's traditions should be promoted by the media. Others imply such a promotion. The Broadcasting Act of Japan insures that Japanese broadcasters uphold their culture. Article 44 of *Japanese Broadcast Law* says:

> The Japanese Broadcasting Corporation shall . . . strive to the upbringing and popularization of new culture as well as to the preservation of past excellent culture of our country.[5]

Japanese Broadcasting Corporation's (NHK) own standards for overseas broadcasts says:

> . . . a current understanding of the nation's political, economical, cultural, scientific and tourism phases be made known and thus cultivate due recognition along these lines.[6]

In Islamic countries such as Pakistan, anything unacceptable to Islamic culture is excluded from the mass media. Pakistan radio and television do not broadcast anti-Islamic information. Even secular countries such as Great Britain, the United States, and India have certain laws to insure that the countries' cultures are respected by the media.

The British Broadcasting Corporation's charter says that the BBC's programming should be designed to fulfill its audiences' cultural needs. BBC's Broadcasting Councils have that responsibility:

> The Councils are required to exercise this control with full regard to the distinctive culture, language, interests, and tastes of the people of the countries concerned. They may render advice to the Corporation on any matter relating to its other broadcasting services which may affect the interests of the peoples of Scotland and Wales.[7]

Individuality, including the freedom of expression which is a part of individuality, is a primary value in all American cultures. Americans believe each person should be given an opportunity to express himself. This value has become an integral part of American politics. To insure that American mass communicators respect this value, the First Amendment to the Constitution guarantees the individual's right of freedom of expression. Section 315 of the Communications Act of 1934 says:

> If any licensee shall permit any person who is a legally qualified candidate for any public office to use a broadcasting station, he shall afford equal opportu-

nities to all other such candidates for that office in the use of such broadcasting station: Provided, that such licensee shall have no power of censorship over the material broadcast under the provision of this section. No
obligation is hereby imposed upon any licensee to allow the use of its station
by any such candidate.[8]

The United States Federal Communications Commission went a step
further in guaranteeing such rights in all areas of public interest, necessity
and convenience. The FCC's Fairness Doctrine says:

Licensee editorialization is but one aspect of freedom of expression by means
of radio. Only insofar as it is exercised in conformity with the paramount
right of the public to hear a reasonably balanced presentation of all responsible viewpoints on particular issues can such editorialization be considered
to be consistent with the licensee's duty to operate in the public interest. For
the licensee is a trustee impressed with the duty of preserving for the general
public radio as a medium of free expression and fair presentation. [9]

American laws in the area of mass communication are designed to give
freedom of expression not only to the general public but also to individual
mass communicators such as newspaper editors and radio station
managers.

In India, which has declared itself a secular republic, there are government guidelines for radio and television officials. The so-called nine-point
code prescribes what they can and cannot broadcast, including prohibi-
tions against attacks on religion, obscene information, and programs that
might incite violence. In addition, the government-controlled broadcasting organization has programs for training its officials to work within
the framework of the peoples' cultures. There will be broadcasts of
Hindu, Muslim, Christian, Sikh and other religious songs, prayers, stories and talks.

We have mainly discussed government control over the so-called public
media of radio and television. Whether or not the public media are owned
and operated by private business organizations, governments have realized that these two media need more regulation than the others in public
interest and necessity.

The media of print and film are regulated more by public pressure than
by government regulations. Although there are laws to regulate these
media, so-called community standards control them. Even legal decisions
are based on cultural standards of the community the media are serving.
There is the famous example of a film which was not shown in an American city because the members of that city rallied against the film, which
they considered obscene and un-Christian. The judge of the local court

agreed with the citizens' opinion. The U.S. Supreme Court in 1973 upheld the community standards as the deciding factor.

In socialistic democracies such as India, governments control the contents of the press and film by such means as censorship laws and press councils. Indian film censor boards carefully review all films before they are shown to the public. A classic example is that of a commission formed by the Indian government in 1972 to recommend whether or not kissing should be allowed on the movie screen. Until the commission recommended that it should be permitted, the film censor boards would not approve any film that showed kissing, because the cultures of India do not approve any show of intimacy between males and females in public. This is true of most Asian cultures, so as a result, Asian governments legally prohibit showing scenes that go against cultural values, beliefs and customs.

Cultural Content of the Media

We said earlier that a main function of the media is to transmit the cultural heritage of their audiences. Since radio, television and film are more popular than print, we will discuss the ways these three media try to include the culture of their audience in the information they give.

In pluralistic countries such as the United States, Great Britain, and India, the media try to transmit the cultural heritage of the majority. In the United States, it is the white man's culture. Wright mentions a study done in the United States that showed white Americans have the edge over foreigners, providing proportionately more (83 percent) of heroes and fewer of the villains.[10] The study also showed that heroes were typically evaluated as having personalities that conformed closely to the ideals of our culture. Villains had typical personality patterns that were almost the direct opposite of the heroes.[11] Stereotyping of characters was measured in terms of degree to which the apparent personality of the members of each group conformed to the typical pattern for that group.[12]

Before the time of this writing, in television shows such as *Hawaii 5-O* and *Mannix,* the heroes were whites. McGarrett, the main character of *Hawaii 5-O,* was white and his subordinates, who were Chinese, Hawaiian and Samoan, addressed him as "boss," while his white subordinates called him by his first name, "Steve." The main character in *Mannix* was white and his secretary black, thus promulgating the American myth of the white man as all-powerful and of unquestioned authority, with a black secretary who places the security and welfare of her white boss over that of her own son and herself. This value is a residual of the master-slave relationship that survives the slavery institution in America. During the period of slavery the Negro slaves who worked in the white master's home were called "house niggers." It was commonly known that the house niggers identified closely with their master's household and its welfare, while the "field niggers" did not do so. Mannix's black secretary is the exact personification of the house nigger.

The above observation is on American commercial television, but even in educational media the trend is to educate audiences in American values. Although it does not define American values, the Carnegie Commission in 1967 submitted its recommendation for a public television setup in which it definitely said that foreign cultural patterns were not to be copied by American educational television:

> . . . this is a proposal not for small adjustments or patchwork changes, but for a comprehensive system that will bring Public Television to all the people of the United States: a system that in its totality will become a new and fundamental institution in American culture.
>
> It is not patterned after the commercial system or the British system or the Japanese system. . . . But when such a system was successful it met the special needs of society in terms of that society's culture and tradition, and there was little or nothing we could expect to import. We propose an indigenous American system arising out of our own tradition and responsive to our own needs.[13]

The Carnegie recommendation was later used as the basis for the Public Broadcasting Act of 1967.

When the media broadcast cultural programs, they include cultural values of the majority. A columnist of *TV Guide* magazine says:

> Prime-time commercial TV, in short, is no place for minority tastes and nobody's making any bones about it any more.[14]

The emphasis on cultural values of the majority is not the characteristic only of the United States. Great Britain is made up of several cultures, while the British Broadcasting Corporation's programs reflect mainly British cultural values. This is evident in BBC overseas broadcasts and English-language lessons. The special broadcasts directed to immigrants from Asia and Africa are designed to acculturate them. *BBC Handbook 1971* says:

> Two regular weekly broadcasts in television and radio are directed to immigrants of Indian and Pakistan origin. The programs are in Hindi/Urdu and their purpose is to help the integration of Asians into the life of this country. They include, among other items, stories of success in community relations, answers to personal problems, information and advice about life in Britain,

musical items specially recorded in our studios and also an element of English teaching, designed particularly to assist house-bound mothers and young children.[15]

Some Americans contend that Canadian and American cultures are not much different, but Canadians disagree. They believe their culture is different and want to maintain the Canadian character of their media. Henry Comor of the Association of Canadian Television and Radio Artists has observed:

> Canada is in contact with United States along a great and undefended border and by the process of osmosis America is destroying not only our television, but our values and our very culture.[16]

The Canadian comment tells us something about American values that are unacceptable to them. The result is a Canadian craving for radio and television programs that reflect their own culture. Several committees appointed by the Canadian government for reviewing broadcasting in the country have noted the need for a broadcasting service that is "basically Canadian in content and character."[17] The Canadian Radio and Television Commission appointed in 1968 stressed this concept further:

> . . . Broadcasting in Canada can and must express the originality of Canada and Canadians. The Commission is determined that the hope and spirit embodied in the Broadcasting Act of 1968 will be successfully achieved.[18]

A casual look at program guides of broadcasting stations around the globe shows us that each station produces programs to uphold the culture or cultures of its audiences. As one UNESCO report says:

> Each country has tried to meet this demand for cultural broadcasts according to its social structure and its traditions. The significance of this conference has been reports of efforts made to this end, in the various countries represented at the meeting.[19]

All countries evidently endeavor, through legal acts and popular pressure, to insure that their mass media transmit the cultural heritage of their peoples. While supporting their own culture, they sometimes give information that creates negative images of other cultures. When the media messages do not support cultural values, chances are the messages have little effect. But when they support the values, they may even bring about social change. Studies conducted in many cultures support these assertions.

SUMMARY

Cultural institutions are organizations which originate and reinforce values, beliefs, expectations and customs. They also accept or reject values from outside cultures. We have identified four such organizations: the family, the church, the school, and mass media.

Reinforcement of values tends to be prescriptive in the family and the church, and descriptive in the school and the media. Although the general tendency of all four institutions is to reinforce their own values, the mass media are more liberal than the other three. In industrialized cultures, mass media have successfully introduced new values and beliefs. Reinforcement and introduction of values are accomplished by effective communication.

NOTES

1. Frederick Douglas, "Narrative of the Life of Frederick Douglas, An American Slave," *Growing up Black* (New York Pocket Books, 1969), p. 100

2. Katherine N. Handley, *Four Case Studies* (Honolulu: University of Hawaii Press, 1961), p. 24.

3. Wayne N. Thompson, *Quantative Research in Public Address and Communication* (New York: Random House, 1967), p. 3.

4. Charles Wright, *Mass Communication, A Sociological Perspective* (New York: Random House, 1959).

5. *NHK 1973 Year Book* (Tokyo, Japan, N H K Theoretical Research Center, 1973).

6. Ibid.

7. *BBC Handbook 1971* (London: British Broadcasting Corporation, 1971).

8. Federal Communications Commission, *The Communications Act of 1934* (Washington: U.S. Government Printing Office, 1961).

9. Ibid.

10. Wright, *Mass Communication, A Sociological Perspective.*

11. Ibid.

12. Ibid.

13. Carnegie Commission, *Public Television: A Proposal for Action* (New York: Harper and Row, 1967).

14. Richard W. Lewis, "Why Shows Are Cancelled," Television, ed. Barry G. Cole (New York: Free Press, 1970), p. 126.

15. *BBC Handbook 1971*, p. 59.

16. Henry Comor, "American TV: What Have You Done to Us?" *Broadcasting and the Public Interest,* ed. John H. Pennybacker and Waldo W. Braden (New York: Random House, 1969), p. 86.

17. *Report of the Canadian Radio and Television Commission,* Ottowa: Canadian Broadcasting Corporation, 1969.

18. Ibid.

19. UNESCO, *Cultural Radio Broadcasts* (Paris: UNESCO, 1953), p. 58.

10

Principles and Ethics of Intercultural Communication

In the preceding chapters, we have tried to show the need for intercultural communication, the factors which affect such communication and how the peoples of the world express their ideas. It should now be possible for us to arrive at some guidelines to help us communicate with peoples of other cultures.

The Personality of Culture

Each culture has its own personality. The personality of one culture is different from that of another; it is unique, distinct and identifiable. The Eskimo culture, for example, is characterized by people who look like Orientals and whose values and habits are shaped by their environment. Because their environment is almost always covered with snow, their dress is appropriate to the cold weather. In order to survive in that climate, cooperation has become a primary value. Because of the weather, they cannot develop the type of agriculture that mainland Americans have. Eskimo food therefore consists of fish, seal and other sea animals. Even their language centers around the snow culture. Hence, when we hear someone mention the Eskimo, we immediately identify them with a culture that has the above characteristics. By personality we mean the general characteristics which personify most Eskimos. We are not trying to stereotype the Eskimo, since stereotypes are not general characteristics that have been observed in a people for several generations. These characteristics, or personality of a culture, are evolutionary. When a person is born into a particular culture, part of his personality is by definition already decided for him because it is identifiable with his culture. The personality of any culture is unique in the sense that each differs from the other. When members of two different cultures interact, their differing cultural personalities affect their interaction.

Most people in a culture are not aware that their personality is influenced by that of their culture. An individual's personality does not develop in a vacuum; it develops in a culture. The overall personality of a culture influences those of its communities, families and its individual members.

We do not mean to confuse the reader with cultural personality as distinguished from the individual's own personality. Psychologists are well aware that the individual's childhood experiences and family situation affect his personality development. We are not talking about individual personality differences within the same culture but the commonality of cultural influence on personality development, contradicting the common notion that an individual's personality develops independently of his culture.

It is imperative that a person in a given culture know his own personality before he tries to interact with a person from another culture. Knowing one's own personality means relating the self to the personality of the culture. This statement applies to intracultural and interethnic communications as well, since each subculture and ethnic group has its own personality.

Self-realization

Most of us do not know why we communicate the way we do. We have not tried to find out what factors influence our communicative behaviors. If we want to communicate effectively with others, we should first of all know about our own communicative arts. Before trying to know others, we should know ourselves. A student of intercultural communication should begin with an understanding of himself. As mentioned earlier, a person's behavior is largely the product of his culture, although he may think his behavior is his own. But with some effort on his part, he will realize that his self-concept is shaped by his culture's values, beliefs and expectations. An American says "I stand up for what I believe in." He also says, "You be you and I be me." These statements are the results of the value of individuality. An Asian would say, "I would sacrifice my own happiness for the welfare of my community." For an Eskimo, cooperation is a greater value than individuality or responsibility. In the Eskimo's environment, food is a scarce commodity. If one day an Eskimo finds food, he shares it with the others in his community. When another Eskimo finds food another day, he will also share his hunt. Today, Eskimos who live in cities such as Anchorage do not have to hunt for food; they can buy it in stores. But the value of cooperation is still basic to them. One Eskimo expects another to cooperate, although he might not know his expectation originated from the old culture of the igloo days.

In an intercultural communication class in an Illinois college, the students were asked to mention at least five values as defined in chapter three. Most of them found it hard to mention them. This is not unusual, since the concept of self-realization is new in studies of communication.

Self and Meditation

Everyday from morning till we fall asleep we spend hours thinking about a lot of things. We think a great deal before taking a certain action that would affect our lives. We also think and decide what words to utter before we say something to another person. We probably spend more time thinking within ourselves than in interacting with others. Sometimes we would very much like to retire to a lonely and quiet place to think. Philosophers, holy men and yogis enjoy being alone because they believe they cannot find answers to their questions by interacting with the people around them. They want to find answers on their own through meditation.

There is presently a great interest in transcendental meditation in the United States. Universities and private research institutes have conducted experiments on the effects of one type of meditation on the individual meditator. These experiments have shown the following results.

PHYSIOLOGICAL: TM produces a deep state of restful alertness which rejuvenates and normalizes the functioning of the nervous system.

PSYCHOLOGICAL: TM eliminates mental stress, promotes clearer thinking and greater comprehension; it enriches perception, improves outlook and promotes efficiency and effectiveness in life.

SOCIOLOGICAL: TM eliminates tension and discord and promotes more harmonious and fulfilling interpersonal relationships.[1]

We are not saying that each intercultural communicator should become a yogi. Our emphasis is on the individual's trying to understand himself in a quiet atmosphere. This type of communication is called intrapersonal communication. In the hustle and bustle of life today, one seldom finds a few minutes for himself. When he does find time, he seeks the company of mass media or of another person. Instead of spending all his spare time in front of the television set or with someone else, he could spend a few minutes alone for self-realization.

What is there to realize about oneself? A great deal. If the individual finds, say, one hour in the evening for himself, he could retire to his own room with a notebook and pencil and write down his day's activities. What did he do, where did he go and about what did he talk with the people he met? What kind of letters did he write to others, if he wrote any? Does he think that everything he did that day is right? Did he hurt anybody? Would what he did hurt himself in any way? Would the things he said achieve their purpose? By saying what he said, did he insult anybody? Answering these questions in his own mind or writing down the answers and reading them over will help him be a better person the next day. The way he interacts with people the next day could be different, with better results. The hour or so the person spends discussing things within himself is the act of meditation. Regular meditation of this sort helps the individual understand himself better.

When the individual asks himself why he did things the way he did, he might relate his own actions to some source he does not know. Take the case of a young university professor who has just received his doctoral degree. He is asked by his dean to teach a new course because the community has asked the university to offer such a course. The dean feels this is an opportunity for his university to establish a good relationship with the community, so he asks the young professor to develop and teach the course. But the young professor feels his academic freedom has been violated by the dean's asking him to teach something only the professor has the right to decide. He writes back to the dean that he has no right to ask him to teach the course. This starts a battle between the dean and the young professor.

If the young professor asks himself why he handled the situation the way he did, he might trace the origin of the whole battle to his belief in his individual freedom. In this case, he interpreted his individual freedom as the freedom not to teach a course the dean asked him to teach. Then, if he asks himself who told him that only he has the right to decide whether or not he should teach the course, he might not be able to find an answer. His entire culture—his parents, his school, mass media and others—has reinforced his belief that he has individual freedom, or in this case academic freedom. He therefore believes the dean has no business asking him to teach the course.

The young professor could also ask himself how else he might have handled the situation. Could he have avoided the confrontation with his boss? Did he go too far in interpreting his so-called academic freedom? It would be easy for an Asian professor to answer the above questions. His primary value is individual responsibility instead of freedom. His responsibility is to teach the course in the interest of the university. The Asian believes his responsibility to his university is more important than his own academic freedom. The American professor might think the Asian is stupid. The Asian will think the American is selfish and ungrateful to his institution.

Meditation, or self-realization, would have helped the young professor act less emotionally. He would have found several ways to handle the situation and avoid the confrontation.

Let us add another dimension to the problem. If the dean happens to be black and the young professor white, the professor should ask himself the question, "Would I have protested against the dean if he were white?"

At the University of Hawaii, it has been the practice of some Oriental professors and instructors in a certain department to get together for lunch every day. A few years ago a young white man from the mainland was hired to teach in the same department. Every day he used to see the Oriental professors going for lunch. He wanted to join the group, to get together with them and learn about the Hawaiian cultures; but they never gave him a chance. One day he said, "I would like to join your group, or if you have a club I would like to become a member of it." The Oriental professors looked at each other and one of them told him, "You can join us if you want. Today we are not going out for lunch. We are going to get it here." They were about to send a secretary, also Oriental, to buy lunch from a lunch wagon. The white professor gave her some money for a fish burger. She said they did not have any fish burgers at the wagon. The mainlander went out to eat his lunch while the others ate in the department coffee room.

The Oriental professors could ask themselves the question, "Would we have left him out, if the new professor were also an Oriental?" This dimension points out that we identify ourselves with people of our own color.

An unemotional pondering over the actions one takes on a given day may lead one to realize his actions are based on a set of beliefs. Deeper pondering may also lead him to the realization that those beliefs are not absolute truths, but he has acted as if they were. Because they are not absolute, there could be other ways of handling the same situations. Another case in point is an editorial that appeared in a midwestern newspaper. The editorial was published one day in January 1975 on the Middle East situation. It was clearly against the Arabs and in support of the Israelis. The next day another editorial in the same paper was highly critical of the Arabs' investing several billion dollars in the United States. It said that Arabs might eventually buy this country. If the editorial writer asks himself whether what he wrote was right, he might find out that he was either writing for somebody or was acting emotionally. Perhaps he does not like Arabs because he thinks they are bad guys. His stereotype of Arabs is of men with swords drawn to kill men and steal their women. Therefore, he has written a series of editorials against the Arabs. Was his comment on the Arab investment in his country's interest? Probably not. If the United States does not want the Arab money, the Arabs will invest it in another country. The other country gains and America loses. Therefore his comments on the Arab investment was not right. His belief that Arabs are bad guys is also not true; it is only a belief. If he goes to the Arab countries, he may find many good Arabs. Again, some meditation on the part of the editor might have helped him handle the editorial in a different way.

The Self

In the case of the white midwestern professor or the Oriental Hawaiian professors we noticed that each seemed to consider people of another color undesirable. Does this mean that the so-called self has any color? We say, "I am black, he is white, my neighbor is brown." We identify ourselves with our skin color. But the so-called "me" is not black all over. Our blood is red; we all have the same number of chromosomes; our bones are white or brown, so to identify the self with any one color is not right. However, we interact with people as if the self of each of them had a particular color. Color is one variable with which we identify the self.

Nine Postulates of the Self

Voice as Self

Suppose the reader does not know how his speech sounds. He makes a tape of his own voice and asks a friend to listen to it. The friend says, "That is you." Then is voice the self? Speech specialists say that each person's pitch patterns are unique. Each of us has a certain voice pattern, but we also identify ourselves with people whose voice patterns are similar to our own. People of the same accent identify with each other. Therefore, voice is another variable with which we identify the self.

Appearance as Self

Each of us has an image of himself. Anyone knows what color looks good on him. When we see a suit of our favorite color in a store, we imagine ourselves in that suit; it is a reflection of ourselves. We like to wear the latest fashion and comb our hair the popular way. In each culture certain types of dress and certain styles of hair are fashionable. The John F. Kennedy hair style was popular for some time. Then long hair, beard and moustache became fashionable. In Asia, however, the Kennedy style was considered funny. Asians liked to comb their hair toward the back of their heads. Even long hair is not fashionable there. Only poor men who can't afford haircuts or real philosophers are supposed to grow long hair. Styles that are fashionable in New York or Paris are not equally fashionable in New Delhi or Tokyo. Although a stylish person in Asia will wear an expensive wool suit, it is usually loose, not tight as it is in America. Good looks as imagined by a man in America are not the same as that imagined by a man in Asia. In each culture, a person's self-image tends to agree with the latest fashion in that culture.

Psychologists say that a person's image of himself is what others say he looks like. If a person is told he is good-looking, he imagines himself as good-looking. But psychologists have overlooked the fact that people in each culture have certain standards to measure good looks. If a person comes up to those standards he is told he is good-looking. A Japanese would not imagine himself handsome according to American standards, nor would an American like to be the image of a handsome Japanese.

In any case, we identify the self with the way we think we look.

Intelligence as Self

When Jensen published the results of his tests on intelligent quotient (IQ) of American whites compared with IQ's of blacks, there was furor in black communities.[2] According to Jensen's tests, blacks had IQ's much lower than those of whites. Blacks and other minorities did not like the Jensen findings. They questioned his methodology and pointed out innumerable cases of higher black intelligence when blacks are provided equal educational opportunities.

Each person and members of each culture would like to achieve a high IQ. A person's social status is based partially on his intelligence. He would not like to be branded as one with a low IQ. A culture's honor depends upon the overall IQ of its members.

Each person is identified with his intelligence in one subject, and each culture is identified with intelligence in a certain area. For example, Germans are associated with high intelligence in science, American blacks with music, Indians with philosophy, and French with fine arts. We associate the self with intelligence.

Conscience as Self

Despite associations with several factors such as voice, looks and intelligence, we cannot say that any one of them alone is the self. Each person has his own conscience. We have heard individuals say, "My conscience doesn't permit me to do that." Even if a person is highly intelligent, we do not say he is highly conscientious. Intelligence and conscience are different factors. When we say a person has a good mind, we do not mean that he has a good conscience. Conscience is something inside a person that tells him what is right and what is wrong, what he should do and should not do. Values are not the same as conscience since they are originated and reinstated by an institution that has existed for centuries before an individual's birth. Conscience and cultural values are, however, closely related. When the eldest son in an Asian family has to choose between his own marriage and the education of his brothers and sisters, he would choose to educate his brothers and sisters. He is satisfied to sacrifice his own happiness for their good. He might say, "My conscience did not permit me to marry the girl I loved and neglect my family members." The oldest son in each family is expected to look after his brothers, sisters and aged parents. The value of responsibility affects his conscience. His conscience guides him to do what is valued in his culture.

It is not uncommon to find the oldest son assuming responsibility in some Western sub-cultures also. The oldest son or daughter in black and Mexican families may neglect his or her own comforts and aspirations in favor of younger brothers and sisters. The Western belief in the individual's right to happiness generally preempts this type of responsibility. In exceptional cases Westerners assume such responsibility, but not as a rule.

In discussing Hindu and Buddhist theories of perception, we referred to the final stage of perception as cognition. At that stage the self decides what is right and what is wrong information. Hindus do not associate conscience with the self. They believe a person's conscience is his own, colored by what the individual thinks is good and bad or right and wrong, while the self is that part of the divine light that is in the individual. Somewhere deep inside each individual there is the divinity. That divine portion is the self or *Atman*. When a person dies, his conscience dies, but his Atman leaves the body either to join the Lord in Heaven or to enter another human body.

It is not our purpose to discuss the philosophical aspect of the self. Suffice it to say that there is something inside each person, whether called the mind or conscience or Atman, which guides the individual in determining right and wrong in his culture. That inner portion is the self.

Mental Health as Self

Under this postulate we include much more than mere absence of disease. It signifies, rather, the progressive maximization—within organic limits—of the individual's ability to exercise all his mental functions, and to achieve his maximum sensory acuity, strength, energy, coordination, dexterity, endurance, recuperative power, and immunity.

Without good mental health, interpersonal episodes often diverge in outcome from wanted ends. Fatigue is a common example. While it can be and often is a symptom of complications in living, with certain other people it may also cause difficulties. The individual, in an intercultural situation, has to have patience in critical periods while attempting to communicate. Endurance of strain makes mental demands, but the capacity to bear strain is not constant; it can be cultivated in advance of use. A striking example is the frequent recovery from despair and breakdown of interpersonal relations through vacation and rest, hygiene and recreation. On the positive, nontherapeutic side—in terms of optimal development—a benevolent spiral seems to extend from radiant mental health to a cheerful mien, from a cheerful mien to a friendly response, and back again to adequate intercultural communication.

Knowledge as Self

This postulate presupposes the individual has a scope of perception suitable for determining relationships between events; the capacity to abstract and symbolize experience, to manipulate the symbols into meaningful generalizations, and to be articulate in communication; skill in mobilizing the resources of his environment, and experience in the services of a variety of goals. It is significant that the construction of measures of intelligence is as controversial as ever, and that in any particular research project, the appropriateness and validity of measure adopted is always a question of judgment and interpretation.

Understanding as Self

This postulate is crucial to intercultural communication. People differ in their ability to interpret correctly the attitudes and intentions of others, in the accuracy with which they can perceive situations from others' viewpoints, and thus anticipate and predict their behavior. This type of social sensitivity depends on what we call the empathic responses. Empathic responses are basic to taking the role of the other and hence to social interaction and the communicative processes upon which rests social integration. They are central to the development of the social self and the capacity for self-conscious behavior. The sign of its absence is misunderstanding and insult; the sign of its presence in the positive sense is improved intercultural communication.

Autonomy as Self

Our use of autonomy suggests a sense of physical as well as mental independence. Physical independence refers to a minimum amount of freedom to move in and out of one's own culture and thus have the opportunity to meet members of other cultures, or at least to having access to members of other cultures while they visit yours even if movement outside your own culture is restricted for whatever reason. Restrictions preventing travel out of one's culture can include economic, political, or personal reasons. By mental independence we mean essentially that the mind must be open to new experiences. That is, a value must be perceived from contact with members of other cultures. It must be understood and appreciated that interacting with members of other cultures provides an opportunity to develop mutual benefical, and reciprocal types of relationships. Hopefully the relationships will leave each party more fully enriched through sharing and exchanging. Fundamentally, autonomy connotes a healthy atmosphere under which a self-governed individual has a sense of physical and mental independence to explore with others different from himself those things of mutual interest without interference of superfluous minutiae.

Judgment as Self

This last postulate perhaps undergirds those preceding. It is critical, and found in varying degrees among people. It is understood to be acquired slowly with experience, more or less according to age, but its operational definition and measurement is still a difficult task. Certain educational psychologists have gone furthest in differentiating this ability from intelligence and in analyzing the conditions under which an educational or other agency can cultivate judgment among people.

We define judgment as the ability to estimate the consequences of one's acts, to determine options and to make the best possible decisions. Some people are noted for good judgment while others are noted for the opposite. In an intercultural situation, judgment or the lack of it can mean the difference between success and failure in intercultural communication.

Self-concept and Communicative Behavior

One's self-concept affects his interaction with others in many ways. If a person has a high self-concept, he interacts with confidence. His expectations will be high. In a group consisting of one person with high self-concept and others with low self-concept, the former dominates the interaction in that group. Persons of low self-concept are less confident and their expectations are not very high. This does not mean that those with high self-concept are always the most successful. One with high self-concept may try to dominate everybody else and incur their displeasure. He may even act carelessly. On the other hand, one with low self-concept may be less domineering and more pleasing than the other. The person with low self-concept may act cautiously.

Each culture has much to do with its members' self-concepts. One's cultural values shape his self-concept in that he acts according to his cultural expectations. A person from an aggressive culture may act arrogantly with a person from a less aggressive culture. An aggressive person sometimes goes out of his way to achieve his goals. In his culture, not achieving the goals is considered failure, and failure demotes a person down to a very low status.

The resume an American job applicant submits to a prospective employer is an example of aggressiveness. An American believes in boasting of his achievements however minor they may be. Consequently, his resume tends to be several pages long and includes every minor achievement. An Asian's resume tends to be much shorter. The modest Asian might overlook many of his achievements. If both the American and the Asian apply for the same job in America, chances are the former will get the job, while it could be the other way in Japan.

On the basis of the foregoing, we might say that a person needs a high self-concept in aggressive cultures and a modest self-concept in less aggressive cultures.

Understanding One's Own Culture

If a person knows his own culture, he can relate most of his actions to cultural values. Understanding one's culture includes knowing the cultural value system, the artistic traditions, the technological achievements, religious beliefs, philosophical concepts, and the communicative techniques used by the people. It also helps a person to know the genetic characteristics of his people, the geographic origins of his ancestors, and the age of his culture and how it has changed during the centuries.

A Chinese student in an American university attended a party given by his foreign-student advisor. At the party, an American woman asked him about the significance of the Chinese dragon dance. The woman asked him so many questions about his culture that he felt stupid not knowing anything about what the woman asked. Americans might face the same situation in foreign lands. An American newspaper correspondent in Sri Lanka was talking with an old Sinhalese newspaper editor. The Sinhalese suddenly asked him, "Do you remember the name of the newspaper that Peter Zenger edited?" The American did not know who Peter Zenger was in the first place, let alone the name of the newspaper he edited. When he went to the American embassy library, he found that the Zenger case was a classic in American history of freedom of expression. Had he known about Peter Zenger, he could have interacted more efficiently with the Sinhalese. The feeling that he did not know much about his own culture chilled his enthusiasm for talking with the foreign editor.

Minority Cultures

Understanding their own cultural heritage is particularly important for members of minority cultures in multicultural countries such as the

United States. It helps them realize the value bases of their expectations and understand the origins of their conflicts with other minorities and with the majority. Sometimes two people from different ethnic groups do not feel easy communicating, without knowing the reasons for their uneasiness. As an example, two Americans who were eating lunch at a university cafeteria started talking without introducing themselves. A few minutes later one of them said, "Excuse me, I did not introduce myself, I am. . ." The smile on the other's face suddenly vanished. One of them was of Jewish origin and the other of Arab ancestry. Although the parents of both had arrived in this country more than fifty years ago, both had last names which clearly indicated their parental origin. Now, both did not know why they had to dislike each other. They were Americans. If they had not introduced themselves, they could have communicated very well. Had they known something about their parent cultures they would have known that the origins of their hatreds lay in Israel and Arabia. It should be possible for both of them to be friends and to like each other in the new land where they now lived.

Sometimes, a minority member feels ashamed of his parent culture. He may even try to conceal his identity. By identifying himself with the majority culture, he might improve his life in multicultural countries such as America. In some cases a person cannot hide his parentage since it is so obvious in his physical features, as with a Japanese American, for example. Some Japanese Americans do not want to talk about Japan and deliberately avoid anything Japanese. If they face reality, they will always be considered Japanese. All the stereotypes of the Japanese are associated with them even if they are full-fledged Americans. Another case in point is the unreasonable dislike of some Japanese Americans for Korean Americans. Both may not know they dislike each other because their grandparents in Japan and Korea disliked each other for historical reasons.

Knowing one's cultural heritage and its greatness stimulates confidence and helps one communicate better in his society.

Understanding Other Cultures

After learning to understand one's culture and oneself, a person is ready to take the second step in intercultural communication, that of understanding the audience culture. The communicator should remember that each culture differs from all others and should therefore try to understand each audience's culture. There is no such person as a universal communicator. Each time a person tries to interact in a different culture, he must begin his preparation all over again.

To understand another culture one must know as much about it as he does about his own culture, including the value system and all other factors that are components of the audience culture.

Understanding Values

In chapter eight we mentioned some primary, secondary and tertiary values of the major cultures of the world. That list was by no means exhaustive. There may be several more values in each culture that no one has yet recognized. Based on the values, there may be many more beliefs, expectations and customs. Since the area of cultural values is quite new, there are not many studies which gives us information about them. No one should try to change another culture without knowing that culture. Just because another culture is not like ours, or because that culture is not industrialized to our standards, we should not try to change it to our standards. Sometimes we declare that another culture is underdeveloped without knowing much about that culture. A case in point is that of a group of American women who visited a European country to teach the women of that country how to liberate themselves, but when the Americans talked with the women they found these women were more liberated than the Americans. But before they left America for that country, they were under the impression that European women were backward.

In some cases we might not even be able to know that the people of another country are not as backward as we think them to be, perhaps because of a language difference. If those people speak a language we do not know, we may make an incorrect judgement of that culture. It is imperative that a communicator learn the language and read about the culture in that language. Reading books and other materials in the native language are indeed necessary. In an international broadcasting class in an American university, two students were asked by the teacher to read articles written by representatives of Moscow Radio and Radio Television France and report to the class. Neither student read the articles; instead, they read books written by an American university professor. After they presented their reports, a student in the class asked them where they got their information. The two students gave the source of their reports. The other student said the information given by the American author was not accurate, since he had visited both Russia and France and knew better. He said the articles written by the Russian and French authors gave more, if not entirely accurate, information on their broadcasts.

Although each author is biased to some extent when he writes about his own country and culture, it is better to read an ethnocentric book by a native scholar rather than a book by a foreign scholar. By reading a book in the native language, or even one written in English by a native scholar, we will know how a native perceives his culture and why he does so.

There are other ways of understanding a foreign culture. We should see movies, listen to radio, and watch television broadcasts from that culture. Talking with people from another culture is very helpful, but we should be careful in selecting our informants. Foreign students studying in American universities are not always representative of their cultures. They are generally the cream of the crop in their homelands, the upper-class members and intellectuals. They are not average people, and sometimes look down on their cultural traditions. Movies, radio, and television can give better information on the life and culture of a people than do the foreign students. We should make particular mention of movie directors and commentators such as Kurosawa of Japan, Satyajit Ray of India, and Alistair Cooke of Great Britain, who not only accurately depict life in their cultures but also create films that are excellent pieces of art. We should also mention novelists such as Kawabata of Japan and Hemingway of America, both of whom have been Nobel laureates and are known for the moving stories they have written of their people.

While reading a novel, listening to a radio broadcast, watching a television show or seeing a play from another culture, the student should try to understand beyond what is written, said, or shown. He should try to locate the cultural values, beliefs, and expectations of that people in their actions.

Let us take as an example the movie *My Fair Lady* which is based on the play *Pygmalion* by George Bernard Shaw. The movie depicts the British values attached, in those days, to the colonies and the monarchy. In those days ambitious British men went to India to make a fortune and earn a reputation. Reputation was of high value if it was recognized by the British majesty. In the movie the semanticist who believes he can make anybody speak "King's English" trains an uncultured girl to speak excellent English and behave like a lady of high society. In the movie we can locate many British values, beliefs, expectations and customs. Some of these have not changed even today.

In the story *The Old Man and the Sea* Ernest Hemingway describes the life of an old Cuban fisherman called Santiago. This old fisherman is a representative of the western cultures so much characterized by aggressiveness, adventurism and achievement orientation. When the old man catches many fish and kills several sharks he says to himself, "But a man is not made for defeat. . . . A man can be destroyed but not defeated."[3] This tells us a great deal about western cultural values and beliefs.

Kabuki, the dance drama of Japan, tells us a great deal about Japanese art, beliefs, and communicative behaviors. By closely observing a Kabuki play, we can identify many Japanese customs and gestures which are used even today.

By listening to radio music from another culture, we can become familiar with that culture's tunes, so that when we actually visit a person's home in that culture, we will not be shocked to hear "a bunch of noise" as the Oregon music teacher. Music is an important part of the daily life in all cultures. In most Asian cultures musical systems have been developed over many centuries. People practice diligently and have high respect for their own music. If a foreigner wants to communicate in those cultures he should learn to appreciate that music. An American music lover would certainly be happy to have somebody in a foreign land tell him, "I love your Boston Symphony Orchestra," or "I have a great respect for Eugene Ormandy, your great conductor." That would bring the American and the foreigner closer. Many Americans know about Indian music only from having heard an instrument called sitar. They may not be able to pronounce the name of the man who made sitar popular, but if somebody mentions "Ravi Shankar" the Americans will say, "Yes, I have heard him on the radio."

Reading a foreign newspaper tells us a great deal about a culture. Other people's traditions and aspirations are reported in their newspapers. Their communicative techniques and their everyday language can be understood by reading the papers. In 1955, Wilbur Schramm studied how fourteen newspapers from fourteen countries reported the Suez canal incident when the British took over that canal from Egypt. Each of the fourteen newspapers Schramm studied was in the predominant language of the country and reflected quite well the views of its people. It is interesting to read how the fourteen newspapers perceived the same incident depending upon the beliefs and expectations of their peoples.

Learning the Language

Learning to read, write and speak the language of the audience is necessary. Because language is developed by a people to make life easy and meaningful for that people, it becomes an integral part of that culture. Language tells us much about the history and life of its speakers.

When a student in a foreign country decides to go to an American university for higher education, he learns English. If he has already learned it, he refines it so he can better interact with the Americans. But when an American student goes to a foreign university he usually goes to one where English is the medium of instruction. American students who learn the language of their host country are exceptional.

A foreign language should be learned from its native speaker. The native speaker knows the heart of his language and can develop expressions that are unique to the culture of its speakers. The American Foreign Service Institute (FSI) has set certain standards for Americans who learn a foreign language. The FSI standards are established for those who go into foreign service. The highest grade an American can achieve is FSI-5, which is the level of speaking noticed in the best speaker of the native language. We would like to raise this level to a grade higher, say 6, to identify the level of a native scholars or poets who create new expressions and enrich their language. It is not easy for a foreigner to acquire the level-6 unless he reads, writes, and speaks the foreign language for many years. A rule of thumb is that if one can make jokes in a foreign language and understand the native jokes, then one has achieved level-5. If one can write stories and books in a foreign language, then one has achieved level-6 in that language.

Some languages other than English consist of more phonemes and native speakers use those phonemes more frequently. Although the number of phonemes known to linguists are limited, all of them are not used in the English language. In Sanskritic languages, sounds such as "th" and "t" are not one and the same. When an American learns a Sanskritic language he tends to use the sound "t" for both "t" and "th." When a native speaker hears an American speak his language he just smiles and says nothing. The American probably believes he is doing fine. Americans are also unable to pronounce certain retroflex sounds in Asian languages. It is not easy for an American to say the retroflex sound "l" frequently used in south and southeast Asia. When an American Peace Corps Volunteer (PCV) visited an Indian village she tried to speak the native Kannada language as she had learned it from an American. She was trying to tell the Indian farmers, "If there are no rains, there will be no crops." With that introduction she was going to impress upon them the need to take other jobs, raising poultry for example, to make extra money. She could not pronounce the retroflex sound "l" and substituted the dental "l" and gave her speech. The Indian farmers said nothing, although they seemed amused at her speech. Several months later the PCV learned that instead of saying "no rains, no crops" she had actually said "no breasts, no value."

Many foreigners who speak English see no difference between the English sounds "v" and "w." They say "wote" for "vote" and "wictory" for "victory."

It is clearly necessary to learn a foreign language from a native speaker and speak it the way he speaks it. It is important to recognize that some Americans today at least attempt to learn a foreign language while many do not bother. Most would put the burden of learning another language on the foreigner.

Facing the Audience

We come now to the third step in intercultural communication: actual interaction with members of another culture. The key word here is *adaptation*. We define adaptation as the technique of changing our communication in order to create mutual respect and understanding between ourselves and the audience of the other culture. Our communicative technique should be adapted to each culture in which we want to interact. Initially, adaptation may look like a game to the communicator. When it becomes his way of interaction, he will realize its benefits, and it will no longer be just a game. We shall consider adaptation under three situations: (1) a situation involving only two individuals from two different cultures; (2) a situation involving a person from one culture and several people from another culture; and (3) a situation involving a person from one culture and a large audience from another culture.

One-to-one Situation

In a situation involving two persons from different cultures, communication will be facilitated by extreme honesty and openness on the parts of both. We said earlier that eye contact indicates honesty. In cultures where eye contact is considered important, it is imperative that both persons establish such contact. The eye tells many things. If one looks deeply into another's eyes, one can detect any dishonesty the other person is trying to hide. In cultures where eye contact is not an important factor or where it is bad manners, however, it is hard to tell whether or not the other person is telling the truth. Conversely, if the person trying to establish communication comes from a culture where eye contact is considered unnecessary, he may not read anything in the other person's eyes. If on the other hand the person happens to be from a culture where eye contact is bad manners, he may misinterpret the other's looking straight into his eyes.

Americans often ask questions that others do not like to answer. Americans generally begin by asking the other person, "Are you from. . .?" The moment a person with a different face appears, an American tries to stereotype him. He might ask, "In your country do people. . . .?" People from other cultures usually do not like questions of a personal nature. When the American asks questions beginning with "In your country. . .," the other person might think, "This Yankee does not even want to say the name of my country." Further, the other person is not an expert on his country. He may hesitate to answer any question about his country for several reasons. Forcing the other person to answer questions he really does not want to answer may create dislike for the American.

Some Americans ask questions on religion. For many people religion is an entirely personal belief. They do not like to discuss their religion with foreigners. Politics is a similar area. Most foreigners do not like to answer questions on their country's politics. Many students from foreign countries are studying in American universities. Some of those countries are torn by wars; others may still be fighting. Those students do not like to be asked anything about wars in their homeland, but many insensitive Americans do ask questions. Students from other cultures, Asian and Latin particularly, are too humble to say, "I do not like to talk about the war in my country." They may answer the question, but they are hurt by the American.

Another question a person from a foreign culture has been asked many times is, "Do you know . . ., he is from your country?" The foreigner secretly laughs at this question. How could he know everybody from his country?

Americans cannot understand why some persons from a foreign culture "act big." It may happen that the foreign person is not just acting big, he is "big" in his culture. Americans are born and raised in a society where social hierarchy generally does not mean much, but in most cultures there are social levels and each person is placed in one of them. Sometimes a person may move up and other times he might not. It is not for the American to change that social system when its people are not interested in changing it. How, then, should an American communicate with one from another culture whose social position is high? In order to communicate effectively, the American should recognize the other's high status. Conversely, what should an American do when a foreigner shows him respect that other Americans do not show? Many American university professors have confronted this situation. Asian students show them great respect and generally stand at a respectful distance. The Asians also expect to be patronized. American professors who are ignorant of the fundamentals of intercultural communication think the Asian is trying to curry favor. In the interest of a good relationship, at least in the beginning, the American professor should accept the Asian's respect. Then the Asian should be informed that in America he need not be so formal. We have seen many Asian students happy about being informed of local customs and have liked the professors who told them even more.

In short, understanding the other person's culture, respecting it, and adapting one's communication to that culture are the key steps for successful interaction in one-to-one situations.

Listening

Listening to the audience is important in any situation, but it is most important in one-to-one situations. At a university in New York a young American professor was talking to a young man from Japan. The American introduced himself as an instructor in broadcasting and said, "I am the only one who can teach color television at this university." The Japanese smiled and said, "Is that so?" Without giving his Japanese acquaintance much chance to tell about himself, the American talked about the greatness of color television. Later on he found out that the Japanese had tremendous experience in teaching color television in the Japanese Broadcasting Corporation and was a visiting scholar at the same university.

Listening is not emphasized in western universities. Listening to a person from another culture is preceded by respect for the other person's culture and patience for that person's slow expression. Most Americans lack both, and learning respect and patience would facilitate intercultural communication. We have seen a few Americans listen patiently to a foreign person and even cleverly correct the person's speech.

On a city bus in Los Angeles, an old white woman asked the black driver where to get off to go to a certain street. The driver said he did not know. His attitude told everyone he was impatient with the old woman and did not even clearly hear the name of the road. Most passengers in the bus knew the street she was asking for was on the route, and, in fact, that there was a bus stop on the street. The bus driver's attitude was considered racist by the passengers. It is possible he was not a racist, but merely did not have the patience to listen to the old woman.

If a person does not listen carefully to one from another culture, he may miss many points. The reader may well feel that listening is important in one's own culture, and wonder why it is especially significant in communicating with one from another culture. Another culture is special because the person from that culture may have an accent, or may use certain words to express an idea where we might use entirely different words. In many Asian cultures, there is one word for write and draw. A person from one of those cultures will say, "write a picture" instead of "draw a picture." Japanese use the sound "l" for "r," and their pronunciation of the English word "rice" sounds like "lice." The Japanese does not think he is saying "lice," but the American ears are trained to hear it as "lice." Careful listening and understanding the context of the conversation will indicate the Japanese is really saying "rice."

Culture and Credibility

Many communicologists say that in the final analysis it is a person's credibility that accounts for his success or failure as a communicator. They also say that credibility consists of two dependent variables: trustworthiness and expertise. Trustworthiness is the result of such variables as the character of the communicator. If a person advocates that a certain action be taken by his audience, he should have no vested interest in advocating the action. There have been instances where politicians suggested rezoning farm land to construction sites and after their suggestions were approved by the legislature people found that several hundred acres of that land was owned by the same politician. Even if the land were useless for agricultural purposes and useful only for construction, the politician did not advocate rezoning with good intentions, so the people no longer trusted him.

A person may be honest and of excellent character, but if he is not an expert in the area of his communication, too many people do not accept his message. Trustworthiness and expertise are therefore two variables which decide the communicator's credibility. This holds true only in the communicator's own culture. Trustworthiness in one culture may not be so in another. Variables such as character, on which trustworthiness depends, are highly cultural. A person of good character in one culture may not be so in another.

In many non-Western cultures trustworthiness ranks above expertise, while expertise is more important than trustworthiness in Western cultures. Business and governmental organizations hire experts. A person may be of high character, but if he lacks knowledge of his job, he does not have a good chance of being hired for the job he is seeking. Sometimes, even when his personal character is somewhat questionable, a great expert will be hired. This is not true in Eastern cultures. There, character places high and sometimes a person who lacks basic knowledge in his area will be appointed on the basis of his high personal character. It seems, then, that a trustworthy person can do better in an Eastern culture and an expert can do equally well in a Western culture. We have seen many ambassadors of Eastern cultures fail in the West because they were more trustworthy than expert.

This does not mean that communicators in Western cultures are untrustworthy and those in Eastern cultures are inexpert. The point we are trying to make is that in Western cultures expertise is more important than mere trustworthiness and in Eastern cultures trustworthiness is considered more important than mere expertise.

Discussion in One-to-one Situation

Often, two persons from different cultures discuss problems of common interest and arrive at an acceptable solution. It is more difficult to conduct discussions in intercultural situations than within the same culture. When a discussion takes place in America and the discussants are black Americans, both may have a basic understanding of democratic processes and other customs. But if one of them comes from an authoritarian culture, he will tend to impose his views on the other person. Conversely, the American tends to be democratic even in authoritarian cultures. In authoritarian cultures, the mention of democratic attitudes results in laughter, because those peoples do not believe there is such a thing as complete democracy. They believe a certain degree of authoritarianism is necessary to arrive at a conclusion.

Ethnocentrism is another problem in discussion. Each person views life in other cultures using his own life as a standard. An American might say the Chinese are tyrannical because officials in China impose their views on their subordinates no matter what the subordinates think. The American is judging the Chinese bosses according to his own cultural beliefs. He is saying the Chinese bosses are not democratic, as are American bosses. A Chinese, however, might think everyone is a boss in America. He has no reason to think otherwise. Sometimes an inexperienced and ignorant young man is elevated to high status and accorded high honors he really does not deserve. The Chinese believes that subordinates, and young men, should be guided by senior and more experienced authorities.

Again we can apply the same rule. In non-Western cultures, the discussant should accept a senior person's authority and show respect to that authority.

One-to-few Situation

In a one-to-few situation where a person from one culture tries to interact with several members of another culture, the communication problems are much different from those in a one-to-one situation. An example of a one-to-few situation is the small-group discussion. In industrial disputes the negotiator must meet with representatives of the workers and the administration who may belong to several subcultures, ethnic groups and races. In international conferences, a diplomat from one country must meet with representatives of another country. In this case, although the conference is of an international nature, the members also act as members of their own cultures. In business negotiations, a businessman from one culture will have to negotiate with representatives of business organizations in another culture.

Small-group communication occurs in several forms. It may be as casual as a social gathering or a scholarly seminar. It may be negotiations between government departments of different countries or business organizations of different cultures. Communication tends to be casual and two-way in social gatherings and seminars. In some negotiations it will be two-way. In meetings and problem-solving groups, communication is not always two-way; members of each culture tend to stick together. The fair-minded chairman will have a hard time pulling the two cultural groups together. Often even the chairman joins his own cultural group. In such meetings all the variables which affect small-group communication in the members' own cultures do not affect the group at all. In an intercultural problem-solving group, for example, there is no cohesiveness; each member represents his own culture. Even in cases where members of subcultures or minorities sit in small group, it is not easy for the chairman to bring about cohesiveness.

Small-Group Discussion

Discussion in a small group consisting of members of different cultures will be successful only if the members make certain adaptations unique to such groups. In monocultural groups, members adhere to group norms. In intercultural groups, however, members act as representatives of their own cultures. Their own values affect the nature of communication. It has been the experience of many negotiators that members of another culture feel insulted if the negotiator makes suggestions which oppose the cultural values of those members. A classic example is that of certain Western agricultural experts who visited an Asian country and suggested the Asians change their food habits and eat American wheat. One American even suggested the Asians slaughter the cows that wander their streets, considering them a nuisance to the public. Both wheat and beef had not been parts of the Asian diet for many centuries. They were not ready to eat the new foods just because the Americans suggested it. It was not the intention of the Americans to insult the Asians; it was merely a suggestion they thought was in the Asians' best interest. The Asians perceived it as an insult to their culture, but did not tell the Americans so. From that point on negotiations did not go very well, and the Americans never knew why.

An Indian scholar was invited by an American university to participate in a seminar on Mahatma Gandhi. Many American specialists on Gandhian ideals also spoke at the seminar. Their speeches were highly analytical, comparing Gandhi with many Western political philosophers. The Americans speeches were considered scholarly by those who listened to them. But the Indian had brought many original books written by Gandhi. Each time he made a statement on Gandhi, he quoted a line or two from one of those books. He did not agree with anything the Americans said, and spoke as if the Americans had no right to speak on Gandhi. At the same time, the Americans who participated in the seminar and those who were there as observers expected more from the Indian scholar. They expected to hear his own views on Gandhi, possibly comparing Gandhi's views with those of other Western political philosophers; they did not expect him to read from Gandhi's books. Since the Indian was in a Western culture, he should have tried to discern the expectations of the seminar participants and observers. Conversely, if the Americans had participated in a seminar on Gandhi in India, they should have planned to meet the expectations of Indian scholars.

In small-group communication, the communicator should adapt to the cultural values and beliefs of the other members. In intercultural group discussions, whether a scholarly seminar or business negotiations, the participants act as members of their own culture. Such behavior tends to be habitual and not deliberate.

In problem-solving group discussions consisting of persons from different cultures, many cultural variables affect the problems. In some cases the problem itself is cultural. It may also be true that what is a problem in one culture would not be so in another culture. For example, the food problem and population explosion in many Asian countries are results of many cultural beliefs and expectations. In many Western cultures, such problems might not exist. If such problems come up, Western people may solve them more easily since their cultural values and expectations will not stand in the way. In fact, many western values and expectations encourage solving such problems using modern know-how. In situations where cultural values affect the nature of the problems, the group discussants should convince the other members that the problems are cultural. It has been our experience that people of all cultures do not like to blame their own cultural values for their problems.

We are not advocating that the discussants should try to change the cultural values to bring about change. On the contrary, we suggest they try to solve the problem within the cultural framework. Sometimes the cultural system does not lend itself to the particular change the discussants have in mind. Then, our suggestion is to wait until they can come up with a practical solution that does not require drastic change in the culture.

One-to-many Situation

In a situation where a person has to speak to many members of an entirely different culture, as in a public speech, communication tends to be one-way. Because there are many listeners, sometimes several thousand, it is not possible to establish two-way communication. An example would be a speech given by the American president to a Japanese audience, which tends to be both international and intercultural, or a speech given by an American agricultural expert to a group of Thailand villagers on modernization of agriculture. Chances are in both the above cases, there will be an interpreter to translate the Americans' speeches into Japanese or Thai.

Two points to remember are to learn the audience's language so you can say a few words to them, and to consult a cultural advisor. It is important to speak the audience's language correctly. Even if one understands the language but cannot speak very well, he will know whether the interpreter is translating his ideas clearly.

The idea of a cultural advisor is not new. Governmental and business organizations in many countries have cultural advisors on their staffs. These experts advise the organization on matters related to other cultures.

Every culture observes several traditional customs in public speeches. An Asian participated in a televised seminar in an American university. He took too much time to speak, and interrupted the others whenever they expressed opinions relating to his own area of specialization. Once the moderator of the seminar, an American, was forced to say, "You certainly dominate the show." The Asian thought this was a compliment, and continued to be "dominant." He went home believing he had done an excellent job speaking in the seminar. In his Asian culture his domineering attitude would have been considered impressive, since shutting off the opponent is a quality of a good speaker; the same attitude is considered bad manners in America. Some homework and consultation with American friends would have helped the Asian scholar create a better impression of himself.

Whether communication is one-to-one, one-to-few or one-to-many and whether it is in an interpersonal or media situation, the most important rule to be observed is *adaptation* to the audience culture.

In summary, the intercultural communicator should remember the following fourteen principles.

DO'S

Know yourself

Know your own culture

Know your audience's culture

Treat your audience's culture as equal to your own

Be sensitive to the audience's values, beliefs and expectations

Learn that audience's language

Adapt your communication to the audience's culture

DON'TS

Don't manipulate the audience of another culture

Don't ask questions about the audience's religion

Don't ask questions about the political situation in the audience's country

Don't stereotype

Don't be ethnocentric

Don't be arrogant

Don't ignore your audience's customs

A Code of Ethics

From the beginning of history we have seen in man a need to develop some form of understanding between himself and others. To do so he has developed many forms of interaction, which grow directly out of his culture. We learn early in our educative process that the need for understanding is directly related to the intensity of man's relationships. That is, the sparser a population, the fewer understandings needed, and conversely, the greater the density of a culture, the more understandings are needed. As noted earlier, there are four basic cultures, generally classified as hunting and gathering, agricultural, industrial, and technological, but it is not uncommon to see elements of all in one culture.

The more people involved, the more materials, and the less space, the greater the complexities. These complexities, which necessitate intricate understandings and relationships, stem directly from the nature of involvement. As a culture's technology advances, the expansion spills over into other cultures, creating a need for intercultural intercourse. Just as there is a need for order and civility within a given culture, so does that need exist between cultures. Conditions and understandings must be established so that each culture will have its own set of rules by which its members will live. This is an evolutionary process, as new insights and problems are constantly being uncovered. As a culture becomes complicated, due to internal development and external influence, human interaction also becomes complicated.

The morass of legal entities that have evolved through court and legislative procedings represent man's attempt to work out understandings. They are national and international in nature, but attempts have not been too successful at bringing them down to cultural and intercultural levels. The statutes, documents and writings, though complicated and monstrous, all serve a unique purpose in helping man to understand his relationship to others.

Man's attempts to establish codes of professional ethics are not new. As early as the eighteenth century B. C., Hamurabi developed a code of laws. And Hippocrates, in the fourth century B. C., developed his code of ethics for physicians. From time immemorial man has tried to influence others through physical and psychological methods of persuasion. In the area of persuasion, Aristotle mentioned ethos as an important characteristic of the communicator, although this was limited to persuasion in one culture and Aristotle did not develop a code of ethics for intercultural communicators. Although the practice of physicians tends to be intercultural in nature, Hippocrates did not include a code for intercultural communication. As a result, many physicians, psychiatrists and others in the medical professions often do not consider knowledge of intercultural communication as an integral part of their practice. This problem is not limited to the medical profession, but extends to the professions of diplomacy, business, the military, and education.

Our purpose here is to establish a code of ethics for all intercultural communicators.

We believe the following thirty-five points cover almost the entire area of intercultural communication. We believe the intercultural communicator should abide by the following code when communicating in, translating from, or conducting research in other cultures.

CATEGORY	*CODE*
	The intercultural communicator shall:

Understanding Other Cultures		
	1.	Recognize that he does not set world standards
	2.	Treat the audience culture with the same respect he would his own
	3.	Not judge the values, beliefs and customs of other cultures according to his own values
	4.	At all times be mindful of the need to understand cultural bases of other's values
	5.	Never assume superiority of his own religion over that of the other person
	6.	In dealing with members of a different religion, try to understand and respect that religion
	7.	Endeavor to understand the food habits of other peoples which were developed on the basis of their particular needs and resources
	8.	Respect the way people dress in other cultures
	9.	Not treat with contempt the unfamiliar odors which may be considered pleasant by people of other cultures
	10.	Not use the color of a person's skin as a basis for the nature of his relationship with that person
	11.	Not look down at another person because he speaks with an accent different from one's own

Communicative
Techniques

12. Recognize that each culture, however small, has something to offer the world and no one culture has a monopoly in every aspect

13. Not take undue advantage of one's superior position in the hierarchy of his culture to sway the actions of members of his own culture

14. Always remember there is no scientific evidence to prove that one ethnic group is superior or inferior to others

15. Not manipulate his communicative techniques to bring about change in the behaviors of peoples in another culture to suit his own needs

16. Not create an atmosphere to reinforce stereotypes of another people

17. Not employ preconceived notions of others in attempting to communicate with them

18. Make honest attempts to learn the language of his audience in preparing to interact with them

19. Make honest attempts to learn, respect and adapt the customs of his audience of another culture in preparing to interact with them

20. Recognize that the primary values of one's own culture are different from those of other cultures, and not communicate in such a way as to impose one's own values on them

21. Be aware that the nonverbal symbols used in one's culture, if used in another culture, might be insulting to members of that culture

22. Refrain from speaking one's language with another of one's culture in the company of those who cannot understand that language

23. In using mass media of another culture, use communication techniques to suit their media system and format

24. When using mass media, not create false, inaccurate, insulting images of another people in order to suit one's own interests, necessities and conveniences.

Recognizing
Other Sources

25. When using written and unwritten information from the minority cultures in one's own country, give recognition to the source of that information

26. When using written and unwritten information from other cultures, give due recognition to the sources of information in those cultures

27. When communicating at the intercultural level, not impose on the person from the other culture one's own national interests

Conducting
Research

28. When conducting research in another culture, not surreptitiously collect data from members of that culture

29. When conducting research in another culture, not misrepresent the details of one's research to the people of that culture

30. Not use psychological or physical coercion to force one's subjects of another culture to participate in one's research

31. When interpreting the results of research data from another culture, refrain from doing so to serve one's own or others' needs

32. Not misuse the data from another culture to serve one's personal, cultural or national needs

33. Recognizing that data one collects in another culture may be used for malicious purposes, refrain from releasing those data to unscrupulous individuals

34. When involving members of other cultures in experiments such as simulation and role playing, inform those

members of how the data are going to be used

35. Use data from another culture only for enhancing and enriching human knowledge

SUMMARY

Because each culture has a personality, the way in which members of that culture communicate has a definite pattern. In order to communicate effectively in another culture, one must adapt to the personality of that culture. Understanding one's own culture and that of his audience precede adaptation. Self-realization and knowledge of values are part of understanding one's own culture.

We have identified nine postulates of the self. One's self concept affects his interaction with others. Understanding the audience's culture, including that of minorities, is essential for effective and efficient communication. Talking with members of the audience's culture, learning their language, reading their books and viewing their films and plays are some ways to prepare for interaction with members of another culture.

Adaptation is necessary in interactions involving one-to-one, one-to-few and one-to-many persons. Adaptation is also necessary in face-to-face and mass media situations.

While a communicator's credibility is probably the most important factor in all cultures, the variables on which credibility depends differ from culture to culture. Although adaptation is necessary to each culture, subculture, or ethnic group, one should be aware of some general principles of intercultural communication.

Intercultural communication involves some ethical considerations. A communicator must abide by a code of ethics when he tries to interact with other people, translate their works into his own language, or conduct research in foreign cultures.

NOTES

1. *Scientific Research on Transcendental Meditation* (Los Angeles: Maharishi International University, 1972), p. 17.

2. Arthur R. Jensen, *Educability and Group Differences* (New York: Harper and Row, 1973).

3. Ernest Hemingway, *The Old Man and the Sea* (New York: Charles Scribner's Sons, 1952), p. 103.

Index